Joys *of* Joy

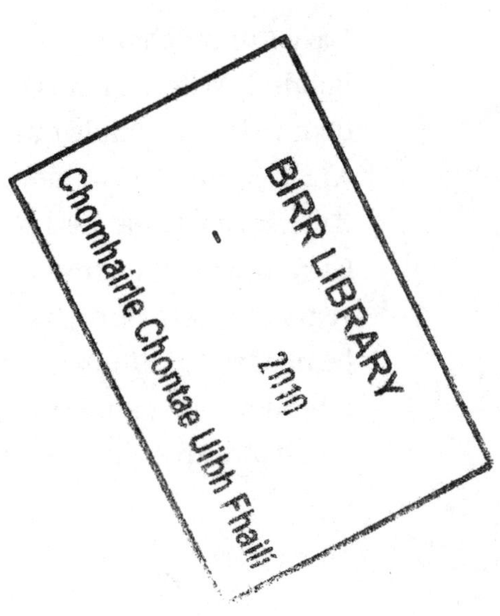

About the Author

Gary Cunningham is a painter and decorator by trade, and a budding writer. A man who has battled addiction to alcohol and depression, he made one extremely stupid mistake in his life, which in turn led to his incarceration. But it was during these darkest times that his love for the written word began to grow. Gary won the Listowel 'Writing in Prison' competition two years in a row (2013/2014), and this was the encouragement he needed to complete this memoir. Gary has done numerous interviews on radio and keeps a regular blog which can be found at https://garcunningham.wordpress.com/

JOYS *OF* JOY

Finding Myself in an Irish Prison

Gary Cunningham

The Liffey Press

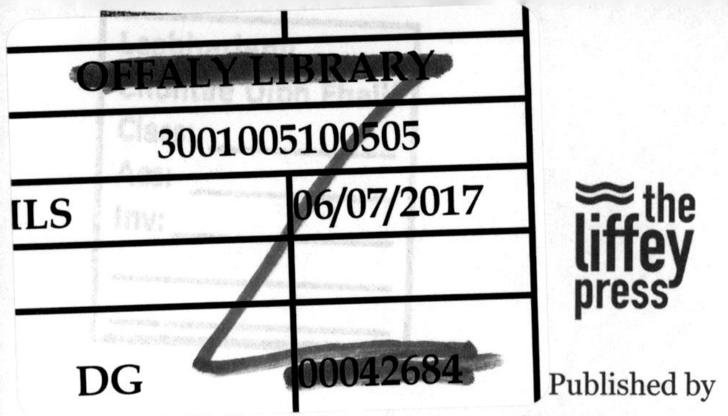

Published by
The Liffey Press Ltd
Raheny Shopping Centre, Second Floor
Raheny, Dublin 5, Ireland
www.theliffeypress.com

A catalogue record of this book is
available from the British Library.

ISBN 978-1-908308-97-9

Printed in Spain by GraphyCems.

Contents

Contents

Dedication

To the loving memory of Daithí, an amazing friend and mentor. R.I.P.

And to Lily and Annie – your love, support and encouragement are simply breathtaking

PREFACE

I have never written a book before, or anything else for that matter except an essay for my Junior Cert., as you will probably be able to tell after the first paragraph, but I wanted to push myself, challenge myself, and so what you have in your hands is the result of a lot of blood, sweat, tears and tantrums!

This book is an absolutely true account, well, with a bit of creative story telling thrown in, as I take you inside one of Ireland's most famous jails and guide you through what was the most frightening and exciting rollercoaster rides I have ever been on. In no way will I try to glorify prison life, nor will I regale you with tales of bloodshed and torture. This is just my honest telling of how getting myself in serious trouble with the law and ending up in Mountjoy, and subsequently Loughan House, was a truly life-changing experience for me.

Being locked up is a horrible experience for anyone, although as prisoners we do realise it is of our own doing, and Mountjoy is a disgusting place in which to do your sentence. I spent the beginning of my incarceration with a false air of confidence, afraid to lose face. But some of the things I witnessed shook me to my very core. When I was 'doubled up' (sharing a cell with another prisoner) I would have to keep this facade going at night once we were locked in a cell together, not wanting to appear weak. But I can tell you that on more than one occasion, once I was alone, I wept like a baby longing to be home with my loved ones, so sick of living in this vile dungeon.

But I had no intention of writing a tale about those feelings, or of the drug use, attacks, feuding or intimidation in jail – all of which does go on – since that's been done before. Instead, I wanted to try to highlight some of the more positive aspects – and they do exist – of ending up incarcerated. This is despite feeling ashamed, remorseful, frightened and a huge sense of failure as you lose everything, which in my case was over one stupid, disgusting mistake. I hurt so many people as a result of my incarceration, but the idiot and liar I was before I was locked up caused even more pain and hurt. So I knew I needed to use the time I was under lock and key to totally change every aspect of my life and come out a changed man, and I hope I have achieved this goal.

Not only did I ruin my own life, but that of my family, too, as I brought shame raining down upon them. I also lost contact with my son through this process, which is nobody's fault but my own and is something that I have to live with and regret for the rest of my life. But I had wasted a major part of my life drinking, taking drugs, being deceitful and letting people down. As a result, getting locked up was actually the best thing that could have happened to me. I soon became a believer, and coined a phrase that *'It's not the time you do ... it's what you do with your time.'*

I had so many ups and downs, met so many amazing people and forged true friendships that I hope will last a lifetime. So for the people who think jail is a 'holiday camp' I hope this book will prove it's not! At the same time, for people who think Mountjoy, or any of Ireland's prisons, is like the prisons we see sensationalised in American movies, it's not. It's not a nice place, but it is what you make of it.

In the time I spent writing this tale of two prisons, firstly on A4 sheets kindly given to me by the truly outstanding teaching staff in Mountjoy, to sitting in Conn's IT classroom in Loughan House frantically typing away, I looked for feedback from my fellow inmates who, quite patiently, would read over what I had just written and give me either their seal of approval ('Spot on Gar, yeah? On the fuckin' button pal!'), or their damning critique ('No! Are ya for real bud? That's a load of *shite*') and I would try to take on board what they said as I'm telling this story for those lads too.

So when Gooners, one of the men with whom I travelled through this 'whack', came to me and said, 'Gar, everyone is too fuckin' nice in this book,' it staggered me a little. For you see, my account of the people in this tale is true and from the heart. Not all men and women locked up in Irish jails are 'animals' or 'scumbags' – they're mainly lads and ladies who, like yours truly, made catastrophic mistakes which they were paying for dearly.

The book starts with my sentencing and subsequent move to Mountjoy, and follows the next couple of days as I tried to find my way. It then breaks off into a series of notable events, since if I was to describe every day I spent in jail it would get very boring very quickly. It then finally transports you to Loughan House Open Prison after I finally got transferred there. I hope you will find the humour in what was at times a very dark episode in my life. But I also hope I can show that housed inside Ireland's jails are some of the most intelligent, creative, amazing people that you will meet who just made an 'arse' decision which left them ashamed, broken and imprisoned. But a very wise man once told me, *'The man who never made a mistake, never made anything at all'*.

So, hopefully, you will see that *yes* there are some bad people locked up, but there are also some very, very good ones too.

So come join me as we embark on a 'mad auld tale' of the true Joys of Joy! This one is for 'The D Wing lads' – stay strong and do your whack!

Author's Notes:

1. All the names and identities of the prisoners, prison officers and others in this book, except as indicated otherwise, have been changed or disguised to protect their privacy.
2. Please excuse the 'colourful' language that appears in the following pages – I was in prison after all!

Chapter 1

THE SENTENCE

'I sentence you to three and a half years, Mr. Cunningham,' bellowed the immaculately well-kept Judge Bolan as he peered at me from atop his skinny glasses. His perfectly groomed silver hair reminded me of the male model black and white photos you would see in a Dublin's barber shop, circa 1980. It was March 27, 2012 and my world was crashing.

Thank you VERY much Judge Bolan, ya sanctimonious prick were the words that came flooding into my mind as the magnolia-painted walls of Court 5 came closing in on top of me, but who was I kidding? Our good judge here didn't force me to go and collect copious amounts of grass off Billy the Greek (who in fact hails from Dingle!). And I am not talking about the grass you cut with the lawnmower on a sunny midsummer's day! No, I'm referring to the fuckin' grass you fuckin' smoke which, ironically enough, I don't. I just agreed to go and collect it for the very people who are *not* sitting here today receiving three and a half years in prison, but sure, I'll 'take it on the chin, like a good right hook', as me aul' grandda would say, the fuckin' legend. Better to be a gobshite and take full responsibility than to be a rat!

Let me introduce myself. My name is Gary Cunningham, a.k.a. 'The Voice', a nickname bestowed upon me by my fellow inmates, who you will meet in the following pages, for two reasons: (1) Because I became a spokesperson for many prisoners, and (2) Because I am extremely fuckin' loud!

I'm an average looking, not at all attractive, 33-year-old with mousey brown hair and horrible teeth, which are the sad result of never listening to my loving mother as a young lad when she'd bellow at me to 'scrub those gnashers'. Now I say 'average looking', but I was 18 and a half stone with a massive 'beer belly', one which had put many a barman's child through college, and it's clear that my love of Guinness and occasionally a certain white powder – combined with my lack of income to truly embrace and abuse them both – was a massive contributing factor as to why I was sitting here facing a prison sentence for, according to the judge, my *'integral part in a well organised criminal gang's militarily executed drugs run'*.

Eh, no Judge 'Bolo', me auld flower, I must strongly disagree with you there my good man. The first I heard of this 'militarily executed drugs run', as you so colourfully put it, was the day before I was caught when James 'The Sap' Foley – so named because he's a complete *sap*, a skinny soul whose face would remind you of Skeletor from the He-Man cartoons – rang my phone, slurring, 'Here, I'm up to me bollox in the mornin' yeah? And I'm meant to be meetin' someone, yeah? Can you do it or wha'?' Well, it's pretty safe to say that I saw the euro signs and the Guinness tap as my selfishness and greed kicked in, and I duly replied, 'yep!' And that was how I got caught with the grass by armed Gardaí, and how I was sitting here in a black suit that's too big for me, hearing the faint sobs of my ever loving mother in the background, listening as the judge tells me I'm going to prison for three and a half years. No, I hardly think it was an 'A-Team-esque' plan, your honour!

The sun had decided to peek through the massive bay window facing me, as I sat behind a glass screen feeling every gaze from the gathered court crowd pierce right through to my soul. The court's officer appears and takes hold of my left arm. He starts me towards a door, *the* door that is the confirmation that, yes, I'm going to prison! I turn to see that my mam, a beautiful woman, small in stature who looks nowhere near her age, has now burst into tears. (*Well done, Gary, ya self-centred arsehole!*) I blow her a kiss. 'I'll be grand ma,' I stutter. If only I believed that!

The court 'screw' is a six foot odd, balding, lumbering, stout neanderthal who seems to be enjoying his job a little too much today. 'Jaysus, your poor mother. Fair play to ya for leavin' her in that state,' he bellows at me.

'Mind your fuckin' business,' I'd say on any other day, but not today. The *fear* has gripped me, so I stare at my feet as he leads me through a maze of white-walled corridors.

I am presented to another officer, who searches me and removes everything from my person. I'm then led into a room which consists of a steel chair bolted to the concrete floor, and a massive perspex glass dividing the room in half – the beginning of 'us and them'. I take to the seat just as my legal team enter the room from a door on the other side of the perspex, and they're smiling! Massive, wide-grinned, smiles! 'Well, Gary, that went well.' For fuckin' who, I'm thinking, Judge Bobo?

'And how do you work that out?' I enquire.

'Well, we were full sure you were getting the ten (years),' replies one of the team, who up on until this very point I was convinced was a deaf mute as he never spoke *ever*!

'Really?' I say startled. 'Thank you for sharing that nugget of information with me.'

'I know it looks bleak now, Gary,' says my Barrister, an immaculate man from head to toe, I mean fuckin' perfect! Even his nose hairs looked like they got groomed in the Grafton Barber. 'But you'll come to see in time that this was a good result. Now we're off to another case, take care.' And like that they disappeared, like the new Marvel Agent Super Fuckin' Team, and I'm left on my own. Great!

The primate officer returns, and he now seems to be enjoying himself as he takes his time leading me to my holding cell. When we finally arrive outside he proceeds to write my name on a chalk board mounted to the wall, under that of another inmate I don't quite catch. He then undoes the massive lock and ushers me in. 'Get comfy pal, yeah? Next bus to The Joy won't be for a few hours,' he slurs as he slams the door closed. I turn to see my cellmate is fast asleep, a strange bore-like snort transmitting from his nasal passage every now and then. The holding cell is white, very white, with a stone cold bench bolted to the walls and floor. I tip-toe over to the bench, park my fat arse down upon its cold surface, and bury my massive head into my chubby hands.

Just as I'm asking myself over and over, *What have ya done, ya fuckin' arsehole?* sleeping beauty stirs to life beside me. Now, as I've said, by no means would I describe myself as attractive, in fact instead of taking after my mam or dad in the looks department, I took after our dog and he was a boxer! I was told growing up that the only way the dog would play with me was if my mam tied a piece of steak around my neck first. But in comparison to this guy beside me I was stunning! This fella made your man out of the *Nightmare on Elm Street* films look like Brad Pitt!

'Story, bud?' he drools, 'did ya get a whack?'

I assumed he meant did I receive a sentence and not a spanking over the skinny knee of Judge 'Baba' – which our friendly Judge just might like – so I crack into my 'hard man', in other words 'shit head', mode and reply, 'Yeah bud, three and a half year.'

'No way, yeah?' he replies, 'drugs, buddy, was it?'

'Yeah, mate', I reply. 'Few pillows of grass.'

He studiously absorbs my posture and asks, 'First time locked up pal?'

'Yeah,' I reply, a bit more sheepishly.

'Joy's a fuckin' kip,' he begins screaming. *'Full to the fuckin' top with giant poxy cockroaches, fuckin' huge ones! Fuckin' food is muck. Bad auld jail, man, havin' to slop out an' all! I'd fuckin' hate to be goin' there! Now, my first night in the Joy? Battered I was. Ha ha ha! Owed some bloke a score or somethin'!'*

He has roared this at me without taking a breath, which was actually quite fuckin' impressive, but *now* my pot hairs are tingling. The *fear* is taking over.

'I'm in the Midlands bud, yeah?' He seems to have calmed down a little, thank fuck! 'Grand auld jail it is, yeah? School is deadly an' all. *Tomorrow mornin' go to the poxy fuckin' governor* ...' Uh oh, Mad Bastard is back, '... *in that poxy kip and tell him you want the Midlands*, grand auld jail it is.'

Me head is fuckin' racing, a million insane thoughts bombarding around my brain like a pinball, when my new 'guidance counsellor' hits me with, 'Are ya stuffed?'

Now, this throws me a bit, but I did think it nice of him to enquire after my food intake, so gobshite here replies, in a hard man's voice of course, 'I had a bit of fuckin' brekkie, but ya know yourself I couldn't ...'

'No, ya fuckin eejit,' he laughs, 'is your arse stuffed with *drugs*!'

I start to laugh, which in turn makes him go into fuckin' convulsions, this strange, high pitched shriek bellowing from his toothless mouth every three seconds or so. 'No, mate,' I reply, 'I couldn't be doin' that, that's an exit, not an entrance!'

'Well,' he says, 'I'm about to lose what's inside me ... argghh ... ahhh ... *jaysus* ... ahhh ... here, keep your eye on the hatch there bud, will ya?'

Before I can say, 'Are you for fuckin' real?' his black Nike tracksuit bottoms are around his ankles and there are noises coming from him that are reminiscent of the auld German porn VHS cassette you used to find in your da's toolbox in the shed! Next thing I know, he's vertical, smiling from ear to ear, holding what just looks like a massive lump of excrement in his hands.

'Any skins, bro?' he enquires, to which I duly reply with a curt *no*!

'Might have some here,' he continues as he rummages around the pockets of his tracksuit bottoms. 'I'll get an auld J (joint) goin', yeah? Sort ya out bud.'

As I've said before, I don't smoke the stuff, but I most certainly don't want a joint of fuckin' shite! 'No thanks, man, I'm alri',' comes my reply.

'No bother, bud, sure I might leave it meself, I should be out of here soon enou',' and with that, there is a rattle of keys in our lock. My new BFF shoves his hands containing whatever it fuckin' is down the back of his tracksuit bottoms. He then does whatever it is he needs to do, drops into a sitting position, and remains there with a massive, innocent, toothless smile etched across his face.

An officer opens the door, waves his hands in front of his face to swat away the stench and says, 'William, are ya right?'

William, or Wills as I like to call him now that we've shared this magical moment together, slowly gets to his feet, readjusts himself and says, 'No bother officer. Here bud?' He turns to me as he's walking out of my life, probably forever, and with a twinkle in his crazy eye he says, 'Remember, come to the Midlands yeah? The Joy's a fuckin' kip. See ya after bud, yeah?' And with that he's gone, and I'm left sitting in the stench as the *fear* begins its decent from my frontal lobes down towards my toe nails. Shittin' I am, excuse the pun.

Chapter 2

On the Bus

I was left on my own for what seemed like an eternity, the fear now truly choking my subconscious into submission. My mind was in the middle of another horrible scenario, played out like that of a true Hitchcock classic, when I was jolted back to reality by the sound of keys rattling in the blood red cell door.

'You right, Gary?' came the words from a friendly, grey-haired officer, who looked like he has been in this job since he could walk. *(Not really, I thought, for you see there has been a heinous mistake, one which this Court should feel* really *embarrassed over, for you see, I'm fuckin' innocent!*)

'Yes, guard,' I reply, noting a slight quiver in my voice.

'I'm not a guard son, and don't go calling the officers in The Joy guard neither. We're officers son.'

'Sorry ... thanks,' I reply.

'Ah, you're grand. Now, put the hands together Gary, I have to put the auld bracelets on in case ya try to do a runner!'

I raise both my hands, and realise for the first time that I'm trembling, a small bead of sweat beginning its descent from my hairline.

'First time locked up son?' asks the officer in a real aul' Dub's voice.

'Yeah,' I reply.

'You'll be grand son, don't worry. Keep the head down and just get on with things,' he says in a calming tone. There is something about this officer ... a warmth. I wouldn't insult him by guessing his age, but his grey hair and worn face tell the tale of a man who has seen a lot of comings and goings in this place, so I find some comfort in his words. He clamps both of my wrists with the cuffs, taking care not to make them too uncomfortable, and then leads me down a brilliant white corridor, which after several twists and turns brings us into a large open area where the prison vans await ... wait to bring the cattle to the *slaughterhouse*... Jaysus, my head is racing with crazy, and most probably ridiculous, thoughts.

I'm led on to a bus. Now I must point out that this is not the 19a bringing you into town (although the stench of urine is somewhat similar), no, it's a fuckin' mobile prison, a cell on wheels. It is depressingly grey inside, with very little light. Small doors line its corridors, both left and right, each a holding compartment for its unwilling passengers. 'You're holdin' us up there mate,' jokes an officer behind me. *Wanker*, I think to myself.

I'm put into the second last 'cell' on the left. It's smaller than a toilet cubical, but again the smell is the same! As soon as the officer slams and locks the door (which I don't quite get, as I'm still fuckin' cuffed, not even Paul fuckin' Daniels could escape this one) the uncontrollable shaking starts. A chill has entered my body and is having its fun with me. I look to my left to see if I can spot anyone else, but all I see is the torso of the officer, as he turns and heads back up the bus. Then, silence. An eerie, deathly silence. I look out the window to my right, but see nothing but black. The silence seems to linger forever before it's broken by a low murmur as the officers chat among themselves. Then ... *bang*! A door slams shut, shuffling of feet, a key rattled into the ignition, the engine turns over and ...

'*Here, is there any young wans on this yolk?*' roars a male voice from one of the cells.

There is a slight pause, then, 'Yeah! There's two of us!' comes the reply of a female.

Then another male voice, '*Here*, anyone got a light?'

'Yeah,' replies yet another male, 'I'll get this *wanker* of a screw to open me up and give it to ya, yeah? *Officer, Offficer* ... give your man a light here, will ya?'

Fuckin' hell! It's like my fellow passengers were all hot-wired to the bus's engine, and when the officer turned the key they all sparked into life.

'Here, young wan, what's your name?' asks the first voice I heard.

'Which fuckin' one of us?' comes the sarcastic reply.

'Whichever one of yas is goin' to write me an auld filthy letter,' answers our Don Wan.

This brings half a grin to my face.

'Amy,' shouts out one of the female passengers.

'Here, Amy? I'm John, yeah? Are ya good lookin' Amy?' John seems to be in full swing now.

'I'm fuckin' massive,' laughs Amy.

'Ah, I'm not into fat birds Amy!' says John. Now I'm laughing.

'Fuck off ya sap, I meant massive gorgeous!' counters Amy.

'Good stuff Amy,' says John. 'Will ya write to me?'

'I might,' says Amy, trying to play hard to get.

'Have ya a fella?' asks the ever-so-subtle John.

'Yeah, but fuck him, poxy prick never even showed up in the court today. Bleedin' pox!'

'Ah, did he not Amy? I'd never do that to ya chicken,' replies John.

Amy's laugh begins to ring through the dank bus. I have to say, John and Amy's blossoming romance is a welcome distraction.

'Where ya from Amy?' asks John.

'Finglas,' says Amy proudly.

'Yeah?' asks John, 'Do ya know Debbie O'Nail?'

'Yeah I do ... fuckin' auld bitch she is!' The whole bus erupts into laughter at this response from Amy.

'That's me ex,' says John through stifled laughter.

There is a pause then. 'Oh ... are you Johnner Smith?' You can sense the anticipation in Amy's voice.

'The very one Amy,' replies an extremely proud Johnner.

'Ohhhh ... you're a bleedin' ride,' gushes Amy. Again the laughter erupts, this time accompanied by wolf whistles.

'I'd say you're fuckin' gorgeous Amy, are ya?' asks Johnner, hopefully.

'Well I'd get plastic surgery to look whatever way you wanted me to Johnner!' she replied. This time I even think I hear the officers joining in with our chorus of laughter, as one of them opens the cell facing me and takes a lighter for one of the other lads.

'Here officer, will ya throw on the aul' radio?' asks the recipient of the lighter. And before you could say 'prison romance' the silky smooth bass line from 'Sexy Thing' is flowing from the bus speakers.

'There's your song now Johnner,' shouts Amy.

'You're mad,' replies Johnner.

'I'm mad about you,' counters Amy.

This has been so distracting that when I look out the window to my right and see the Mater Hospital, I'm shocked to realise we've arrived.

'78876555, that's me prison number Johnner, yeah? Write to me now, won't ya?' shouts Amy.

Johnner suddenly replies with an uncharacteristic and curt, 'Yep.'

The bus comes to a stuttering halt as an officer comes down to unlock Amy's 'cell' door, and the door of another female. 'I'll write ya filthy replies Johnner ... so make sure ya write!' gushes Amy.

Johnner has gone very quiet all of a sudden. Amy begins her final goodbyes, and as her voice becomes more faint, Johnner pipes up, '*Jaysus*! Very fuckin' clingy lads, wha? Fuck that! It would be like havin' me mott fuckin' write to me!'

The remainder of us again join together in laughter. Noel Gallagher is telling Sally she can wait on the radio, as the bus comes to a stop for a second, final time. We have arrived at my new home for the next three and a half years ... *The Joy*!

Chapter 3

Cunny

We're taken off the snow-white prison bus one by one, as dusk begins to settle across the cool Dublin sky. We're then ushered into a port-a-cabin, four of us in total, with me the last in. What strikes me about the other three lads is that they all seem quite young. Nobody is saying anything, a real uncomfortable silence. A middle-aged officer, with bright orange hair, is taking our details and issuing out our prison numbers, all except for the guy just in front of me. He's been asked his name.

'Ya know me fuckin' name officer,' comes the response from this extremely confident young man.

'*Name*?' asks the impatient officer again, his face now glowing, kind of matching his hair actually.

'John Smith, yeah?' So this is the bus Adonis, the romantic Johnner. He's not bad in fairness. Ah, here, wait just one second, I'm not even in the main building and already I'm starting to find an attraction to the lads. Cop on now Gary!

Johnner is processed and taken away, and now it's my turn. I give off the air of a total confident super-fuckin'-hero, but inside I'm shittin'. After I give my name and date of birth, the orange-haired officer says, '77615, Gary. Memorise that, as that's you for the foreseeable future.' And with that I'm led by another, younger officer through a massive old, rusting, arched door that brings us on to a corridor inside the main building of Mountjoy.

The first thing that hits you is the stench! I can safely say that this aroma would be somewhat similar to Bigfoot's arse if he'd just spent the day on the Guinness, finishing up with a curry. As the officer leads me down a small flight of stairs of faded white walls and dark blue skirtings, I ask him for the time. 'Just after half seven,' he replies in a thick country accent, maybe Kerry. 'Don't worry,' he continues, 'the palace is on lockdown so they can't get at ya until the morning!' He laughs a cold, sinister laugh reminiscent of a haunting Vincent Price. A right comedian this fella is all right, fuckin' prick.

At the bottom of the stairs we turn right onto a narrow white corridor which leads to Mountjoy's reception area. Ahead of me is Johnner. 'Alri' Mr. Burke, ya auld bollox?' asks Johnner to a bald officer with crimson red cheeks.

'Well, how was court today Smith?' Officer Burke offers as a reply.

'None of your fuckin' business,' laughs Johnner, 'but let's just say we'll be seein' a bit more of each other for the foreseeable, now let us back up will ya? I'm fuckin' starvin'.'

Johnner is strip-searched and then asked to sit on The Boss, a massive grey and white chair that can detect phones concealed up one's bum! He's then sent into an adjoining room, and I'm left with Mr. Burke and two younger officers, who are not paying anybody any attention as they discuss Wayne Rooney's future with Man. United.

'Name?' asks Mr Burke.

'Gary Cunningham,' I reply, again noting the quiver in my voice.

'Ah, yes, 77615, Mr. Cunningham. Well, welcome to Hotel du Joy. Have you anything on ya or in ya that ya shouldn't?' Again with the stuffing of one's arsehole! I wonder how Will from the holding cell back at the court is doing?

'No officer, just this chain 'round me neck.'

'I'd leave that here with us son, it'll be put into your property. They'd fuckin' whip that off ya in no time,' replies Mr. Burke. What is it with everyone trying to put the fear of God into me? 'Right Gary, strip off everything, cacks, socks, the lot. We'll keep your clothing here.'

Straight away my mind goes into overdrive as I begin to picture myself being led through the wings of Mountjoy *naked*! I enter a cubical and begin to strip, as the two football fanatic officers watch. Footy Fanatic Officer Number One tells me to hold up my arms. He then asks me to turn around and bend over. Now I've been in relationships with females who have never seen me in this position and what happened next? Well, let's just say his fuckin' gloved hand was freezing, enough said! I'm then turned back to face the officer who concludes his rather intrusive search.

Footy Fanatic Officer Number Two then takes the lead, and asks me my measurements, right down to my shoe size. I can feel the faded yellow walls and low ceiling of the reception area grow closer to me as I realise I'm bollock naked in front of three men as they ask what fuckin' shoe size I take! I'm then instructed to turn right and go in to have a shower.

As I nervously make my way toward the brilliantly white shower room, Footy Fanatic Officer Number One hands me a pillow case with everything in it. I mean it's incredible. It's like they've just handed me Dunnes Stores in a fuckin' pillow case! I find an ice cold blue bench and set the pillow case down and start to unpack. First come the clothes. Prison issue blood red jumper, blood red shirt, white vest, fake looking denim jeans, two pairs of lemon socks, two pairs of blindingly bright Y-fronts and a pair of runners, without laces, that I'd say came straight off the top shelf of Fred's Fashions. Next there is a see-through bag with toiletries – comb, soap, toothpaste, toothbrush – then a hand towel, a normal sized towel, a bed sheet plus a 1970s-designed duvet cover, all in a fuckin' pillow case!

I shower, dry off, and put on the prison jocks. My Jaysus, they make Bridget Jones's cacks look like expensive French knickers! Next are the lemon socks, then the vest, then the red shirt, the red jumper, the fake ass jeans and finally the ridiculous runners. All I'm missing is a fuckin' neon sign 'round my neck with New Gobshite flashing on it.

I head back into Mr. Burke who hits me with an important question. 'Are ya fighting with anyone, Gary?'

To which idiot here replies, 'Yeah, me and me brother went at it this mornin', though I can't blame him, he's worried 'bout me ma, as am I, and deep down I know he's worried 'bout me too. We're close, ya know? But it did get hairy, Mr. Burke, there was nearly digs! Sure I ...'

Mr. Burke is in convulsions of laughter, his belly shaking like Santy's. 'As much as I'd love to hear more about your current domestic situation, what I meant was, are you fighting with anyone in here, or outside. Are you gangland?'

I reckon it's safe to say that the colour of my face matched my brand new jumper as I offered, 'Sorry officer, no I'm not officer.'

He's still laughing as he says, 'Keep me up to date on the latest comings and goings with the brother though, yeah?' I feel like a fuckin' sap! Mr. Burke composes himself, and asks, 'Do ya know anyone in here?'

As it turns out I did. Word was sent in to a bloke locked up in here to keep his eye out for me. This man is like a member of my family. I haven't seen him in a couple of months, but we're like brothers and I know he'll have my back. 'Peter Cunning,' I answer.

'Cunny the painter?' replies Burke.

This sounds right. Firstly, Peter's nickname has always been Cunny, and secondly he, like myself, is a painter and decorator. In fact, he served his time under my late father. 'Eh, yeah, I'd say that's him alri' Mr. Burke.'

'Right,' says Burke, 'I'll go check that out, see if he'll take you up. You park your pretty little hole down in there,' and with that he undoes the lock on a door which leads into a large holding cell, reminiscent of a large football changing room, with its white walls and dark-coloured benches, although not many football changing rooms have graffiti of this nature!

Inside are the other two young lads who came on the same bus as me, both deathly quiet, their heads facing the cold grey floor. As I take a seat on one of the benches, I look up to see Johnner at the other end of the holding cell, talking away to some other bloke who is in the middle of doing push-ups! 'Yeah, I'm goin' back the gym meself tomorrow, yeah? Just been flat out on the Zim Zims lately,' says Johnner.

The 'press up man' jumps to his feet and stands towering over Johnner with his massive muscular frame bulging, his eyes pinged in his head, his jaw like a fuckin' typewriter. 'Ah, yeah, yeah, I know what ya mean, yeah, deadly, yeah.' As he says this, he stretches his arms above his head, and his body shudders as a rush runs through him. 'These yolks (Ecstasy tablets) are fuckin' rapid!' he says as he drops back down to continue with his push-ups.

'Ya mad bastard,' laughs Johnner.

Neither have noticed me, which suits me down to the ground, as the lock turns and the door opens to reveal Mr. Burke. He looks at me and says, 'Yeah, Cunny is goin' to take ya up on to his floor, let's go.'

He leads me out of the cell, out of reception, and down a long narrow white corridor. We arrive at narrow ascending stairs, and as I step up I can see that it leads to Mountjoy's famous Circle. Its high-domed ceiling seems endless, and as your eyes follow the cages down, you can feel the history of this ancient jail whisper in your ears.

There is an officer's station in the middle of The Circle, bright brown in colour, and busy as a beehive. All of Mountjoy's wings feed off from The Circle, so as I come up the stairs to my immediate left is C Wing, which seemed closed off for construction, and a little further left is D Wing. To my immediate right is B Wing, and a little further right, A Wing. I am engulfed by the sensory overload that is taking place before my eyes. The Circle seems so bright, and the wings so dark and gloomy in comparison.

I am led toward D Wing, with its battleship grey walls and dark blue skirtings and door surrounds. As the place is on lockdown it's quiet, with the odd inaudible shout coming from the cells. As we pass through the first blue gates, I notice above a door on my right the word Kitchen in red stencil. How important that place would become for me! We go through a second blue gate and we are now on D1. Each wing in Mountjoy has three landings. In the centre of these landings are stairs, which are caged in right around. Above me is mesh, and on either side are the landings, all lined with dark blue cell doors. We head for the stairs and as I look above me to my left, I see Cunny on the next landing, D2. He's wearing a huge smile on his face and has his arms out-stretched. God, am I glad to see him!

Me and Cunny embrace on the landing of D2. 'I'll leave him with you so, Cunny,' says Mr. Burke, as he turns and heads back to reception.

I follow Cunny into his cell, its dark grey walls brought to life with pictures of his wonderful partner and his kids and, of course, Cheryl Cole! The cell consists of a steel-framed bed on the right with a small MDF locker beside it. There is a small wooden table on the left accompanied by a light grey plastic chair. A small portable TV is sitting on a corner shelf showing a Champions League game involving Chelsea. I turn to look at Cunny. I can see he's been working out, his arms are the size of my fuckin' legs and he hasn't lost that massive, warming smile. He's a tall lad, over six foot, and is still rocking the same tight, brushed forward, dark brown hairstyle that he's had since his fuckin' confo!

An officer appears at the cell door. 'Right lads, we done?' asks the young, geeky-looking officer.

'That's us,' replies Cunny.

With that the officer pulls closed the cell door. It is such a strange feeling when you first get locked into a cell. You immediately realise that you are now on their time. A sense of foreboding washes over you and stays with you for a couple of days. It's very unnerving.

'Jaysus, Gar, how are ya?' beams Cunny.

'I've been better, Cunny,' I reply.

'So what did ya get?' he asks through that massive smile of his.

'Three and a half year,' says I.

Cunny has begun pulling a blue plastic mattress from under his bed. He turns to me and says, 'That'll fuckin' fly for ya, once ya do it right and keep yourself busy all the time. Every day this kip will challenge you and push you to your limits so it is up to you to do all you can to survive and that process starts now!'

It's not my place to say what anybody else is in prison for, but I can tell you that Cunny received five years a couple of months before I did. He is one of the nicest, kindest blokes you could ever meet, but he had a massive addiction to cocaine, which led him to do stupid, stupid things in order to feed his habit. But you can see he's clean now, in fact I've never seen him look so healthy.

'Have ya a smoke?' I ask.

'Yeah, work away, me dust is on the table,' he kindly offers.

'Dust?' I ask confused.

'Me tobacco, ya gobshite,' laughs Cunny.

Bollox! I haven't a fuckin' clue how to roll. 'Eh, can ya roll me one buddy?' I ask coyly.

'No bother me auld pal,' laughs Cunny, 'but ya better get to practicing. Dust is a lot cheaper than buying a box of smokes, or straights as they're called in here, and money is fuckin' tight. Plus you only get to the shop once a week. So start rollin', rollin', rollin',' he says, as he breaks into a raucous rendition of 'Rawhide'.

I accept his perfectly rolled smoke and lay down on the deep blue mattress. I whip out my funky '70s-inspired duvet cover, although I doubt I'll need it as it's like a sauna in this cell. 'What's the story with the fuckin' heat, bud?' I ask.

'That's on 24/7, fuckin' 365 days of the year, my friend,' laughs Cunny. 'Listen, Gar, I'll get ya sorted in this place tomorrow for a job and what have ya, but for now you should try to sleep, ya look bolloxed!' I felt bolloxed all of a sudden, my eventful day finally catching up to me. 'We're up early, so try to get a kip into ya. It's great to see ya, Gar.'

'And you Cunny,' I reply, 'I just wish this was a sleep-over in one of our gaffs, like the old days, and not in this kip.'

'Don't worry,' comes Cunny's sleepy reply, 'you'll be grand.'

I rest my head on the mattress. There is a radio blaring some 1000 BPM dance track coming from one of the cells, and every now and then you'll hear lads shouting to each other. After a while the din of locked up prisoners kind of becomes second nature, like that of a noisy neighbour. I find that I am beginning to drift away, when all of a sudden that scrawny little wanker Will from the holding cell back at the courthouse pops into my head: *'Full of fuckin' cockroaches!'* Well, fuck him anyway! Cunny is now snoring his head off, while I lay dead still wide awake readying myself for the attack of the giant cockroach!

Chapter 4

BREAKFAST

The roaches never came, but thankfully the Sandman did. I was dragged from my slumber by the rattling of keys and the throwing open of the cell door. A fresh-faced, red haired officer, who would kind of remind you of the ex-Ireland football player/manager Steve Staunton, stood at the foot of my mattress. 'Ah, sure, you're after settling right in aren't ya?' he said in a half Dublin, half some other part of Ireland accent.

'Fuck off, Mr Dannon,' grunts Cunny.

'Now, now, Cunny, I'm not here for you. It's breakfast time, Gary. And after that you have to go on the Governor's parade, so make sure you are in the prison issue clothing.'

'I'll sort him out, Mr Dannon,' says a slightly more alert Cunny. All the while I haven't a fuckin' clue what is going on, so I just nod.

'Grand so,' says the officer over his shoulder as he goes to unlock the next cell.

The main thing that strikes you on your first morning waking up in this shithole is the noise. Shouting, banging, more shouting, crazy! I rise up from my mattress wearing the prison vest and jocks, and this stirs Cunny into life. 'Ha ha ha, the fuckin' state of ya, looks like a big nappy on ya!'

'Fuck off Cunny,' says I, laughing.

'Right, come on and we get our breakfast,' starts Cunny. 'Now, look, I have clothes boxed off for ya, as in "normal clothes", some are mine, some the lads donated to ya, just till ya get your own. But you're not meant to have your own till after your first visit, and you've to see the Governor this morning, so just lash on the prison chats for now.'

'Prison chats?' I ask, slightly bewildered.

'Yeah chats is, well, fuckin' everything really, like, "Here, check out me new Nike chats", or "I was caught in a Volvo chat",' explains Cunny. 'Now, in the prison chats,' he continues, 'everyone knows you're new, and some will want to know if ya came in stuffed. Just tell 'em no – no big conversation, just fuckin' *no*!'

We step out of the cell and it's as busy as a train station at peak time. There are fellas on each of the three landings roaring at each other: 'Here Jay, *Jay*, get fuckin' Jay will ya,' or, 'Here Snotz, where's the fuckin' dust ya owe me?' The smell is inhuman as lads bring their chamber pots to be slopped out. Daylight streaks down through the barred windows way above our heads. It's such a surreal feeling knowing that you are now a cog on this massive wheel, and from right this moment you have got to adapt to your surroundings and try to get on with it. Prison does not give you the time to adjust and prepare, it just kicks you right in the back of the head straight away.

I put my head down and walk closely behind Cunny. The landings are narrow so there's a lot of moving out of people's way as they too try to navigate a path. It is so unnerving as your mind begins to play games with you. Who am I walking past here? What is he in for? I think I know that fella's face, don't make eye contact! We head down the caged stairs onto D1 ('the ones') where the food server is. As we approach the queue, I look over the counter and see an officer in kitchen whites, a tall, burly man with a huge white moustache, and a prisoner, also in kitchen whites. 'Kitchen is a good job, Gar,' explains Cunny, 'or ya could get a job as a painter just, eh not with me, sure I'll explain that later but I'm gonna try get ya into the kitchen. I worked there when I got in here first.'

'I've a pain in me bollox paintin', Cunny,' says I. 'Been doin' it all me life. While I'm here I wanna try to learn, ya know? Absorb some new skills and information.'

As we get closer to the top of the queue, the prisoner working behind the server addresses Cunny. 'Is this your mate you were tellin' me about?' he asks while tossing his head in my direction.

'Yeah, Fitzer, this is Gary, gonna try to get him sorted in the kitchen,' replies Cunny.

'Top of the morning to ya, Ted,' barks Fitzer to me, in a put-on Culchie accent. 'Welcome to The Joy.' The first thing that strikes you about Fitzer is his good nature. He's about six foot, stocky, with tight fair hair, and he's kind of dancing as he serves the lads their breakfast! You can tell he's a bit of a character, but you can also feel the positivity radiating from him. Little did I know, on that first morning meeting him, how important he would become in my life.

'What'll ya have, Gar?' asks Fitzer, 'the rashers and sausages will be ready in a few.'

'Really?' replies gobshite here.

Everyone begins to laugh, with the odd 'fuckin' brand new he is' getting thrown in for good measure. 'Weetabix please bud,' I say whilst taking a massive 'redner'.

Fitzer is in stitches as he hands me a bowl with a small packet of Weetabix in it. 'See ya later, boys, oh, and Gar, come up to the kitchen later, yeah? I'll put in a good word for ya,' laughs Fitzer.

'Nice one, Fitzer,' I reply as I take my bowl and some milk and exit the queue.

Just as I walk away this thing approaches me looking like the Hunchback of Mountjoy. 'Alri'?' he slurs, 'did ya bring anythin' in with ya?'

'No bud,' comes my reply.

'Ya fuckin' did, ya lyin' pox,' he replies angrily.

'Fuck off 5 Cent, will ya?' says Cunny.

'Ah, is he with you Cunny? Sorry bud, sorry Cunny, yeah?' and with that Quasimodo turns and walks straight into a fuckin man-mountain, a foreign lad. I mean this chap had muscles *on* muscles.

'Watch yourself, ya Polish prick,' says a rather brave 5 Cent.

Smack! Such a fuckin' dig the Polish lad gives him. Poor auld 5 Cent folds like a nervous poker player. There is a roar. 'Go *on* the big fella.'

'Fuck sake, did ya see that Cunny?' I ask excitedly.

'Yeah, but it's fuck all to do with us. Don't get involved. Even look at the wrong person and ya risk gettin' a stripe.'

'A stripe?' says I.

'Yeah, a dirty big cut down the side of your face is common practice in here.'

We make our way back up onto 'the twos' and into Cunny's cell. 'It's not always like that, Gar, in fact it's very seldom ya see any fights, but they do happen. Just worry about you and your business. Keep your head down and you'll be fine. This place is filled with some of the hardest fuckin' headbangers you are ever likely to come across, and if you want trouble you won't have to wait too long to find it, it will come and find you!' It's day one, and although I know Cunny is not saying any of this to scare me, already I am shittin'.

'They're gonna bang us out now (lock us in the cell),' he continues, 'for an hour, then it's Governor Time for you. Just be honest with him. Tell him you want to work, do the school etc., and you will be no trouble. You'll be grand with him, he's all right. Then, when ya get back, I'll sort ya with clothes and, eh, we'll have a chat about my painting job and this cell!' He says all this with that 'cheeky fucker' smile forming across his face. What's me auld mate up to?

Chapter 5

New Friends

When the officer opens up our cell again, I head back down to D1, past the food server and, facing the aforementioned door with Kitchen written above it, I arrive at the Governor's Parade, which isn't much of a parade as it's just me. I'm brought into the office (a cell which has been converted) and Governor Farrell, a tall, haggard-looking, grey-haired man in a grey suit, and an officer with a hat on resembling a drill instructor we see so often in American war movies, are sitting waiting. 'Name and prison number?' asks the man in the hat.

'Gary Cunningham, 77615, officer,' I reply.

'It's Chief, not officer!' comes the stern reply.

'Sorry Chief,' I say sheepishly.

'How long did you get Gary?' asks the Governor, as he studies his computer screen, not making any eye contact.

'Three and a half years, Governor,' I say.

'Drugs was it, Gary?' he enquires.

'Yes Governor,' says I.

'*Well I bet ya feel like a silly little prick now!*' roars the Governor.

'I sure do,' I reply.

'Look,' says the Governor, 'it's now up to you how the time that you have to spend here goes. There is an excellent school available to you, and, there are plenty of jobs on offer. Now, you don't have to do either, but I wouldn't recommend that!'

'I've worked all my life, Governor,' I say, 'and I'm not one to sit on my backside' (I'm being polite so I don't say 'hole'... I'm even using my posh voice!) 'so I intend to take full advantage of all amenities available to me, in fact, I'm hoping to start in the kitchen.'

'Good to hear Gary,' replies the Governor. He then asks, 'What did you work at on the outside?'

'I was a painter and decorator, Governor,' comes my reply.

His face lights up like a Christmas tree. 'Really?' he says with a massive grin plastered on to his face. 'Well, then, I'm going to have you painting, Gary.'

'Thank you Governor,' I reply, 'but I've been painting all my working life. I'd much rather spend this time doing, and maybe learning, something new.'

'Well ... go see if you can get a start in the kitchen,' he says, a little wounded, 'but if I want you painting then *that's* what you will be doing! Anything you want to ask?'

There was about a trillion things I wanted to ask, like maybe could he see to it that I get released ... *today* ... but instead I just reply with, 'No, thank you Governor.'

'Right Gary, I hope we never have to talk again. Good day.'

Well that wasn't too bad Gar, now was it? I leave and start heading back up to Cunny's cell, feeling like every eye is boring into my soul as I rock my wonderfully chic Mountjoy attire. You can almost feel the tension coursing through the air as I navigate a course back up to D2. Cunny is sitting having coffee with some bloke, both of them wearing workers' clothes (wine overall bottoms, old t-shirts).

'This is FunTime,' a cheeky lookin' fucker, and when he smiled, it showed his fanged teeth, 'me and him are the painters here ... we have this place sewn up!' They both start to laugh and before I can answer, Cunny says, 'Right, your new chats are on the bed. Get them fuckin' prison yolks off ya. FunTime is after getting ya a pair of runners.'

'Cheers FunTime,' I say.

'Not a bother me auld pal, any friend of Cunny's is a friend of mine. If you're stuck for anything just say the word ... ah, here comes Handsome. What's the story buddy?'

Handsome is the prisoner who has just walked in, small in height, with perfectly white teeth and immaculately combed black hair. 'All right bud, they don't call me Handsome for nothing,' he says as he turns to me, which makes us all laugh. 'I'm the cleaner here on D2 yeah? Anything I can do for ya just let me know. Here, Cunny, where's your complan ... I'm poxy starvin'!' Handsome comes across as a real character but straight away you can tell he's a nice bloke, as is FunTime.

'Right,' says Cunny, 'I have a surprise for ya Gar, turn around.' I rotate to see No. 2 standing behind me. No. 2 is a stocky, bald, intimidating lad, with a full beard and a menacing grin. He is from our area and only called No. 2 because the lad known as No. 1 is just a little bit more of a mad fucker! I know this guy's mam, dad and brothers, all fuckin' sound.

'Fuck sake, Gary, the whole estate is in here now!' says No. 2 as his smile grows wider.

'No. 2, ya auld bollox, I didn't know you were in here?'

'Yeah,' he says, 'got two year.'

We hug ... like ... well, like men do, and Cunny says, 'Right get dressed and we'll go get ya that job in the kitchen. You and No. 2 can catch up later ... sure yas will be banged out together!' He kind of throws this comment at me like he's embarrassed. I don't bring it up, I just get dressed into my 'normal' clothes. So far, Fitzer (from the kitchen), FunTime, Handsome, No. 2, and of course Cunny have alleviated my fears a little, and made me feel welcome. Maybe it will be okay. After all, there is safety in numbers!

Chapter 6

THE KITCHEN

I get dressed into a pair of dark grey, knee-length shorts and a white Adidas T-shirt and immediately feel rejuvenated. No longer do I have the 'fresh meat' look about me. I ready myself to head down to the kitchen to try to bag myself a job, when Cunny calls me back into his cell for a chat!

'Right, Gar, look, ya know you're me mate an' all, and I'll always do *anythin'* for ya ...'

'But?' I say.

'Well, ya can't stay in me cell tonight,' he starts, 'but I'm after gettin ya sorted ... you're doublin' up' with No. 2. Now I know ya think I'm a prick but let me explain,' he says, kind of embarrassed. 'Ya see,' he continues, 'it's nothin' personal ... well it kinda is ... but it's not your fault'...

'Just spit it out Cunny,' I say laughing.

'Well, my cell door is left open, because I'm a painter ... I don't get banged out ... as I work for a few hours along with the cleaners while the rest of yas are locked up. Someone has to keep this kip fresh and clean! And this luxury of being out with just a select few, albeit only for a couple of hours, is fuckin' deadly! But with you in me cell, well, they will bang me out so ...'

'Say no more, Cunny,' I say reassuringly, 'it's no bother, but know this, I'm gonna tell everyone that ya fucked me out into the Big Bad Joy on me own after only one night!'

'Ah fuck off Gary,' he says followed by a playful dig in the arm then, 'right, since you're been so understandin' an all, ya can't come painting with me neither!'

'Jaysus, Cunny, don't go out of your way for me or anything,' I say sarcastically.

'Ah, it's not like that ya bollox ... well it kinda is like that ... but ya see me and FunTime have this place sewn up. We get to go all over the jail painting, but there's only room for two. FunTime is hopin' to get a move to Shelton Abbey (one of two open prisons in Ireland, the other being Loughan House) so when he does, if ya still wanna paint ...'

'Ah, so you'll take me on then Cunny, will ya?' I say sarcastically. Again we're united in laughter. 'No worries,' I say, 'sure I'm off down the kitchen to see if I can get a start there. I'll pack me pillow case when I get back, might be best if you're not here ... too painful sayin' goodbye after all we've been through ...'

'Fuck off ya bleedin' sap,' laughs Cunny.

'Right, I'm off to become a kitchen worker. See ya later ya back-stabbin' prick.' I say this with a laugh over my shoulder as I walk out of his cell, his own laughter ringing in my ears.

I travel the short trip from D2 down onto the 'ones' where the entrance to the kitchen is located. I approach the blue-barred gate and catch a quick glimpse of Fitzer, the lad from breakfast this morning, as he's bouncing along singing what sounds like a song from The Script (bloody good singer too!).

'Fitzer,' I shout.

'Ah, good man Gary ... hang on ... officer... *officer... gate*!' he roars. 'Hang on bud,' continues Fitzer, 'he's comin'... ah, here he is now. This is the fella I was tellin' ya about this mornin', Mr. Haycorn.'

Mr. Haycorn is a colossal man, with a crew cut hairstyle making him look like he's come straight from an army roll call.

'Howya young man, you looking to start in the kitchen?' he asks in a booming, flat, Dublin voice.

'I'd love a start officer,' I say.

'Right, are ya in here for violence?' he enquires.

'No Mr. Haycorn, drugs.'

'Are ya a messin' little bollox?' he asks with a cheeky grin.

'No, Mr. Haycorn, I'll work me bollox off for ya.' I say. 'I just wanna get me head down and get on with things.'

'Name?' he asks.

'Gary Cunningham,' I reply.

'Right,' says Mr. Haycorn, 'come on in, interview over, you're hired!'

That was pretty painless. He unlocks the large gate and ushers me in. The Kitchen in The Joy is huge and is what I assume any large industrial kitchen looks like – white ceilings, white walls, with a wide range of ovens/hobs, food preparation areas etc. There is also a Tunnel Wash room, a small canteen for ourselves, and toilets with showers, which I'll soon find out is a major perk of working in the kitchen.

'Fitzer, get him sorted with whites (a white t-shirt, with Kitchen printed in red on the back, and a pair of snow white trousers) and a pair of steel toe boots. Let him have a cup of tea or whatever, introduce him to the lads, then get him started on the pot wash,' orders Mr. Haycorn.

'No bother Mr. Haycorn, come on Gar, this way,' says Fitzer as he brings me into a tiny tearoom, our canteen. Inside sit five lads, who in time will become five of the greatest blokes I've ever met. 'Right boys, this is Gary. Gary this is The Little Fella, Beasey, BC, Budgie, and Natoman. I didn't know it at the time, but these fellas, along with Fitzer and another guy who comes along later in this story, help change my life forever and become lads I can hold my head up with pride and call my friends.

'Howya, lads,' I say kind of nervously, if I'm honest.

'Alri' Gar, welcome to The Joy's kitchen, or as we like to call it, *the fuckin' kip*,' says The Little Fella, so named because he is ... well ... vertically challenged! Approaching the wrong side of 40, The Little Fella has a real deadpan voice, which makes him even funnier, as does his bald patch which somehow assists in highlighting his funny nature!

Beasey, who is the size of the Incredible Hulk, with a completely bald head and a massive body-builder frame, speaks next, 'Howya Gary, you'll be grand in here, anything I can help with just say the word.' You can tell this guy has got a heart of gold. A true gent!

Next it's Natoman, a half-caste lad with stylish facial hair and tattoos strewn across his arms. 'Story, bud? Natoman yeah? I'm lovin' your J.P.,' he says in a north Dublin accent. My J.P.? Now, I'm confused, but don't want to make a show of myself, so I just say 'Thanks,' but Natoman can tell I haven't a fuckin' clue what he's talking about. 'Your Jesus Piece ... round your neck,' he says laughing.

'Ah, me rosary beads,' I say.

'Na man ... your J.P.!'

We both start to laugh when BC joins in, 'Don't mind him Gary, I'm BC. The kitchen is *bleedin' deadly* you'll love it here ... it's *bleedin' great*.' Already I can see that BC is just a bundle of positive energy, a small, red-haired little pocket rocket with wide eyes and an infectious smile.

Lastly Budgie, a short, stocky, dark-haired lad with a similar deadpan tone to his voice as The Little Fella. He says. 'Well hi ... how are ya Gar, where ya from?'

'Finglas bud,' I say.

'I'm from Ballymun meself. Welcome to the kitchen. Stay away from the pricks in this room and you'll be flyin', especially The Little Fella, he's the boss's pet.'

'Fuck off Budgie, ya bollox,' replies The Little Fella. Already I can see these lads are a close unit.

'Right, do ya wanna cup of tea, Gary?' asks Fitzer.

'Love one bud,' comes my grateful reply.

'Well, there's the fuckin' kettle, make it yourself,' he laughs, followed by, 'only messin' me aul' mucker.' So far, all these lads hail from different parts of Dublin, but I'll end up meeting lads from so many walks of life during my time here!

'So, what ya in for, drugs?' asks The Little Fella.

'Yeah, got three and a half year for a few pillows of grass.'

'Like us all bud,' he replies with a slight shrug. 'Well, except Fitzer and Natoman ... they'll be here for fuckin' years!' says Budgie. The laughter starts again and I find myself joining in. I'm only in the gate and already these lads have put to bed any fears or nerves that I had about interacting with fellow prisoners.

'Yeah, ya little bollox,' says Fitzer, 'me and Natoman are hardcore, we got a bang of eight (years), not like yous with your pansy five year whack.' Fitzer says all of this in a sarcastic tone with a massive smile on his face, and in time I will begin to think that his smile is in fact tattooed on, for he never seems to be without it.

The rest of the day I spend inside this tiny tearoom chatting with these lads, and some others who come and go. Fitzer informs me to, quote, 'Fuck workin' today, we'll get ya started tomorrow,' so I just sit and have some crazy conversations with the lads. Natoman is filling me in on who's who in the kitchen, The Little Fella is coming out with some of the driest one-liners, as is Budgie, which has me in knots of laughter. BC is filling me with so much hope and optimism for a brighter future, while Beasey is constantly asking if I'm okay or need anything. And Fitzer is just smiling and putting an amazing spin on absolutely everything. I think I've landed on my feet here. I think I'm going to like working in the kitchen.

Chapter 7

Anti-Clockwise

After my first day's hard graftin' in the kitchen, I return to Cunny's cell to find that my pillowcase with all my worldly belongings had been transferred into No. 2's cell next door. No. 2 greets me with a steaming cup of coffee and a pre-rolled smoke. I think this is going to work out just fine.

We head out for a walk around D Wing's yard, which is pure craziness! We make our way through D1 towards a massive iron gate, which leads to a metal scanner and then on to an arched door. I find as I walk along D Wing that I am terrified to raise my head in case I catch the eye of someone looking for trouble. And I will find in time that, although my confidence grew with each passing day, I still walked with my head down so as not to draw any unwanted attention.

One day, though, I did pay the ultimate price as my confidence allowed me to drop my guard and I ended up annoying the wrong person, receiving a major dig for my troubles. Mountjoy is truly a very scary place. You simply must have your wits about you at all times.

As you come through the arched door and stand at the top of the descending steps that bring you on to the yard's gravel, well, it's crazy. You're inside the walls of Mountjoy! In the corner to your left is a hut, which I soon find out is the Tuck Shop. The famous high walls that you associate with Mountjoy enclose this grey, drab exercise yard. There are goal posts painted on the walls at either end, but other than that? It's grey, though this is the famous yard that the IRA flew a helicopter into and escaped with two prisoners in years gone by. That amazing feat could not be re-enacted today, as the powers-that-be have erected a massive net over the yard, which also prevents magical 'parcels' falling from the sky into the yard. There are guys doing 'laps', which consist of the men walking around the yard anti-clockwise ... *against* time! There are a couple of lads doing the 'pads', which is a form of boxing cardio, while a group stand around them encouraging the next Rocky Balboa in his quest to impress Adrienne.

No. 2 has always been one of those guys who just has it sussed. Straight away he is able to inform me, 'See your man over there, that looks like he fell into a vat of acid? Prick he is' or, 'That there is No. 1, salt of the earth he is. I'll introduce ya to him later. He's a great man to have on your side.' It's extremely intimidating traversing this yard for the first time, so I am grateful to have No. 2 by my side. We do a few laps and I find I'm amazed. I can't help it. I'm in the infamous Mountjoy, walking around one of her three yards (anti-clockwise!) with a bloke from my area, while chaos reigns down all around me. And yet nobody is being threatening, nor do I feel like I am at risk. Organised chaos.

As we head back inside, it's like an extremely busy market on D Wing. There are lads everywhere either standing around chatting, or milling around making sure they have all they need for the approaching night before the screws lock us up. No. 2, Cunny, Fitzer and myself are standing just outside my new cell, and I'm the butt of all the jokes ('fresh meat' etc.). I find I am enthralled by the madness of the goings on around me. I find myself staring, which Cunny notes. 'Just chat away with us buddy, don't mind anyone else.' Not that there is anything in particular happening, I just can't fully grasp that I am here! A small row breaks out between two young lads, mostly shouting and name calling and threats, nothing more. But it is a stark reminder how quickly this place can just blow! After having a bit of banter with the lads, the officers start to shout, *'Right D2, bang it out!'* It's just gone 7.20 pm.

'Is this every night, No. 2?' I ask.

'Yeah, sometimes it's earlier. Ah, sure we have *Corrie* and *Eastenders* on tonight and I think there's a film on TV3.'

I laugh to myself. 'Nice one,' I say.

No. 2 and I enter our new home and the screw bangs the door closed behind us. All cells in Mountjoy are identical in measurements and wall colour, so it takes the flair of each individual to mould them to their own liking. In No. 2's cell, I can see a lot of pictures of his new son, a fine little lad. There are also a lot of pictures of cars, his passion and vocation in life, and of course Cheryl Cole! Straight away No. 2 has the kettle on and he begins to teach me the art of rolling a cigarette. We soon settle down in our bunk beds, me on the top one, and half watch the drama unfolding on Albert Square, while we reminisce about old times and the area we grew up in. The hours seem to fly past and soon we are fighting a losing battle against the oncoming slumber. We say our good nights, and as I drift off I find myself becoming more relaxed, happy that I'm doubled up with such a sound fella. But this is Mountjoy, and just when you're happy and content, the beast that is The Joy will rear its ugly head and try to fuck everything up for you.

Chapter 8

The Gaffer

Next morning at 8.00 am the screw opens our cell door and drags me kicking and screaming from a wonderful dream I'm having about Pamela Anderson, myself, and a sunset on the beach at Dollymount. No. 2 is still coming around as I dress into my clothes. 'You gettin' breakfast, Gar?' he asks in his sleepy stupor.

'I am, big man,' I say, not much more alert.

'Grab us a few Weetabix and a drop of milk will ya?' he asks.

'No bother bud,' I duly reply.

I head down to join the relatively short queue that has formed for breakfast – sometimes prisoners don't 'do' mornings – when Fitzer, exasperated, greets me with, *'Where the fuck were ya this mornin'?'*

I look at him, extremely confused.

'You're meant to start at seven a.m. ya mad thing,' he laughs.

'Ah bollox, are ya serious?' I ask, the plea notable in my voice. 'I sort of remember a screw saying somethin' earlier all right. I'll be in now,' I say flustered.

'Don't worry, just tell them that they never came to wake ya this morning,' says Fitzer.

I grab some Weetabix and milk and sprint like Sonia O'Sullivan back to our cell. 'I was meant to be in work at fuckin' seven this mornin' No. 2,' I say as I throw off my clothes to replace them with my kitchen whites.

'No way, hate that,' laughs No. 2, as he turns on to his side. 'I'll be thinkin' of ya as I head back into dreamland.'

'Fuck ya,' I reply laughing.

I launch myself out of my cell, thunder down the stairwell, and soar like an eagle to the gates of the kitchen, where Fitzer is returning from his stint at breakfast.

'Good man Gary, The Gaffer is in today and he's, well, he's like a fuckin' *nazi*!' We both start to laugh when an officer appears at the gate.

'Who the f-f-fuck is this?' he barks, with a slight stammer.

'Gary Cunningham,' I say with trepidation.

'Well, Gary, next time you're f-f-fuckin' late, you can fuck off back to your cell and walk the fuckin' yard like every other little b-b-bollox in here okay?' His stammer makes this rant funny and frightening at the same time.

'Sorry, won't happen again,' I reply sheepishly.

'Too f-f-fuckin' right it won't happen again, and what are you standin' lookin' at Fitzer, nothing to do no?' he barks at Fitzer, 'Well I'll find yas b-b-both something to do. Now get fuckin' in!'

Mother of Jaysus! He really is like a Nazi! A big man with a beer belly, everything about this man screams 'hater' – in fact, he actually has the look of someone cast to play the role of a German Nazi Sergeant in one of those old black and white war movies, with the small rounded glasses perched on the bridge of his nose and everything. I look at Fitzer who seems to be stifling the laughter, which in turn has me holding on for dear life as my 'giddies' come to the front, but thankfully I find I can smother them.

We enter the kitchen where The Little Fella is standing shaking his head. 'Good man Gar, first proper day and already The Gaffer hates ya,' he says as he erupts into a fit of laughter.

'Fuck him,' says Fitzer, followed by, 'come on, we can get a cup of tea into us Gar.'

As the day continued I kept my head down and washed everything that was sent into the pot wash like my life depended on it! Now, as I pointed out at the beginning of our tale, I have a tendency to be quite loud, well, very fuckin' loud if I'm to be honest! My mother and brothers are always at me to keep my voice down. It's not like I do it on purpose, I'm just a loud fucker! The Little Fella approaches me and warns me, 'Jaysus Gary, I don't think they heard ya in Wheatfield, are ya tryin' to get the eye on ya or what?'

He laughs as I reply, 'I'm always at this bleedin' volume.' We both get a giggle out of this, but when The Gaffer pops his head out of his office I don't even see The Little Fella leave, he's that quick, like a ninja!

'You must be f-f-finished all your fuckin' work, Cunningham, are ya, all the talkin' your d-d-doin'?'

'No officer, sorry officer,' I reply as I catch sight of The Little Fella and Fitzer breaking their bollox laughing at my expense.

'Well get back to it or ya can leave your whites at the g-g-gate.'

Great. The Gaffer does fuckin' hate me! Though it must be a miserable existence being the arsehole that he is.

Whilst The Gaffer and I work on our blossoming romance, I note that a new lad has also just started in the kitchen. He's a tall lad, very tall, well over six foot and just has the look of a big, skinny oaf, though time will soon tell that he is anything but. He talks with a bit of a drool and his unkempt black hair doesn't help his case. God love him, he's only in the door when The Gaffer subjects him to a barrage of insults, mostly about his height.

'Now,' says The Gaffer, 'you go washin' with B-B-Big Mouth (my good self!) over there. I'll have me eye on both of yas!'

I introduce myself. 'Stretch is me name,' comes his awkward reply.

'Well Stretch, let's just get stuck in, keep the eye off us, and we'll be grand.' There is a wonderful innocence about this young fella. As you listen to him speak you'd swear he's not the sharpest knife in the drawer, but I will soon come to learn he's nobody's fool and is in fact very intelligent.

Our day flies as we submerge ourselves in dirty trays and massive cooking pots. I was ever vigilant that my voice did not exceed the allowed decibel limit! Mr Haycorn then calls us both into the officers' canteen. 'Right men, you are now not only workmates, but cell mates too.'

At first I was a bit put out by this as I knew No. 2 for years and we seemed to work well together. But, as I have said, this is The Joy and you just accept what comes your way.

'It's not fair on your cellmate to be woken up an hour earlier when we come to get you for work, Gary, so we try to keep all kitchen workers together.' Makes sense I suppose. We're told we can leave early and get our stuff packed, which for me was my pillowcase.

I lumber up to No. 2 and break the news to him. 'Ah fuck it, is your man alri' you're goin in with?' he asks with concern.

'Ah yeah he seems harmless enough,' I say.

'Sound, so, now I have me own cell ... *deadly*,' laughs No. 2.

I pack my stuff and head over to cell 28 on D2, where Stretch and I will become cellmates ... for now!

Chapter 9

SLOPPIN' OUT!

My first night with Stretch is one I'll remember for a long time. The cell we were given had a telly that barely worked because the cable was too short and there was no remote. Remotes are a massive commodity in The Joy ... you *never* leave yours hanging around! Just before we were 'banged out' I was in the middle of telling Natoman from the kitchen about our telly woes, when John-Joe, a huge beast of a man in his late twenties with an oversized head, narrow slits for eyes, and a massive beer belly, overhears us and stops to address this situation.

'Hang on there bud, yeah? I'll fuckin' sort this in a second!' John-Joe is not a man to be messed with, and has a reputation for being, well, a fuckin' headcase. I'll later discover that he has a calming, even soft side too, he just doesn't portray it very often. Natoman is laughing as he's telling me to just do whatever the man says, just as John-Joe returns, pushing me into my cell.

'See this?' He produces some TV co-ax wire, and then proceeds to wrap it around each of his hands! 'I use this to fuckin' choke any bollox that's got it comin' to em' ... fuckin' dead handy it is!' John-Joe then decides that maybe he's not explaining his torture device clearly enough so he enthusiastically uses me for a demonstration! To say the fear of bejaysus went through me, as this hulk of a man wrapped some TV wire around my neck, is the understatement of the year!

'Ughh ... that's ... ughh ... deadly ... John ... Joe,' I splutter out.

'Not too fuckin' shabby is it Gar?' he replies as his death-grip loosens. 'But here, you get me brown bread outta the kitchen. I love me brown bread, so just keep that comin' and I'll lend ya this. But if I need it back? Well ... you know yourself!'

'Cheers John-Joe,' I say, slightly petrified as Stretch connects the 'death wire' to our little portable. Soon *Nationwide* is being beamed into our cell. Result!

'Now I can't help ya with a remote, but sure your cell mate's arms are fuckin' huge ... he'll be able to reach the telly and change the channels from his fuckin' bed,' laughs John-Joe as he turns and heads back to his cell.

Natoman is doubling up with laughter. 'Ya went fuckin blue in the face there, Gary,' he spurts.

'Fuck that,' I reply. 'I thought that was the end of me!'

The screw starts to roar, informing us that it's time to bang out. Me and Stretch say our good nights to everyone and prepare for our first night together.

Our cell was clean, I have to say, with the same grey walls and of course the obligatory Cheryl Cole poster – I was beginning to think this Gordie lass was sponsoring Mountjoy. We decide that TV3 has the best programs on, thus eliminating the need for a remote. Stretch had gotten to the cell before me so he had the honour of selecting which bunk he wanted. Of course, he opted for the bottom, the driver's seat! We start the ritual of finding out about each other, asking questions about our path to prison, our friends and family and so on. I can tell already that Stretch loves to talk. We decide that, seeing as this cell is our home for, well, God knows how long, we would make it our own. Put our stamp on it. Stretch wants to put a Man. United crest on the wall. Over my dead body! I follow Liverpool! We decide that it would be fuckin' ridiculous to put a football crest on the wall. We do agree that maybe some scantily clad ladies might brighten up the place. Stretch, full of vigour, says he'll have that sorted tomorrow! I offer Cunny's services to give the place a lick of paint. Sure, we won't know ourselves!

Through all the excitement and terror of being choked by John-Joe I had forgotten to go to the jacks! I'm now faced with a bucket in the corner of the cell ... and it's not a piss that I need! I won't go into the next few minutes, but let's just say I never thought I'd be squatting in front of a bloke taking a dump in a prison cell! I apologise profusely, but Stretch couldn't give a shit (excuse the pun!). It's inhumane to have these conditions in a prison in this day and age. It has dawned on me that this stench will most possibly linger for an eternity as we have nowhere to dispose of the shite. Like every other prisoner, we will have to slop out in the morning, which is basically over 200 men queuing to empty their piss and shite into a toilet at the top of each landing. But I'm not going to stand on a soap box and vent about it. It is what it is and we just have to deal with it. It is my fault I am in this kip in the first place.

I clamber up onto my bunk and get ready to practice rolling a few smokes for myself. I offer to roll some for Stretch, but after taking a look at my first effort, he politely declines. I get myself comfortable and pull out my book, a James Patterson thriller which one of the kitchen lads kindly loaned to me, hoping that a read will tire me enough to fall asleep. But Stretch has different ideas. He has found his comfort with me and is regaling me with stories of his madcap teen years. I have a lot of time for this guy, but tonight I just want him to shut the fuck up!

'Listen bud,' I say, almost apologetically, 'I'm just gonna have an auld read and then hopefully get some kip. Sound, yeah?'

'Jaysus Gary, no bother man yeah, sorry bud, work away,' replies Stretch.

I'd say Stretch's ceasefire from talking lasted maybe four minutes when he's off again, reliving a night of passion with some girl at some house party somewhere! I lay my book on my chest, let out a sigh and just let him continue. He's really getting into this story, and feels like some actions may be necessary to fully describe his tale of lust, when all of a sudden he's on his feet, hyped as his story comes to a climax, and although I'm lying flat on my back ... *on the top bunk* ... I'm still looking up at him, he's that fuckin' tall! I burst out laughing and God love him he thinks I'm laughing at his sleazy reconstruction of this fateful night.

I come clean. 'My Jaysus Stretch ... you're fuckin' tall,' I say as he towers over me.

'Yeah, I get that all the time,' he replies and soon we're both united in laughter. 'Ohhh, I need a piss,' he says.

'Ah, I forgot you had gone already! *Jaysus*!'

That's it, I'm now crying with the laughter, tears streaming down my face.

'You can fuckin' slop out in the mornin' Gar,' laughs Stretch.

'Wouldn't have it any other way buddy,' I reply.

Chapter 10

Balls Rough and Doin' Your Whack

Me and Stretch soon settled into a regular routine and found we got along well, which is handy as we were locked into a cell together for nearly twelve hours! The days started flying by as I immersed myself fully into working in the kitchen. Prison life is a complete Groundhog Day experience. There are no 'weekends', as every day is just an extension of the last. It's the same thing day in and day out, so you've got to be creative in order to adapt. You could just sit around and do nothing all day, but that just wasn't me. There are evil temptations and nasty goings-on lurking in the shadows of this historical jail and I wanted fuck all to do with them. I began to find my feet and started to enjoy going in to meet with the 'kitchen crew' in the mornings. Beasey would come in first thing in the morning like he'd been dragged kicking and screaming from his bed, eyes still half shut. The Little Fella would be his funny, sarcastic self. Always good for a laugh. Natoman would be his usual mischievous self. BC and Fitzer would be in incredibly good form, thus putting everyone else in the same frame of mind ... well, nearly everyone!

I'd heard Natoman sounding off about one of the blokes who worked scrubbing the floors – Harry. 'I swear to Jaysus your man Harry is *major* balls rough ... he'd wanna do his fuckin' whack,' he'd bark.

Well, of course, curiosity killed the cat with me, so with some trepidation, as I didn't want to lose face and show my ignorance, I asked Natoman what he meant.

'He's fuckin' balls rough ... he can't do his whack!' came his informed reply.

'Okay ... what?' came my ignorant response.

'He can't do his jail ... do his whack ... so he's doing it rough. And the worse type of rough is *balls rough*!' explains Natoman as he grabs his crotch! I start laughing, which sets Natoman off.

'That's fuckin' brilliant,' I say.

'Sure, watch,' says Natoman, 'in about five minutes he'll be in the jacks smoking smoke after smoke, tellin' anyone that will listen that his mott won't wait for him to be released. Then he'll ask what sentence you got and compare it to his own ... and this is *every day*!'

Well, of course I had to put this to the test, so right on cue I spot Harry going into the jacks. I give it a few minutes then follow him in, with Natoman tailing behind ... he is such a fuckin' shit-stirrer.

Just as Natoman had said, there's Harry, a small guy with brown hair and teeth that protrude from his sour mouth. He is puffing away on a cigarette, which must be his second or third on account of the amount of smoke in the small, drab room, which consisted of three urinals, two toilets and two showers. 'Three and a half year you got, wasn't it Gary?' he asks me.

'Three an' a half year, yeah,' I say.

'Jesus I was caught with the same as you and I got a longer sentence. That's a load of me bollox! Me mott is gonna leave me an' all Gary. Load of me bollox it is!' As he says this, you can almost see the tears forming on his lower eyelids.

I'm stifling the laughter and just about to ask him how he knew how long I got, when he follows it up with, 'You were in the paper this morning Gary. Here look, I cut it out.' He hands me a cut-out story from some tabloid describing my arrest and subsequent sentencing. 'I collect them to give to me solicitor for me appeal,' says Harry.

Well it's enough to make me want to erupt with laughter.

'Ya don't mind me havin' your one do ya?'

'Work away Harry, it's not like I'm proud to be in the paper over this situation.'

I can't take much more, so I make my excuses and leave. Natoman is right behind me bursting his bollox laughing. 'Ya see? Fuckin *balls rough*! B.R.H.!'

'B.R.H.?' I ask.

'Balls Rough Harry,' replies Natoman. Classic! So as I'm sure you can gather it's a sin to be classed as balls rough in prison ... you've gotta *do your whack*!

Chapter 11

Phone Calls and Visits

After a couple of days inside Mountjoy, you are presented with two sheets of paper. On one you will give the names and phone numbers of up to three people you can ring, and on the other you put the names of the people, and their relationship to you, who you would like to come visit, capped at six people, but you can change these lists at any time. After each name is checked and verified, you receive a phone card with a long number printed on it. You need to enter this number in order to make a phone call. Also on the phone card are the names and corresponding numbers of your selected people. You are also informed that you can now request a visit once your prospective visitors have been checked to see if they have ever been in prison themselves, as you cannot visit someone in an Irish jail for a period of ten years if you, yourself, have ever been incarcerated.

I got lucky, well sort of, for you see, we had a prison phone in the kitchen, thus eliminating the need to queue in D yard waiting to use the prison phone out there (of which there was only two for over 200 prisoners), but I did make the effort to work, and in the kitchen I worked my arse off, so it's not so much luck, more I earned it. My first phone call was to my mam. You pick up the phone and dial in the long printed number on your phone card. You are then prompted to press a number between 1 and 4 (1 is reserved for your solicitor and is the only call that is not listened in on) to start ringing your chosen person. After a few seconds the beautiful, soothing, warm tones of my mam's voice came radiating from the phone's receiver, which of course reduces me to uncontrollable sobbing. You get six minutes to talk, so I quickly move to tell her I am okay, and that I can't wait to see her. She informs me that she and everyone at home are okay and that she'll be up on Monday (this was Friday) and will bring clothing and photos of her and my son. An intrusive beep cuts short our chat, and tells us both that this talk is over. We say our goodbyes, I hang up, and head straight into the toilet for a good auld cry. Fitzer has spotted this, follows me in, and is just 'there' for me.

The weekend seems to fly past, as I eagerly await my first visit. On Monday, I set about my kitchen duties, but my eye is constantly on the blue barred gate that locks the kitchen away from the rest of the prison. This is where an officer will appear holding a sheet containing the names of the lads who have a visitor. He will then roar your name and duly escort you to the visiting area. Soon it's my turn. A roar goes up from the kitchen lads as I embark on my first visit.

I'm taken out of the kitchen. We head left, into The Circle, and make our way towards A Wing. Just before we arrive at A Wing's gate, we stop at a door on our left to which the officer gives a couple of kicks with his black steel-capped boots. The door is unlocked from the other side by a very young-looking officer. I am led through a metal detector, then into a narrow corridor, where we turn left and start to traverse. There are three doors, with a number on a square plate jotting out and above each of them. As I walk into box 2, I notice a massive wooden bench which dissects the bright room in half, us on the right side, our visitors on the left. Straight facing you is a large window, behind which lies a small corridor, where the people who have come through the rigorous search procedure await the arrival of their loved one or friend. Behind the corridor is a massive window that shows the building the visitors must come through. It's sunny today, and it feels strange to gaze upon an outside view, other than D yard. At either end of the fairly long visiting room is an officer, perched up high, keeping his eyes on the goings on. There are wooden benches on the visiting side for them to sit upon, while us prisoners, wanting to get as close as possible to our loved ones, would usually sit on top of the bench. I stand in front of an empty allotted visiting area, and turn my head right, frantically wanting to catch a glimpse of my mam.

It's not long before I see her, being aided by my brother Noel, as she makes her way towards me. My heart breaks, as my mam is awaiting a hip operation, so this is taking a lot out of her. It was that precise moment that I knew I had to wake the fuck up and change every facet of my miserable existence, solely for this lady. As she made her way, slowly, into the visiting box, my 'hard man' facade shattered. I did not care who saw me cry that day. I embraced my mam like I never had before, and constantly repeated, like a scratched vinyl record, how sorry I was. Noel was next, and even his embrace was enough to bring a tear to a glass eye. We soon settle down and I'm fully aware that I only have about 20 minutes to absorb this visit, absorb my mam's true beauty, with her perfect, bright brown hair and lady-like smile.

I quickly inform them both that I am 100 per cent okay. I fill them in on exactly what my day entails, and this seems to calm my mam down. After a short while, Noel is bringing humour into the proceedings, as he mocks my prison photo, which was attached to the sheet he was given as he entered. My mam informed me that she brought all I had asked for (clothes, pictures etc.), but she was worried as, God love her, she thought she could hand them straight to me. I explained that they must be searched and that I will get them on my next 'reception day', which came round once a week in order to collect clean towels or anything that's been left in and cleared by the prison staff. The rest of the visit, as did all my subsequent visits, flew by, but I came to cherish this time every Monday, for my mam never let me down. I am actually crying as I type this, but every Monday, sometimes accompanied by someone, but mostly on her own, she would struggle up to see me without fail. Due to my guilt of seeing her suffer with her hip, I begged her to stop coming, to which she'd sternly reply, 'Shut up, you are my baby son, and I want to be here.' After all I had done to disappoint this woman, her love for me never wavered. It was the most humbling experience of my life.

Chapter 12

Kitchen vs Bakery

I woke one morning and slopped out as usual – this became my 'job', so to speak, in our living arrangements – but I had an excitement coursing through my veins and butterflies fluttering in my stomach, for today all the waiting had come to an end, today the kitchen took on the bakery in a game of football, played out in D yard ... on our break! There has always been a rivalry between Mountjoy's kitchen and bakery, apparently going back years, and this collection of prisoners were no exception. Talk had begun early of the impending game, positions were being finalised, and tactics were being argued and discussed at a feverish rate.

A new, wonderfully polite gentleman had recently become a welcome addition to our staff in the kitchen. Auld Bill was a soft, caring man, in his mid-fifties who had such a warmth about him. Now, he didn't come into Mountjoy of his own free accord ... the auld bollox had robbed a bank! You'd never have thought it, but trust me! Although Auld Bill had from day one fit into our little family, we were even more excited to have him with us today, as he was a football coach too.

I spoke up as the lads were arguing about whether or not to play with width or straight up the middle. 'Let Auld Bill take the helm, he knows what he's on about.' As this was my first game playing for the kitchen in this hotly contested match, I hoped I wasn't stepping on anybody's toes by nominating

Auld Bill. But my suggestion was met with a unified agreement from the other lads.

Auld Bill wasted no time in finding out the lads' preferred positions. Beasey was our man between the painted-on posts, a huge intimidating man with a hunger for victory that was second to none. Fitzer informed Auld Bill that he would control the back line, with a view to pushing forward when needed. The Little Fella (who, as it turns out, was a fantastic footballer) took the role of centre mid – our general who would control not only the pace of the game for us, but also conjure up majestic passing not seen since the days of the great Pelé. I was to play the part of the lone striker, making myself readily available and getting into positions that would ultimately contribute to our total and utter annihilation of this bakery team. We also had Budgie playing alongside Fitzer at the back and Natoman tucking in just behind The Little Fella in the centre of the park, well, concrete yard.

We got on with our kitchen duties but could hardly contain our excitement as the hour of kick-off approached. Fitzer was in full voice, boosting us with words of encouragement. 'Lads, we were close last time ... *this is our time!* We can fuckin' do this, we can wipe the smirks off their fuckin' faces ... *come on the kitchen!*'

Beasey, always a level head but with an appetite for victory that almost matched his appetite for food, was being more practical. 'Just play the way you're facing, no need to try to beat every fuckin' player, simple balls all the time.'

I can only imagine this is how the Irish team felt in Stuttgart in '88 as they prepared to face England. I have been captivated by the lads' belief, sucked in by their enthusiasm ... *We can do this!* The Little Fella, though, is being extremely quiet, perhaps steadying himself as he leads us out to battle.

The clock in the kitchen crept closer to kick off. (By the way, being able to see a clock whilst in prison is a luxury, for there are none anywhere and you can't wear a watch! Being deprived of the time is a head-fuck.) Auld Bill assembled us in the canteen to give us our final instructions. Fitzer then instilled in us the confidence to go out and fear no one ... to take our chances ... to make this *our* time ... *our* day!

The bakery is situated below the kitchen in The Joy, and the lads who work in there must come through the kitchen in order to leave. As they started to appear, decked out in their football attire, the banter began ... all coming from us! *'Yas haven't a fuckin' chance'... 'No point in yas even turnin' up boys!'* The bakery lads didn't take the bait. They just stood, silently, waiting for the officer to open the gate.

Word had spread through D Wing that this mighty battle was to take place, and as we walked out on to D yard, it was surrounded by what seemed like every prisoner from the wing, some cheering for us, others for the bakery, others just hoping to see a good match ... and maybe a fight! The sun beat down on D yard, which let us know even Mother Nature couldn't wait for this fixture. Fitzer asked one of the officers on yard duty to keep time (30 minutes a half). The time had come ... no turning back ... *'Let's fuckin' do this, lads ... Do it for the kitchen!'*

Final score: Bakery 16, Kitchen 1!

They were fuckin' amazing and we were *shite*! The Little Fella, who was an astounding player, even on this score line, and who had been quiet all day, simply said, 'Fuckin eejits ... they're *super* fit, we're a pack of fat, lazy fuckers!'

Our one goal? I scored ... well it hit off me arse from a clearance and went in!

While there were some questionable tackles and a bit of pushing and shoving, at the end of the match we all shook hands. The bakery had won the game ... *and* the slagging rights.

Well, what an anti-climax that was! Maybe next time ...

Chapter 13

Smithwicks and the Birth of The Offenders

Once again, the days slowly started to blend into one another. I soon realised that if you let it Mountjoy would consume you, so you have got to try to be productive, which can be hard to do in such a hellhole. In prison, routine is king, it's everything. Although you may do the exact same thing every day – it becomes a necessary tool in your survival kit – I was always on the look-out for something to stimulate my creative side. I'd get up, slop out, go to the kitchen at 7.00 am, do the same jobs as the previous day, leave the kitchen at 5.30 pm and then flute around until it was time for the officers to bang us out at 7.30 pm. Some of the lads would go to the gym, but I had never been in a gym before. Well, that's not true, I did go with my nephew once on the outside, but while he readied himself for an onslaught of total muscle ripping, I got into me togs and waddled me fat arse to the Jacuzzi area, where I proceeded to do a great job of being a fat, utterly unfit slob!

I soon realised that I was becoming very close to Fitzer. How do I describe this bloke? Well, he'd been through a lot before he got locked up. He got married, had a son, and buried his only brother, all in a very short space of time, but not once would you hear him complain, not a hint of balls rough emanating from him. He'd cheer everyone up, either with one of his impressions, all classics, or by belting out whatever song was on the radio ... and what a singer.

We were chatting one day about our biggest passion – music. I told him I played guitar and have done from a young age. In fact, I think the phrase I used was, *'I'm fuckin' lethal!'* which made him laugh.

'No way,' he starts, 'well, I have me aul' fella's guitar in here with me, and I'm after getting meself an acoustic bass. Can't fuckin' play either of 'em like Clapton, or the bass player from the Eagles now or anythin', but sure, fuck it Gar, we can try to have an auld jam if ya like? I can find me way around the bass like!'

'Sounds like a plan, Fitzer,' I reply, trying to bottle up the excitement that I'm feeling.

'Yeah,' he continues, 'the brother, lord have mercy on him, played bass in a band. I used to go watch them and always wanted to play the bass meself. So, I suppose as a little tribute to him, I got the music teacher in here (a man by the name of Paul, a legend, a true gent and an *amazing* musician) to get me an acoustic bass, and I'm gonna give it an auld bash ... sure, why not, Gar, wha'?'

I've never met such a positive person before, and soon it's rubbing off. 'How do ya feel about havin' a jam after work?' I ask. 'I'll play a few tunes and show ya the root notes, just to get ya started.'

'Fuckin' deadly,' replies Fitzer, 'we'll make this jailhouse rock Gary!'

I start to laugh just as The Gaffer appears out of nowhere. I'm beginning to think this prick is a yoga master and can just materialise whenever and wherever he likes. Fitzer had obviously spotted him before I did, as he's nowhere to be seen. The Gaffer, whilst staring at me like I've just farted at a funeral, begins his tirade of abuse.

'A f-f-fuckin' band is it, Cunningham? Well, I can help with rehearsal time if ya like? Oh yeah, you can fuck off and leave your whites at the g-g-gate and spend all the fuckin' time ya want p-p-playin' your poxy guitars or whatever it is you and that other fucker were talkin' about ... talkin', I might add, when you should be workin!'

Now, like Fitzer, I have worked – honestly, not just in illegal activities – all my life and I'm not afraid to get stuck into a 'bit of graft'. But I just seem to be the only one caught by this man, maybe taking five and having a chat with one of the lads. Prisons, I'm sure all over the world, have certain officers that just look at prisoners with contempt, and if they see us having a laugh or getting on with things it riles them. The Gaffer is one such man.

'Sorry boss, won't happen again,' I say through gritted teeth. Nearly all of the lads that this Gobshite had working in his kitchen during my time there were good, hard working lads. We even had a Chinese guy who was a fuckin' legend and spoke 'Dublinese' with a broken Dublin accent, but God help us if we looked like we'd accepted our lot and made a conscious decision to knuckle down and get on with our jail time. There are plenty of lads in Mountjoy who thought we were fuckin' crazy for working in the kitchen – at the end of the day you don't have to – but we did, and no matter what we did it was never good enough for The Gaffer.

I get stuck back into my duties, just as The Little Fella arrives, stealthily by my side. 'Jaysus Gar, it's always you,' he says whilst trying to hold back his laughter.

'Fuck off, Little Fella, though I'm glad I can provide you with some giggles, as I get me bollox chewed off!'

The Little Fella says, 'Fuck this, I'm not standin' here laughing with you ... you're bleedin' red hot!' And with that he turns and leaves.

As I'm watching him go, I catch sight of Fitzer peeking his head out from around the canteen door. 'You're some bollox,' I laugh.

'Dog-fuckin'-wide Gary,' laughs Fitzer. 'Here, I'll see ya up in me gaff after work, we'll have a jam and I'll introduce ya to Smithwicks, me cell mate, coz I'm fucked if I'm gonna be near you for the rest of the day ... you're bleedin' *red hot!*'

Beasey, BC, Budgie, Natoman and, well, most of the fuckin' kitchen seem to have congregated behind Fitzer and I have become the butt of their jokes!

'Yeah, no bother, yas pack of fuckers,' I say as I turn my back to them, stick me arse out and give it an auld slap ... just as The Gaffer reappears *again*! I'm thinking this is it, P45 time, but thankfully I'm saved by the bell, as the black phone in his office is screaming for his attention. The rest of the boys are in fits of laughter as I again return to my duties.

I have my shower (as mentioned, working in the kitchen has the advantage of having a shower, otherwise you share 15 showers with over 200 prisoners on the landings ... loads of fun) and then head up to Fitzer's cell. There are some lads there, most I don't know, but soon as I arrive Fitzer fucks them all out! He hands me his father's guitar. 'Probably a heap of shite Gar, is it?' asks Fitzer. On the contrary, it's a fuckin' fabulous guitar, nice fret board with a lovely sound, all of which I say to Fitzer. 'Yeah? Fuckin' grand so,' he replies, nonchalant. I'll learn in time he's a very tough man to impress!

We get to work straight away as soon we will be banged out for the night. I show Fitzer the basic idea behind playing root notes on his magnificent black acoustic bass, with just a small white trim enclosing its edges, and soon he's loving it as he accompanies me to some Oasis song. 'Ah, this is exactly what I've been lookin' for Gar ... I'm fuckin' delighted you got locked up ... no offence.'

We both start laughing as his cell door opens and in bounds a guy with a shaved bald head and a goatee beard, smiling from ear to ear. 'Well Fitzer, is he "lethal", or just all talk?' laughs this new guy.

I soon cop that maybe telling Fitzer I was lethal was a bit much, until he answers with, 'He's even better, Smithwicks.' Ah, so this is Smithwicks, Fitzer's cell mate.

'No way, deadly,' smiles Smithwicks.

'Gary,' I introduce myself.

'I'm Smithwicks, Gar, pleasure to meet ya man.'

I've heard this guy being referred to as 'Smiley' and it doesn't take long to find out why. I didn't realise it at the time, but these two incredible lads were to help mould me into the new person I have since become.

'*Fair City* tonight Fitzer,' smiles Smithwicks.

'Fuckin' great,' laughs Fitzer sarcastically.

'Sure, just keep playin' the bass and practicing what I've shown ya, fuckin' drown that shite out,' I say, which makes the two boys laugh.

'Here, give us a song there boys,' ask Smithwicks. Now, I've never been shy to belt out a song, so I don't need to be asked twice, and Fitzer has an air that shows he fears nothing. And so on that fateful night we jammed our first song together, 'Melancholy Hill' by the Gorillas, in front of an audience which had just increased to three as Natoman and Stretch had arrived ... and we nailed it. We brought some colour to that drab cell with our little song.

Smithwicks erupts with applause, as Natoman sits back with his hand on his chin, thinking. 'The Offenders, yeah?' he says.

'What?' myself and Fitzer reply in unison.

'The Offenders, that's your name lads, the name of your band.' And so The Offenders were born, and fuck me, do we end up making this jailhouse *rock*!

Chapter 14

So, How Did You End Up in Here?

Q. Did you come from a bad family?

A. Not at all, quite the opposite actually. I had a tough but fair father, who has since passed away, but who worked tirelessly for his family. I have an incredible, loving, caring, kind, *amazing* mother, whose beauty and love knows no bounds. I have three brothers who are fantastic, hard working family men, always on hand if I need them. So ... nope it's not my upbringing that's landed me in here.

Q. Trauma in your life?

A. Well, there was a moment that shook me to my very core, and to this day I'm not fully recovered from it. I had a beautiful daughter who died at a young age. It did lead me to drink heavily, but I was a prick and blamed all my shortcomings on her death, so although I became a heavy drinker and subsequently turned to ecstasy and cocaine, my beautiful angel is not the reason I'm here.

Q. Addiction problems?

A. Well, kind of, I suppose. I was an extremely heavy drinker, who soon included ecstasy and cocaine into this disgusting bingeing I was embarking on. This did have a huge impact on me being locked up.

Q. So, why are you here?

A. You want to know why I'm locked up? Because I was a selfish, lying arsehole who didn't give the most important people in my life the time and attention they needed, and instead concentrated all of my energy on how I'd get my next pint and maybe a bag of coke. I lived in the 'me, myself and I' world of a selfish drinker. I was a disgusting liar and a horrible person to be around, someone who thought this world owed me something! I forgot how to love, or be loved.

I have a beautiful, smart, well-mannered young son (13 at the time of writing) who makes me burst with pride just at the thought of him. He was and still is, in my head, my best friend. But I have thrown away the amazing relationship I had with him by being a dickhead and leaving him when he needed me most (I wasn't there when he made his confirmation as I'd been locked up only a couple of months beforehand). My love for him is never in question, but God knows what he thinks of me at this point. He has an amazing mother, who in turn has a wonderful family, and I know he's thriving. She doesn't want me to have contact with him, and in any other situation I would be up in arms over a woman doing that to a father and son. But I have no right. I fucked up ... I destroyed my life single-handedly.

So when I'm asked what led to my incarceration, I say, 'Me being a fuckin' *prick*! Nobody's fault but my own.' I have done so much work on myself since I walked into The Joy, and I know that the old 'Waster Gary' is long gone. My family has noticed the change in me, even telling me how proud they are of me, which shines a light into my heart. I just hope that one day I can show my son how sorry I am, and how much I love him.

Chapter 15

The Tuck Shop and Getting a 'Dig'

The Tuck Shop in Mountjoy's D Wing is located in a corner of D yard, and it's basically a hatch built into the wall. It's open most days and stocks a wide variety of nearly everything, from shampoos and shower gels to chocolate and crisps. When I first arrived in The Joy, you could only use the shop twice a week, but they have since upgraded to a computer system ... like Spar ... very swanky! But as you can imagine, visiting the Tuck Shop could lead to some quite heated arguments ... almost all over people's positions in the queue.

One morning I headed out as soon as The Gaffer would let me in order to get some toothpaste, some dust and maybe a treat or two! But when I emerged into D's yard, the queue was already the size of one for One Direction tickets, but instead of pre-teen girls, we had (1) fellas out of their minds on tablets, (2) lads trying to ignore these tablet-guzzling zombies, and then (3) some quiet lads slowly waiting their turn to purchase whatever treats would help them as they did their whack! I was in my kitchen whites and joined the queue at the end ... as you do. The banter was flying, except for one bollox who, oblivious to the world around him thanks to his intake of tablets, has taken it upon himself to torment everyone else.

On this particular morning the orders must have been light, as the queue was moving at a swift pace. Tablet Zombie has just made his order and left the hatch. Once you leave, you are knocked off the system, so if you forgot anything, well, tough shit.

Just as I approach the hatch to give my prison number and place my order, Tablet Zombie returns, his skinny frame barely able to hold up his faded blue cotton tracksuit. He proceeds to shove me out of the way and begins with something like, 'Here, ya prick (to the screw) where's me tea cake? And me Turkish delight? Fuckin' like Nazi Germany here, yas pack of knob-jockeys!'

Now the screw, myself, and most of the fuckin' queue knew he didn't order any of those items, and even if he did it's too late now as he's been taken off the system. As he's informed of this, and told to get away from the hatch, he turns to me and slurs, 'Here, you, get us a Turkish ... and a tea cake ... a packet of polos ... and a Freddo' (gorgeous little chocolate bars ... only 10 cents!).

Now, by no means am I a mean person, but this fuckin' yolk can ask me bollox if he thinks I'm getting him anything. I try my best to ignore him and proceed with my transaction, but of course this infuriates Tablet Zombie. With that I get a thump on my left ear ... fuckin' hurt too! I let out a roar – remember, I'm *very* loud – and turn to retaliate until I look at what I'd be hitting. One dig could quite possibly kill this cretin.

A lad by the name of Doggy, whom I don't really know but is good friends with No. 2 and is the kind of bloke you don't mess with, intervenes, clearly with a pain in his hole from waiting in the queue. 'Fuck off ya little pox ya, and get out of the queue ... *now*!' he bellows.

'Ask me bollox ya big fuckin' ... sa ... pri ... ya ya fucker ya!' comes the highly intelligent reply. He's so intoxicated on account of his ridiculous intake of tablets that he can't even manage a sentence and it's enough to make us all laugh. One of his tablet-taking buddies arrives and ushers him away. Do you know what the funny thing is? He will have absolutely no recollection of these events ... in about ten minutes!

I thank Doggy. 'Not at all pal, sure, ya couldn't hit that ... a fuckin' dig would kill 'em!' he replies.

I get my order. Well, not entirely, no toothpaste in stock, no cherry bakewells (which Smithwicks has me addicted to), and *no Freddos*!

Chapter 16

The Magical, Mystical, Maybe Mythical C Wing

Once upon a time, in the kitchen of Mountjoy, The Little Fella sat all the kitchen workers down and spoke of a landing straight from the pages of a fantasy novel. A magical, mystical and maybe mythical landing with ... drum roll please ... sanitation *in* cell! Yes folks, C Wing was this very place. The old C Wing had closed not long after I started my sentence, to be refurbished into single cells with a sink and toilet built in! The powers-that-be thought that in the year 2012 AD having a proper sanitation system might actually be a good idea!

You would have to meet certain criteria to avail of this luxury: (1) Be drug-free, and (2) Work in some capacity.

As kitchen workers, we were to be the first to test drive the new single cells. No more would I have to listen to Stretch tell me about his sexual conquests or about the countless 'wankers' he's panned out. No more filling countless bottles with water to see us through the night, and no more doing your business in front of each other! I'd have my own fuckin' *toilet*! It would be like winning the lotto ... with the bonus ball!

Every week we'd be told by The Gaffer to 'pack your stuff tonight, you're moving onto C1 tomorrow', only for no such thing to happen. This went on for months and became very much the boy who cried wolf, until one day, Mr. Tansy, a sound kitchen officer with a heart as big as his belly, pulled us to one side with a sheet in his hand. 'Right lads, this is your cell number, no arguments, no swapping, just be fuckin' happy you're heading around ... *today*!' Nobody gave a shite where they were put ... the day had finally arrived ... 16 April ... *C Wing*!

I got cell 25, and when I walked in I think I may have wept. The sight of that magnificent white porcelain bowl was enough to floor the hardest of men. I had a piss ... and didn't even need one! The cell was painted a soft yellow, as were the landings. It seemed so fresh and clean compared to the dank, dark conditions of D Wing. In each cell was a steel-framed bed bolted to the wall, in my case to your left as you walk in. A narrow window, with a turning mechanism which allowed the window to open a couple of inches, was above and slightly to the right of the bed. Also to the right, and raised up a step, was the aforementioned toilet, which was semi-enclosed for some privacy, with tiny saloon-styled swinging doors hiding you from the waist down.

Beside the toilet was a sink, yes, a sink with running water! Fitted to the wall above the sink was a small mirror, and to the right of that a large notice board. Any pictures you wanted to put up had to go there, and not on the newly painted walls. There was a cheap MDF desk on the right as you entered, which would become my entire universe, and this desk came accompanied by a grey plastic chair. To your left as you came in, fitted into the corner, were two white plastic shelves, one holding your telly and the other for a kettle. There was also a small bedside locker, made of the same shite MDF to store your clothes. In the prison world, this was the fuckin' Hilton. Yes, the cell was the same size as the one on D Wing, but it was your cell and there was a fuckin' toilet and a sink!

The excitement and buzz that night was electric. C1 was to house kitchen workers and two landing cleaners (Jimmy and Mick), and Paddy the Painter. Now, you may think that I'm overstating the sanitation point, but we're not fuckin' animals. We've made terrible mistakes in our lives and are serving our time, as set out by the judge who passed a sentence he deemed appropriate. Most of us accept this and get on with it, and hope to learn from our mistakes and try to better ourselves. Making a grown man slop out first thing in the morning is fucking degrading, and extremely unhygienic, so it was about time Mountjoy got a proper sanitation system. (All of Mountjoy's wings now have sanitation similar to C Wing.)

Okay, rant over.

The Little Fella and Fitzer were on the same side of the landing as me, and both popped their heads into my cell. 'Is your heating on Gar?' asked The Little Fella.

'It's fuckin' not lads,' I say. 'Poxy fuckin' freezin' it is ... but fuck it, I'll sleep in me jacket if I have to!'

'Too right Gary,' says Fitzer.

'Ah, me bollox, they reckon it's only our side of the landing will be fixed tomorrow or somethin', I'll be fuckin' frozen ... me little body will go into shock,' says The Little Fella.

'Whingin' little fucker isn't he Gar?' says Fitzer, which makes us all laugh. 'Here, we'll have some jams in here, Gar me aul' flower... The Offenders will be fuckin' flyin'!' Fitzer says this with his usual enthusiasm, just as the 'king' of enthusiasm enters.

BC has the biggest smile on his face. 'Bleedin' deadly isn't it lads?' Natoman and Beasey are not far behind, all the lads buzzing with excitement, all looking forward to our first night in our own cell, not knowing that our first night was about to be ruined.

The officer came around at about 7.15 pm to bang us out. We said our good nights and headed into our cells. At first it was strange not having someone to bounce things off, but it was so cold that I soon found that all I was concentrating on was keeping warm! I unpacked the rest of my clothes, put my son's and mother's pictures up on my notice board, and turned the telly on to catch up on the soaps.

I'm not sure what time I heard the first scream, but it shook me to my very core. Soon, it was followed by a constant stream of painful-sounding pleas for help. It became clear that a prisoner in B Base, which was located under us and to the right, was being attacked. I think it was Fitzer who started first, banging on his door to get the attention of the officers. Soon we were all banging and shouting, trying to help this poor bastard. After some time the screaming stopped. We later found out he was attacked by three fellas inside a cell only big enough for two, but on that night housing four. Fuckin' scumbags! Now, attacks of this nature in The Joy are few and far between. But those screams that night will stay with me for a long time.

As I lay in a cell on my own for the first time that night I felt a unnerving chill enter my body. I was actually looking forward to the screw opening my cell door the next morning so I could surround myself with the people I had begun to trust – and all of us thinking the same thing: 'Thank God that wasn't me last night!' Again, the importance of safety in numbers.

Chapter 17

STRETCH GETS SCALDED

We soon settled into life on C Wing. Myself and Fitzer got straight to work honing our silky guitar licks as I began writing songs again. Everyone in the kitchen seemed in great form, besides the usual shower of Balls Roughers.

We had a great crew at that time: Slasher, so called because they found a tiny blade in his cell that he truthfully used to cut his nails, but the screws assumed it was a weapon ... Slasher wouldn't harm a fly for fuck's sake, but the name stuck. Then there was Dotsy, a solicitor who had fallen from grace. We assumed he would be *major* balls rough, but he proved us all wrong by becoming one of the funniest guys I've ever met, and a man who just got on with his sentence. The list goes on and we became like a family. But when one of the family members was attacked, it affected us all.

Stretch was never going to be in the running for employee of the month – truth was that he was a lazy fucker – but he was our lazy fucker. Unfortunately, he was drawing too much attention from The Gaffer and I worried he might get sacked, so I pulled him to the side on one particular morning. 'Listen bud,' I said, 'it's no skin off my nose if ya do fuck all here, but I'd hate to see ya get sacked ... you'll lose your single cell on C Wing.' (The prison had us by the short and curlies – if we fucked up and lost our job in the kitchen we lost our single cell too, and got thrown back onto D Wing.)

'Sound Gar, yeah I'll get me finger out,' replied Stretch. And so we started our day like every other. I took up my residence on the fryers – I had earned a move from the pot-washers – and Stretch worked in the tunnel wash, which was a tough aul' job at the best of times. Every now and then, because of a blockage in the drain, Stretch would have to come out into the kitchen to empty his slop water in one of the other drains. That morning, he happened to use the drain beside Bobby, the kitchen rat!

Bobby was a Romany gypsy, a small little fucker who looked no more than thirteen but was in his twenties. He had coal black hair and a sly grin that showed his golden-capped tooth. He was the officers' pet and would have no bother telling tales on the lads if, say, they like to have a cup of hooch after work, or if they took extra milk or robbed a couple of eggs ... anything to suck up to the screws. Now, even from a young age, you're told that being a tell-tale isn't the right thing to do. Your own mother would state this valuable information to you as you'd run to her, crying that Alison from across the road had kicked ya in the nuts. 'Now, now ... nobody likes a tell-tale,' she'd say, and mother knows best. This goes to a whole new level as you grow up. The reason that the majority of the prisoners in Mountjoy were caught was because of tell-tales ... rats! Now, I'm not justifying the actions that led to any of our incarcerations, but it's disgusting to know that some rat fucker sold you up the river so that he didn't have to be locked up. So, as I'm sure you can imagine, being a rat *in* prison is double trouble! And this prick Bobby was just that ... a dangerous little fucker who you couldn't even give a slap to ... because he'd *rat*!

We knew that Bobby found Stretch to be the weak link in the kitchen, so he took it upon himself to give him a hard time, all the time. In general, bullying is disgusting and not accepted in modern society, and this is magnified ten-fold in prison. Nobody likes a bully. Stretch would never speak up for himself, which just encouraged Bobby all the more. On that morning, I was standing at the ovens with Natoman as Stretch came out with his slop water. As he approached the drain he had selected, Bobby pipes up. 'Here, Lurch, fuck off and use another drain!'

'Don't let that little fuck tell ya what to do Stretch,' came my response.

'Fuck off Bobby,' said Stretch, as he began emptying his slop water. Bobby, losing face here, then decides to push Stretch sending him onto his arse ... in front of The Gaffer, who says nothing as his little pet can do no wrong.

'Leave it fuckin' out,' comes the roar from Natoman. With that, Stretch gets to his feet and throws the remaining slop water, which at this stage is nothing more than suds, at Bobby, wetting him slightly. But this retaliation has been met with great approval from the rest of the kitchen lads, as a mighty roar goes up. 'Go on the Stretch,' laughs most of the lads. 'State of ya Bobby,' from a few others. This is enough to tip Bobby over the edge, but when we all thought he'd throw a dig, he surprised us by picking up an empty bucket and walking away.

We were all too busy congratulating Stretch for finally standing up for himself to notice that Bobby had gone to the industrial water boilers, huge steel containers that held water hot as the fires of hell. He steadily took his time to fill his empty bucket with this steaming hot water, ambled back towards Stretch, and proceeded to throw this scalding water all over him ... it was horrific. I couldn't believe what I was seeing. In shock, Stretch grabbed a sweeping brush and ran at Bobby, but an officer grabbed him. That's when the shock wore off and the pain set in. Me and Natoman rushed Stretch to the toilet to strip him and to try to start the soothing process until the medic could be contacted. A few of the lads tried to get at Bobby, but he ran straight into the officers' tea room where they protected their little rat!

Almost instantly Stretch was starting to blister on his right arm, which he had raised to block his face, which was the area the little fucker was aiming for. His back also got severely scalded, but luckily he had been wearing a standard issue kitchen jacket, which did save him somewhat.

Me and Natoman did what we could, although the fuckin' taps in the toilet in the kitchen only gave out hot water which made the poor fucker worse. Fitzer came into the toilet like a man possessed. 'That little rat fucker ... ya all right Stretch?' Just then an officer came in to take Stretch to a medic. God love him, he was in terrible pain. It was one of the most malicious, premeditated acts that I had ever seen.

As Stretch was taken away talk around the kitchen was centred around Bobby the rat, with the majority agreeing that he deserves to get his fuckin' head kicked in. But, as always, he was protected by the people he provided information to on a regular basis, plus there were no 'hard men' in the kitchen when I worked there. Yes, we'd stick up for people if they were being victimised or bullied, but violence was a last resort. Of course, the powers-that-be had to be seen to do something so Bobby was sacked. But we all made sure word got out that he would not be safe in The Joy anymore, and so they had to move the little rat fucker to another jail.

As for Stretch, he got sacked too, which in my opinion was a fuckin' joke. As myself and Fitzer were heading around to our cells from the kitchen a couple of hours later, we bumped into him, bags packed, being fucked back on to D Wing. The top of his right arm was heavily bandaged, and as I looked at him he had a tear in his eye.

'Ya all right buddy?' asked Fitzer.

'Fuckin' lost me cell an' all lads,' came his reply. My heart went out to him. I grabbed his bags off him and told the officer escorting him that I was going to help him move. As I said earlier, we were like a family in that kitchen, and even though Stretch no longer worked with us, he was still one of us. Natoman had already arranged for Stretch to go in with a friend of his named Rafter, someone Stretch knew too. At least his first night back on the fuckin' kip that is D Wing will be with a sound lad. Poor aul' bollox. All he did was stand up for himself and he ends up with burns on his body, no job and back on D Wing. It's days like this that you realise Mountjoy is a fuckin' hellhole.

Chapter 18

Talking Thursdays

One of my many kitchen duties included the serving of food to the lads at dinner time. We would load up a mobile food server in the kitchen, which kept the food piping hot, gather up the desert, usually fruit or a yogurt, sometimes ice cream if we got lucky, and head on our merry way. I got put on to the A Wing server, so it was my job, along with another prisoner and a kitchen officer, to serve the lads from A Wing their food ... and A Wing was a fuckin' kip! A Wing can't mix with D Wing – ah, it's all a load of bollox to be honest. But there was a small number of fuckin' pricks on A Wing and on more than one occasion I was threatened, for a multitude of reasons, but mostly because they were pricks! I always kept my head down and tried to have a bit of banter with the lads. Most, nearly all, would partake in this form of Irish pleasantry but some were just, well, *pricks*!

Every Thursday and Sunday, after we served up the grub, we had to hang around to clean the serving area which consisted of a counter, fridges, sinks, washable walls, etc., plus the mobile food server. Two lads were required to do this and we took it in turns. Some days it was me and Natoman, on the odd occasion it was me and BC, but mostly on a Thursday it was me and Beasey. And I really looked forward to these Thursdays because whilst me and Beasey scrubbed and cleaned, we transported ourselves outside the walls of Mountjoy simply through the art of conversation. We would reminisce about old times, sexual conquests/failures – mainly failures on my part – nights out, friends, family and so on. But when the talk got on to our future, well, it got very intense, very surreal, very scary!

We would ask one another, 'What's next in your life? Where will the road take ya?' And do you know what? We hadn't a fuckin' clue. We would then begin to fret about how society would judge us when we were released. Could we get a job? Would our family and friends be the same with us? In prison, the one thing you have an abundance of is time, but sometimes too much time to think can be hazardous. The mind is a dangerous thing and these were not the kind of thoughts to be having as it could lead to the incurable state of, yep, you guessed it, balls roughness. But myself and Beasey would reassure each other that we'd be fine ... we're good people after all!

As these soul-searching sessions were taking place, all of A Wing would be on lockdown, except for a few cleaners and painters. Sometimes they would join us, but would soon regret their decision when they realised we were tapping deep into each other's souls. One fella in particular, though, a cleaner, would regularly join in, fully immersing himself in the topics that we would bring up. Showing intense interest, he'd swing the conversation from one point to the next with the grace of a ballet dancer. I fuckin' hated him. He was a dodgy aul' soul. He just had that look about him. He was about five foot, with long, strawberry blonde hair, and no pride in keeping himself clean or tidy. He would talk with an American accent, even though he was from Cavan!

Beasey would laugh and tell me to 'leave him alone, he's a nice lad'. Bollox, he was a wanker! And one fateful Thursday my point was proven as we realised, whilst he was showing his overwhelming interest in our soul-searching conversations, that he was robbing us blind. He didn't really care for our woes, had no time for our fears, he just wanted to rob us!

We usually got left an extra ice cream, if that was what the desert was, or some extra meat to munch on while we cleaned, but Beasey had pointed out that, quote, 'Those fuckin' poxy screws don't even leave us anythin' anymore.'

'Yeah,' says I, 'fuck it, I'm gonna say something when we get back buddy!' Which, of course, I did ... only to be annihilated.

'How dare you question what I do, Cunningham, ya little prick. I always leave something there for yas, ya cheeky little bollox,' was the response from the screw.

That was when myself and Beasey started putting two and two together and realised that our 'Talking Thursday' friend was robbing us blind! He'd feign interest in our conversation, direct it wherever he wanted to, then choose his moment to strike, relieving us of the minuscule bit of a treat we got as an incentive to clean the poxy server! When I pulled him up on it, his face cracked that horrible, sick-looking smile he had, and he said – in a Boston accent? – 'I'm a fuckin' prisoner ... what do you expect? Sure, this place is full of 'em!'

I felt like ripping his head off his shoulders, but he was right, and he got us ... hook, line and ice cream! Still, I always loved my 'Talking Thursdays' with Beasey.

Chapter 19

Weight Loss in the Gym

Before my incarceration I was, to put it mildly, a heavy man. I was 18 and a half stone of stale Guinness and bad fast food. How I ever got lucky to be intimate with two women who bore children for me is fuckin' incredible! To both of those ladies, and any other poor unfortunates who fell for the shite that used to come out of my mouth, I sincerely apologise.

As mentioned, once you're locked up time is all you have, and managing that time becomes a constant quest. The intimidation levels never really subside in Mountjoy, which keeps you constantly on your guard and, if you let it, the boredom that goes hand-in-hand with residing in this kip of a jail could drive you insane. Working in the kitchen was a godsend as you were kept busy all day, but I was starting to get tired of the time I was spending doing nothing after work. I would have to wait for Fitzer to get back from the gym before we could rehearse and jam our new songs. I needed something to change.

Looking around the kitchen one day, I noticed that there was a lack of fatties, and I started to notice lads bringing their gym gear with them in the morning, so they could work out on their breaks or at the end of the working day.

One particular lad was extremely zealous when it came to the gym ... Beasey! With his body-builder's frame he seemed to me the perfect guy to ask for guidance. For I had made my decision ... I, Gary Cunningham, was going to give 'keeping fit' a go!

It was after a hard day in the kitchen that I plucked up the courage to walk into Beasey's cell and request his services. Beasey resided up on D3 at the time. I slowly ambled up the cast-iron stairs that grants access to all of D's landings, and sheepishly made my way towards Beasey's cell. Running through my mind were the words I was going to use to ask for his help, but not look like a girl in doing so! I rapped on Beasey's dark blue cell door and then stepped inside his humble abode.

'Alri' Gar, how the hell are ya?' As intimidating as this guy looks, with his macho frame and massive sleeve-tattoo on his right arm that looks like it came straight from a Brazilian rain-forest tribe, he has got to be one of the nicest blokes I've ever met. He's standing there, drinking raw eggs and farting whilst doing so.

'*Jaysus*, what's that fuckin' smell?' I enquire whilst my hand is firmly clasped across my mouth and nose to try to expel any of the vapours of this satanic stench.

'Wha'?' he asks innocently. 'It's only a fuckin' fart.'

'That it may be Beasey,' I reply, 'but the fuckin' paint is peeling off your walls!' We both start to laugh as Beasey sprays some prison issue air freshener, which is just as vile, to try to dispel the waft which, at this stage, has slowly crept into my soul!

'What can I do ya for Gar?' asks Beasey.

Now's my time, come on Gary, just ask. 'Well, eh, I was, eh ... the thing is I kinda wanna ... will ya show us how to do ... stuff ... in the gym?' I ask this like a child asking Santa for a shiny new BMX.

'Of course I will pal, not a bother,' comes his reply. 'What is it you wanna do?'

That's the easiest question I think I've ever been asked. 'Lose me fuckin' belly ... just wanna feel fit, ya know?'

'Not a bother buddy, you stick with me and in a couple of months you'll be able to see your feet again!' We both start to laugh as Beasey lets rip with another toxic explosion. I turn to run, and over my shoulder I hear Beasey's voice informing me that Operation Transformation will begin the very next evening at 5.30 pm. Let's do this!

I awoke the next day with a spring in my step. I got myself ready for my shift in the kitchen as I did every morning, but on this morn I had an extra bag to pack. One filled with a water bottle, a prison issue vest, Cunny's shorts, Cunny's runners and a prison towel! Watch out Gym of the Joy ... Gary Cunningham is on his way to work his extremely fat arse off!

Work flew by and before I knew it Beasey was telling me to get into my gym attire so I can be ready at the kitchen gate to make the dash to D Wing's gym, which was fuckin' tiny! It consisted of all the gym equipment – machine weights, treadmills, bikes etc. – needed to sculpt an Adonis-like body, but it was slightly bigger than a large garden shed and it had to facilitate over 200 prisoners. So just getting to the gym proved to be as gruelling as what you put yourself through once you got in there!

Once the officer opened the gate from the kitchen, myself and Beasey took off like two Linford Christies and managed to get into the gym before the madness began. I was ready, pumped up, raring to go. I felt I could've lifted the entire gym above my head and spun it on its axles!

'What are we starting with Beasey?' came my eager question.

'*We* are starting on *nothin'*! *You* are getting on that treadmill, putting the incline up to as far as it will go and *walking* for about 30 minutes!'

What? I thought to myself. *Is he insane? Fuckin' walking? I … am … Spartan!* Yeah, right, who was I kidding? I got on the treadmill and felt every eye in the tiny white-walled gym fixate on me, as the radio pumped out a dance tune to encourage the lads as they worked out. So, off I set on my 'walk'. For God's sake, this is easy, I begin to think, this is fuckin'… and after about eight minutes I slip and fall off, much to the amusement of my fellow gym enthusiasts.

'Gobshite ya,' come the laughs and chants from behind me. Beasey ambles over, not able to make eye contact for fear he'll erupt with laughter, picks me up and places me back on the treadmill. Fuck's sake. Now I feel like a right tool. But I solider on, red faced and out of breath.

At the end of the session, and feeling absolutely shattered, I crawl out of the gym into the small barbed-wire yard, the breeze a beautiful welcome on my flushed face. I slowly make my way back into D Wing and up to my cell, with Beasey holding me up. 'Thought it was gonna be easy, Gar?' he asks.

'I never knew walking could be so hard,' I splutter, out of breath.

'Now, that's all you'll be doing for the next few months, hopefully staying on the treadmill next time!' says Beasey.

And do you know what? It worked. I went from nearly 19 stone down to just a little over 14 stone in about 12 weeks. All from walking, and eating less than I had on the outside. Who'd have guessed it? The gym is an integral part of most prisoners' time. It's 'great for the aul' head' is the usual comment made amongst prisoners about it. And I am so glad that I now fully understand this statement and have embraced it. I am still maintaining the weight (I also completed a FETAC in personal training) and … bejaysus … I'm starting to actually look 'all right'.

Chapter 20

The Music Men and Woman

As I write this tale, I sit and think about how I'm portraying prison life. I'll sum up prison life in two words ... *fuckin' horrible!* But as I've already stated, this book is not about glamourising prison life or trying to convey the horrors that people usually associate with prisons ... this is my story of my journey and it is told with the upmost honesty. Hard as I found Mountjoy and the separation from my family and losing my son, I knew I just had to get on with it. But I got through it thanks to some of the incredible people who appear in these pages. Three in particular are the music teachers in Mountjoy – Paul, Brian and Lisa.

When you're locked up you can get up to all sorts of mischief or just do fuck all, basically, but that was never going to be me. I just can't sit around doing nothing, so the auld saying came to mind: *'It's not the time ya do, Gary ... it's what ya do with your time.'* So I fully immersed myself into the school in Mountjoy, attending a computer class three times a week ... if The Gaffer would allow it.

The school is situated upstairs, above the kitchen ironically enough! There is a staircase straight from the film *One Flew Over the Cuckoo's Nest* which steadily winds up a dull, faded yellow stairwell, bringing you into Mountjoy's school. The classrooms were made as welcoming as possible by the incredible staff who turn up every day to try to embrace the lads of Mountjoy, many of whom already feel that society has given up on them. Although there were still bars on the windows of each classroom, with some creative flair from the teachers you were transported, albeit momentarily, over the prison walls. The support on offer was mesmerising. Some lads may have difficulty reading or writing, which can cause confidence issues, but from your first meeting with the head of the school, Mary, a lady small in stature but enormous in kindness, you soon realise that all these people want to do is assist in any way they can. The school offered a variety of subjects and FETAC courses and, if nothing else, it got you out of your cell for a couple of hours.

Fitzer had been attending the music class, and though we didn't realise it at the time, he was honing his bass skills in preparation for the phenomenon that would be The Offenders. Since I had been playing the guitar most of my life, I didn't feel the immediate need to go up to this class with him ... how wrong and ignorant I was! From the second I walked into the tiny music room that day and saw it crammed with amazing electric and acoustic guitars, I knew I had found my nirvana – not the band, more of a 'yoga/hippy' thing. One of the teachers, Paul, who was actually a bass player in his band, was sitting on top of a Marshall guitar amp, playing some amazingly catchy blues riff on a strange looking six string guitar. He then he broke into a solo which I'm confident would make Mark Knopfler put down his bacon sandwich and perk up his ears in admiration. I was transfixed by this man's talents.

He looked up as me and Fitzer entered the 'Music Lab'. He smiled, continued to play, and began to speak whilst not hitting one bum note. 'Ah, Fitzer, how's it goin'?' His silver hair caught a sun beam that was creeping into the room from the barred window above him. Even his attire matched that of a hard working Dublin band member – black leather waist coat, Wrangler jeans, etc.

'Howya Paul, this is Gary ... he's not a bad guitar player, Paul,' answered Fitzer, as I proceeded to pick up the nearest acoustic six-stringer and break into my party piece of 'Roadhouse Blues' by The Doors.

'Pleasure to meet you Gary,' said Paul, followed by, 'ah, "Roadhouse Blues", great track.' He then proceeded to accompany me on our rendition of this Jim Morrison classic, playing these fantastic licks on his guitar, whilst making the funniest facial expressions, each one a representation of the note he was playing. He told me to 'Keep playin', Gar, keep playin' as he instructed Fitzer to pick up a bass. As I continued the steady, memorable blues riff from the song, Paul began to show Fitzer what to do on the bass, and after only a couple of minutes all three of us where jamming the song. I even broke out with some vocals! For about a half hour that day I could have been anywhere, all down to the escape music offers. This was the beginning of a fantastic working relationship with this incredibly talented man. His influence, advice, teachings and encouragement were worth more than their weight in gold.

On the same day I also got to meet Brian, younger than Paul but with his same voracious appetite for music. A tall man, Brian bore all the hallmarks of a 'cool, contemporary, moody musician', and he knew his way around a guitar's neck, like a heart surgeon navigating the path towards the heart. He has played with numerous bands and his experience was invaluable.

Last but not least I met Lisa, a petite, extremely attractive lady with flowing brown hair and a style totally unique to her. She also happened to be an incredible pianist, with such an interesting, quirky taste in music which she was only too willing to share with the group. Again, she made us feel welcome and also offered her skills to try to teach me the piano. I did take her up on this, but that thorn in my side, The Gaffer, would soon put a stop to that, the *wanker*!

Chapter 21

The Offenders Songs/ Poems for the Lads/ Journeyman

In the past I have played in various bands and written some songs, but nothing to sing about ... excuse the pun! But, like most things in my life, I had suppressed what I now realise was a talent that was buried deep in the outer reaches of my soul. I'm actually okay at writing, be it a song or a poem or, hopefully, a book about life in The Joy!

Whilst in The Joy, and being around the positive being that was Fitzer, I was soon to delve into those parts of my soul and start writing, and what began to flow was actually quite good, if I do say so myself. It all started with a joke tune. I've always been able to muster up original songs, tunes and riffs on my guitar, and I had this one that kind of hung around me, somewhat like the band Ash and their style of riff – a catchy little ditty.

I played it for Fitzer, who liked it, but more impressively started to put a damn fine bass line to it. At this stage he was flying with his lessons up in the school with Paul, the music teacher. You could see that music was in him, he was a natural. He was a perfectionist, too, and this only added to his growth on the bass. To this day I have never played with a more accomplished or polished bass player. He navigates the long neck of the bass with such ease. And he learned all of this in jail!

For a laugh I decided to put some lyrics to this little tune, and I used Balls Rough Harry as my inspiration, so of course the song was called 'Balls Rough' (when Balls Rough Harry heard it he twigged straight away that he was the inspiration behind the tune and wasn't too happy ... oh well). Everyone got a giggle out of this song, even The Gaffer liked it.

> It was the start of my sentence, and I was finding it tough / I asked the boys in the kitchen, they said you're doin' it Balls Rough.

As for Me and Fitzer? We fuckin' *hated* it, but it set into motion something that is still going today.

The creative juices started to flow in both of us and the songs, proper good fuckin' songs at that, started to come thick and fast. The Offenders started to write its own material! I penned another 'prison' song entitled 'Doin' Your Whack'. It has a certain '70s funk vibe to it, and to this day is a hugely popular song with inmates all across Irish prisons ... we even named our first EP 'Doin' Your Whack'.

Once Fitzer got sucked up in the hurricane that was The Offenders, his confidence grew, and one day he popped his head into my cell. 'Story Gar? Here I have this song I wrote about the wife and me son ... wanna hear it?'

'Too right I do bud,' came my eager reply.

What happened next will stay with me for the rest of my days. Fitzer picked up the guitar and played this haunting, melodic lament where he speaks directly to his beloved and tells her everything is going to be okay. It is entitled 'Big Kiss'.

> Hello, good morning my dear, I'm thinking of you while I'm sitting here / Wondering what your day has planned, give anything to have you in my hands oh oh woo oh oh.

I was moved to tears. It was just incredible. Of course, Fitzer notices my tears and fuckin' lashes me out of it. 'Ya fuckin' eejit ya, bleedin' cryin' an all,' he laughed, but quickly followed up with, 'do ya like it though, yeah?'

'It's unbelievably good man, but that voice ... *wow*!' I can't stress enough how good this guy is as a singer ... the dark rough tone of Paul Weller combined with the high range of Freddy Mercury. Again, this voice had only came to fruition in jail.

From that moment The Offenders went from being a bit of laugh – a 'prison band' – to being something we might be able to make a shilling out of upon our release. We soon realised that vocally we complimented each other, Fitzer being the all round singer while I was the 'gruff rock singer'. A match made in rock heaven! Soon we had a wide range of original songs and we got to record them in The Joy's school, thanks again to the help of all the music teachers.

Adjoined to the music room in Mountjoy was another, smaller room, 'The Lab'. Inside, the walls were adorned with some beautiful electric, acoustic and bass guitars. To the left was a massive recording board, albeit dated by today's standards, parked on a long wooden bench. Me and Fitzer would spend every minute we were allowed out of the kitchen (most times 'bunking' out like bold schoolboys!) trying to lay down tracks. We had no metronome and yet kept a solid beat, as all the guitar and bass tracks were recorded live. We recorded eight completely original songs, and when all the guitar tracks were laid, the vocals began. I felt enormous pride in the songs we had written. Fitzer wrote a belter, 'All I Wanna Do', and I'll always feel immensely proud when I hear our little EP.

The creative ideas came thick and fast and one day I turned to Fitzer and said, 'I'm gonna write a musical!'

'Fuck it,' says he, 'not a bother to ya Gar.'

And so, after three days or so of straight writing, *Journeyman* was born, my first play. Imagine, some halfwit prisoner who had fuck all self-esteem through alcohol abuse, who had no faith in himself, had just started the hardest working, funkiest rock band *ever* to come out of a jail, and now had penned a fuckin' musical that was well received by all who heard it. Like I said at the start, '*it's not the time you do ... it's what you do with your time!*'

The Offenders provided the music in this play, which tells the story of a man's journey through life from birth to death through the medium of music. It's a sometimes haunting tale of abuse and self-destruction with, of course, some humour thrown in. More about the play later.

I also started to write poems for lads for their loved ones, poems they could put in birthday/anniversary cards, or just to use if they were in the dog house. Some of the lads would tell their ladies they wrote these poems themselves, which I thought was funny. Basically, if a lad wanted a poem, but wanted it to look like it came from him, I would ask him to tell me (1) his nickname for his partner, and (2) a little secret only the two of them would know. I would then write an extremely romantic, sometimes heartbreaking and lonely poem, and would work the information he had given me into it, all of which resonated positivity and hope for the future.

Valentine's Day was my busiest day. I charged a half ounce of tobacco for an A4 poem. If they gave me a photo of their partner, I would scan it in the computer workshop, upload it to a computer and then open the photo in a prehistoric version of Photoshop. I would then tinker with the levels of the photo to get it looking just right, and type the poem I had just created over the picture. I would then laminate it and give it to the always grateful prisoner. Value for tobacco if I do say so myself ... I put a bit of effort into this!

Two things happened that Valentine's Day which to this day makes me laugh. Firstly, I had so many prisoners coming and going from my cell collecting their poems that an officer whom I got on with pulled me aside and warned me not to, quote, 'Fuckin' attempt to be sellin' drugs, they're watchin' ya like a hawk'. In due course my cell was searched, as was I. As the officers ransacked my cell I stood there with a cheeky grin plastered across my face.

'Where are the fuckin' drugs, Gary?' asked one of the intimidating officers.

'I think these are what you are looking for lads,' I replied, as I pointed to the large stack of laminated A4-sized photos with poems strewn across them, and the increasing pile of half ounce tobacco pouches sitting on my desk. After a very short explanation of my budding enterprise, the officers had a laugh and went on their merry way.

The other amusing occurrence that day was when two of the lads from the kitchen had requested poems, but alas the request came just two days before Valentine's Day! I did need a little more time to create a poem, especially two different ones, as I wanted each poem to be unique. But for these two lads, with such a short space of time, I wrote basically the same poem twice, with just the names changed, and each one having that personal 'secret' making it unique. The lads were delighted, but on Valentine's Day they both had their loved ones up for a visit at the same time! When you go out for a visit you very rarely can choose which visiting box you can go to, as everyone would choose box three since it's a bit more private. So the boys were both put into box two, but cleverly they went to opposite ends of the room so as not to be foiled over the fact that they hadn't written their poems.

As any woman who had to visit their partner in Mountjoy will tell you, sometimes you form a bond with another female coming to do the same thing. Unfortunately for the lads, their two ladies, unbeknownst to them, had forged a great friendship, one which talked about the lack of emotion or affection from their men. So on production of 'the poems', well, they had their doubts and comparisons were made in front of the two lads. 'Creative writing class me hole,' I believe was the laughing response of the two ladies. Unlucky lads, and sorry if I put you in the shit house!

I did a fuckin' great poem for Fitzer for his wife, my first one actually. We were sitting in the kitchen one Friday and he informed me his anniversary was next week. I had a tiny little black diary in which I wrote down any ideas for songs or poems. I told him to take me back to Day One, the very first time they met, and tell me everything, which he did. I did most of my writing at that time in the cubicle of the prisoners' toilet in the kitchen. Every now and then I'd run back out to the kitchen to locate Fitzer. I'd recite a couple of lines I'd just written for him, and we would both get excited. I really wanted this to be the best poem I'd ever done, because this bloke always did so much for everyone. It basically told the story of how they met, the birth of their son, their wedding, everything, all told as a poem. I would love to include it here, but it is solely for Fitzer and his amazing wife. I never spoke to anyone about the stories behind prisoners' poems. The information they gave me stays with me forever.

On its completion, Fitzer asked if it could be 'wrote out fancy' instead of just put on top of a photo of the two of them in Photoshop. Natoman offered his services, and it turned out he was an incredible artist. He got a white A4-sized wooden board from the art room in the school and wrote it out in calligraphy, with beautiful floral designs enclosing each verse. Of course, Fitzer being Fitzer, he told his wife I wrote it. She told him she loved it, but to tell me not to do anymore for him as he was to make more of an effort himself ... though I still did the odd sneaky one for him.

Chapter 22

'You've Got Mail'

Writing all of these letters for other lads and their ladies highlighted a deep crater inside my own heart. I had come into prison a single man. I had in fact been single for quite some time and, don't get me wrong, there is a very positive side to being single whilst incarcerated, as you don't have the fear that your lady has 'grown tired of waiting for you', 'it's not her fault that you're in here,' and so on. On more than one occasion I would sit with a lad and listen as he unloaded some paranoid spiel regarding his loved one. The darker side to this is that I know of at least two lads who couldn't take it anymore, who had received a letter or a phone call from their loved one ending their relationship, and tragically took their own lives whilst inside. Such a waste. R.I.P.

But I did crave the love and attention of someone from the outside, someone other than a family member who actually gave a fuck about me. On top of these feelings was the added remorse I had for my son. I would never have allowed him to visit me in Mountjoy, even if the situation with his mam had been different. I have nothing against lads who have their kids up on a visit – in many cases it's essential – but I just wouldn't have liked mine there. But I did long to hear his voice so that heaped more sadness into my heart.

A row had also occurred over the phone one day between myself and one of my brothers, a silly, stupid row, but one that spread like a disease through my family. As a result of this toxic argument, I received no visits from my brothers for about three months. This was a very dark time for me.

I had, quite proudly, been known for my high energy, for my ideas and views on prison life. I was never afraid to fight for 'prisoners rights', and I always tried to be filled with positivity. But, at this particular time, I was fading fast. I was too proud to open up to anyone, and so I bottled up these feelings but they soon started to overflow. It terrifies me to write this, but I was a couple of footsteps away from trying to score some heroin, which I fuckin' detest. But I'd given up.

Then came the suicidal thoughts.

The only one who cares about me on the outside is me ma. Nobody loves me or wants me. Country is on its knees, jobs hard to come by, so who's gonna employ an ex-con? *I hate myself, I hate myself, I hate myself.*

And then, like a volcano that had been smouldering under the surface, I erupted. Suddenly the walls of Mountjoy began to smother me. I started to see the ugly side to this prison more and more. The fighting and slashing of prisoners became second nature to me. I hated it. I was going to end my life, one way or another, either through suicide or heroin, and may have done so except for the intervention of one man – Fitzer.

Fitzer had noticed that I was fading, and he was concerned. One day he made me tell him everything which I did right down to the fact that I had made up my mind to 'check out'. I will never forget his reaction. He grabbed hold of me and verbally laid into me. 'You're a selfish fuckin' prick, Gary, your poor ma, your son who will want to see his da again someday, fuck me, ya prick ya! I fuckin' love ya pal, but ya need to give your head a shake!'

It scared me to see the always happy Fitzer like this. He made me listen and would not let me leave until I 'got' it. But the care he showed for me was enough to start the healing process, plus the fucker gave me a fright which I needed. I promised him I would not do anything stupid, gave my word (which is my bond) that I would not bottle things up and that I would always come to him. To this day I feel I owe my life to Fitzer. If it wasn't for him, well, I don't know to be honest.

Fitzer was keeping a close eye on me, as were the rest of the lads from the kitchen, and of course Cunny. These men were my family in there, and you couldn't ask for a better one. One day in the kitchen, BC, being his ever 'over the top' bubbly self, addressed me as I was manning the fryers, whilst he was beside me cooking a massive vat of coddle.

'Here, Gary, ya have to meet me mott's mate, Antoinette, the two of you would be deadly together,' he says to me, smiling all the time.

'Fuck off BC,' I laughed back, thinking who the fuck would want to get to know a sad waster like me.

'No Gar, I'm *tellin'* ya, she is an amazing laugh, always up for a giggle, great attitude towards life and she's a fuckin' singer in a band, ya see? *Yas are fuckin' made for each other.*'

I have to pay homage to BC and his persistence. Maybe he was trying to help? Maybe he wanted to offload his partner's friend on someone? I don't know, but for the next few weeks he would speak to me about this woman, and I have to say I started to buy into it!

One Friday, around midday, came my weekly visit from two very close friends, Derek and Joe, a father and son I had known for some time who never turned their backs on me. As I was called for my visit, so was BC. We both made our way, under the watchful eye of an officer, to the visiting box and when we entered we each took our place and waited for our visitors. Soon, Derek and Joe came in, and I began filling them in on how I was, lying that I was doing great and getting on with things. I paid no attention to BC and his visitors, until he piped up with, 'Gary, come here, I wanna introduce ya to someone. Sorry lads (he said to Derek and Joe), this will only take a second.'

I looked up to see a beautiful, dark-haired woman was his visitor, and I knew it wasn't his lady as I had seen pictures of her. I put two and two together and thought, *this must be Antoinette.*

From the moment I laid eyes on this woman, I was instantly attracted. She had coal black hair, and was dressed in a dark t-shirt and dark blue jeans. Her smile took my breath away, and her eyes sparkled like stars in a clear night sky. I nervously ambled towards BC, trying to give off an air of confidence, but I could actually feel myself shaking.

'Gary, meet Antoinette, Antoinette, this is Gary,' beamed BC.

As I put out my hand to shake hers (shake her hand? *Jaysus* I was nervous all right!) she smiled straight at me. I was blown away. I knew I only had a few seconds and I remember saying something like, 'Do you come here often?' How pathetic! But I then followed with, 'So you like music?' And she answered with such joy in her voice, with such vigour and positivity, saying she was a singer in a wedding band and that she *loved* music!

BC then quickly interjected, 'So will ya write to him Antoinette?'

'I will not,' came her immediate reply, with a slight grin etched across her face.

'Ah, go on,' countered BC. I was feeling a bit embarrassed and I also feared rejection, so I began to make my excuses and turned away to go back to my visitors.

'I'll tell ya what,' said Antoinette, '*You* write to *me* and if you make me laugh, well, then I'll think about writing back.'

That was enough for me. If I had to take 'comedian' lessons I would, because I now had a mission: *Make Antoinette laugh.*

I returned to my visitors, but couldn't focus on anything Joe or Derek were saying. I would sneak a look down towards Antoinette, absorbing this woman's beauty. I was smitten, I must say!

That evening I set about my letter. I wrote it and then re-wrote it a thousand times, and although I cannot fully remember what the content was, I did feel it was funny if I do say so myself. I remember ending it with a serious of random questions – King or Tayto? Stay in or hit the town? – and signed off with my name, my prison number, my prison cell number and Mountjoy's fuckin' address. I wasn't taking any chances, here, *I wanted a reply*!

Once you have a letter you want to send out, the trick is to give it to an officer who you get on with. He or she will then bring it straight to censors for you, as each letter that leaves Mountjoy, and those that are received, are vigorously scrutinised. It's then an unnerving waiting game. You have no idea when your letter will be posted, and if you receive a reply it can take up to three weeks before you actually get it, which is what happened to me. I had given up on getting a reply as it seemed like an eternity since I had sent my letter, then one afternoon an officer appeared at my cell door with a single, white envelope. Could it be? Is this what I've waited for all this time? My hands shook as I pulled the folded A4 sheets from the faded white envelope, and sure enough it was from Antoinette.

What happened next will stay with me for the rest of my life. The letter was filled with so much humour, so much life, and yet a lot of genuine concern and questions about me – me, she wanted to know about *me*! The letter made me laugh out loud, made me feel alive inside. Here is this beautiful woman, firstly confirming that my letter did in fact make her laugh, then asking about me, telling me all about herself, wishing me well, *wanting to hear from me again*! You could tell from the words she chose that she had an incredible lust for life and was extremely funny. She even signed off with, 'Talk to you soon, take care, Love, Mrs Cunningham!' Mrs Cunningham! Brilliant! I must have read that letter a thousand times that day, each time finding something different.

I have a tear in my eye now as I relive this tale for you. Unbeknownst to this wonderful woman, she had given me back my 'Mojo'. To think that anybody on the outside, who wasn't a member of my family, gave a fuck about me was truly mind blowing. Her simple, kind gesture had taken my breath away. I know to her I was just some fool locked up, but she was inspirational to me. I ran to BC's cell and gave him the biggest hug I could muster, and repeatedly thanked him. This might sound odd, and please don't think that I thought I was in a relationship all of a sudden. I just had someone who cared, someone who was wanted to find out about me. I felt so alive inside.

After going through the darkest few months of my entire existence, Fitzer, with his care and compassion, had begun the healing process. But Antoinette? She cured me.

Chapter 23

Apple Tarts Inc.

Antoinette had really put the zest back into my life, as our letters came to each other thick and fast, well, if you call receiving a letter three weeks after it was sent fast! I began to immerse myself back into the crazy world that is The Joy, and found working in the kitchen something that I, again, began to look forward to. Yes The Gaffer was still a complete jerk, but we did get two days break from him and his headcase ways – the weekend! He didn't grace us with his presence at the weekend, and the seismic shift of the mood in the kitchen, even from some of the officers, was notable.

One Saturday, I mistakenly happened upon Fitzer and The Little Fella who seemed busy and extremely shifty at the same time. I asked The Little Fella what was going on, and he reluctantly replied, 'We're makin' apple tarts, Gar.'

'For the screws?' came my puzzled reply.

'Not a-fuckin-tall,' pipes up Fitzer, 'they're for us and a few others!'

'Ah, nice one, I'll give a hand so,' came my zealous reply.

'Now, look, Gary,' starts Fitzer, 'ya know you're me pal, lovin' the auld music with ya an' all, but this is a highly secretive operation we've got goin' on here. If the screws found out we'd be fuckin' sacked, but we run a very tight ship and we have it sussed. The least amount of fellas that know about it the better, ya know?'

It must have been the puppy-eyed hurt look that my facial expressions couldn't hide that made Fitzer quickly interject, 'Hang on, I'll run it by The Little Fella.' I felt nervous, like you feel as you sit outside the office of a potential employer awaiting your interview. I watched as Fitzer and The Little Fella held their corporate meeting, which was taking place beside the fish refrigerator in Mountjoy's bright-white kitchen. After what seemed an eternity, they returned, smiling. 'Right, you're in,' beamed Fitzer.

'Yeah I was fuckin' *in* whether yas liked it or not, ya saps!' I laughed.

'Cheeky prick,' countered The Little Fella.

And so began our little enterprise. Every Saturday morning the three of us would take it in turns to rob the eggs that were needed to fulfil that day's order, as eggs were like gold dust (similar in value too) in The Joy. We would then source all the materials needed, and begin the slow process of making apple tarts from scratch. Fitzer had obtained the recipe from another lad who had since been released, and *he* had received it from another lad, so this aul' recipe had been doing the rounds for quite some years. We would work at a rapid rate, always mindful of the screws and their movements. We became masters in the art of covering up the rolling of pastry, or the filling of tarts, in the event we were intercepted by a curious screw. We would stay on top of our allocated kitchen duties, or when that was difficult get one of the lads to cover for us with the promise of an extra slice of tart if he complied.

We would make, on average, 15 to 20 tarts on a Saturday morning, and these were cleverly distributed to the 'right' people after we looked after the kitchen lads, and ourselves of course! The remaining tarts were then smuggled out of the kitchen and given to lads from our wing, namely, the cleaners, assuring a top class job done on our cell floors; the painters, thus free painting of our cells, although I'd always give Cunny an extra one just because I liked him; and the lads who worked in Reception, meaning fresh towels every day (which was a Godsend) plus they'd do your washing for you. We would also look after our friends and keep some of the headcases sweet, ensuring that you wouldn't get your head kicked in!

It may seem like nothing, but those apple tarts gave a lot of lads a fleeting feeling of happiness. It was a small treat which would, in some, stir nostalgic memories of home or family in a place that had ripped away any reasons for feeling good. I was very proud to be part of that little enterprise, even on the day we were ratted on by a fuckin' gobshite. This wanker fancied himself as a chef, among *countless* other things, and got a bee in his bonnet over the fact that we didn't want him near our apple tarts. So he informed the screws we were taking eggs in order to make our tarts. It blew up in the gobshite's face, though, as the screws were completely fine about it. They were actually impressed by the fact we made these tarts from scratch. But, of course, they wanted their slice so we'd have to make them an apple tart every Saturday too. Still, it was a small price to pay to keep our tart business afloat. Better luck next time, ya gobshite!

Chapter 24

A Brief Interlude

I've felt conflicted so many times whilst writing this book. The fact I've never written anything before, you would think, would be the foremost concern. But it's not. There are two massive issues that I feel I must address at this juncture of my story.

Firstly, I am not showing you Mountjoy, and later on Loughan House, through rose-tinted glasses. As I've said at the beginning of this tale, this is *my* account, and my coping mechanism was to surround myself with great people who, like me, fucked up, but who had the ultimate goal of using their time to radically change themselves. The short tales you find within these pages describe times that stopped me from going over the edge and falling into a vast crater of depression. Of course, we knew this was all our own doing, but that doesn't make Mountjoy any more welcoming. The place is a kip! The constant stench, the longing for home and your loved ones, the tears shed behind your bolted cell door as the shame you've brought on, not just yourself, but your family, comes to visit and have its way with you amid all the fighting and intimidation, which leads me on to my second issue.

I could very easily fill a book with the vile and atrocious beatings, stabbings and 'stripes' – slashing someone's face – that I witnessed. Whenever there is a major incident in

Mountjoy, an alarm sounds to alert the officers. I remember one day that it seemed the alarm was on constantly, as a feud between two gangs reached boiling point. The list of casualties would fit perfectly into a Hollywood blockbuster depicting a war. In fact, I feel the Special Effects people in Hollywood would find it a challenge to recreate some of the injuries I've witnessed. These images will remain with me for the rest of my life, and it's sad to think that I actually became accustomed to these goings on. I also lost two friends through suicide, and watched as others lost their way only to find drugs as an escape. I'm not into 'macho bullshit', and I'm not afraid to cry or get upset, so I can honestly say that these goings on had a massive effect on me. So this book is an illustration of how I coped, of how I tried to stay positive in a negative world. Because that's what Mountjoy is. It is a world within a world, with its leaders, police force, politics, intimidators and good Samaritans, all combining to create a very strange place.

I have read two books on Mountjoy, both of which I really enjoyed for different reasons, but they both had the same common thread running through them: tales of drug abuse, violence and depression. These are accurate depictions of Mountjoy, but I didn't want this tale to be filled with all of that. I was a very negative person before my incarceration, but through a lot of hard work and soul searching, I changed, so I wanted to try to show a very different side to being locked up, and a different side to me. The statistics show that over 60 per cent of Irish prisoners will reoffend within three years. It is my opinion that this is all down to how they spent their time locked up in the first place. The way I 'did my jail' was to work, study and try to make a difference, not only to myself but to the lads around me. That is not how all lads would do it, and that's perfectly fine for them. But that wasn't for me, and I will *never* add to that percentage of reoffending.

Right, back to the story.

Chapter 25

GOODBYE KITCHEN, HELLO PRINT ROOM!

As I mentioned before, Mountjoy has a way of knocking you off your stride in one swift motion, and my time had come for a stumble. I had become a 'gym junkie', really getting into the exercises I was learning, embracing the new, slimmer, fitter Gary. One day, whilst I was trying my best to sculpt my shoulders like those on Arnie in *Commando*, I was being egged on by Handsome to increase the weight, to not be a, quote, 'pussy'. So of course idiot here piles on the weights and ... *bang!* ... out pops the right shoulder. The white walls of the tiny gym began to swirl. Handsome, stifling his laughter, got me to my feet, and escorted me back towards my cell. The pain was excruciating. I could hear the odd 'Jaysus, look at the fuckin' state of him' as I staggered back towards C Wing.

As we entered through the blue barred gates that guard C Wing, John – a foreign national whose name none of us could fully grasp so naturally we called him John – was standing at his cell door, completely filling the area of the door with his humongous frame. He was a professional body builder, although he never worked on his legs so his massive upper frame seemed to be held up by two matchsticks! He knew a lot about human anatomy, though, as he had attended countless night courses as a free man relating to the world of fitness.

So when he stopped Handsome to check what had happened to me, he then turned to me and said in broken English, 'You come in my cell, I fix.'

I was strangely okay to just follow his lead. We got into his cell and John turns to me and says, 'Lie on your tummy, I need to feel, see if I can put back.' Again I had no issue with this because, at this stage, the pain was making me feel numb inside and out and I knew the best I could hope for off a medic was two paracetamol. I lay face down, and John straddled himself on top of me. After a quick scan of the damaged area, John says with confidence, 'Okay, I'll fix this, might hurt.'

Before I can say, 'Have ya done this before?' John is prodding and moving and pushing me further down into the bed as he tries to navigate my shoulder back into its socket. Just as he finds the sweet spot, I let out an almighty, 'Ah, yeah, that's it, Johnny,' as Officer Dineim appears at the cell door to see what the fuck is going on. I'm sure he got the very wrong impression when he saw 'Big John' atop 'Skinny Gary', who had a look of pure ecstasy etched across his face!

A couple of days later I was brought across to the Mater Hospital, handcuffed to three officers, and I was fuckin' mortified, but after an examination I was informed that Big John had done a stellar job!

This injury stayed with me for quite some time, and I kept it to myself for fear of losing my job in the kitchen, thus losing my single cell on C Wing. But the meds I was prescribed gave the jail doctor cause for concern, and so he scheduled a one-to-one with me. I had fooled him before so I was not too worried, but for whatever reason, as soon as he examined my shoulder area that morning, I let out a painful scream. It was enough for him to recommend I cease work with immediate effect in the kitchen, as 'manual labour should be cut to a bare minimum for the foreseeable'. I begged and pleaded with him to reconsider, but to no avail. I do realise that he only had my health at heart, but I knew this would spell the end of the kitchen for me, the end of time shared with my brothers and the end of safety in numbers.

I sprinted back from the doctor's room on C Wing to the kitchen, but the doc had already made the call. The Gaffer summoned me to his office, and with spiteful pleasure informed me I was no longer a kitchen worker and that I must vacate my cell on C Wing with immediate effect. I felt my world crumble. It may not seem like *that* much of a problem, but to me it was everything so I fought the taking of my cell with all my might.

I had become a popular lad both with the screws and the other prisoners on C Wing. I had a way of talking to the officers with respect and manners, sometimes on behalf of other lads, that stood me well. We had a notorious A.C.O. (Acting Chief Officer, each wing has its own and these are the highest ranked officers in the prison), an attractive blonde-haired lady who would put the fear of bejaysus into ya, but for some reason she liked me. So when I asked for help in not losing my cell, this all stood to me. Good manners and politeness really do go a long way. After some back and forth between my A.C.O. and the The Gaffer, I was informed I could keep my cell for now! I was fuckin' delighted!

But the next morning I realised once again that I was just part of the machine that is The Joy. I had to be locked away in my cell, like the rest of the lads, at four different times each day. I was used to ambling around the kitchen, always finding something to do to pass the time, but now, utter boredom. Plus I got to see, more and more, the truly ugly side of this jail. This was just not for me, so I quickly started to enquire as to what jobs may be available that don't require much manual labour, and was pointed in the direction of the computer and print room located in the bowels of D Wing. It was a drab location, but the lads taking part in learning how to use a computer, or learning how to read and write, could use the pre-loaded software available on each machine to print off positive sayings and the like, to adorn the walls and splash a bit of colour into the place. Basically, the computer room, and the print room for that matter, which is facing it, are made up of four or five cells knocked into one. When you stand at the entrance door and look down, it's like a tunnel, or a military bunker like you would see in the movies, with computers lining each wall left and right. I walked in and made a beeline for the officer's desk at the top of the room.

Mr Dunne was the officer in charge, a grey-haired, middle-aged officer with a country accent, and he seemed taken aback when I opened with: 'I'll do a fuckin' great job in that print room for ya. I'm extremely proficient on a PC, and I was heading into my second year of a degree in Creative Digital Media before my incarceration. I'm a fuckin' legend with Photoshop, as you have seen from my countless visits to your computer room, so as to keep my "poem writing" enterprise afloat I have *massive* OCD and fuss over fuckin' everything so Mr Dunne, I feel it would be detrimental to you and the print shop to pass on the once in a lifetime opportunity of having me on board!'

He leaned back on his leather reclining chair and smiled a smile which showed the youth that his grey hair disguised, and said, 'Go on then, don't fuck it up. Training starts tomorrow.'

I was fuckin' delighted, but not yet finished. 'Ya know Smithwicks, the fella always smiling, well he's lookin' to get a start too, and I feel the two of us would be a fuckin' printing force that could take on the mighty Smurfit!'

'Go on, ya fuckin' gobshite, two of yas here tomorrow after breakfast,' he laughs. Success! I just had to tell Smithwicks he now has a job. Hope he doesn't mind!

He didn't, and we ended up running a very tight ship down in that print room. It actually became like 'our office'. Our duties involved the printing of prisoner information cards that are slotted into cell doors, or the countless different forms and applications that were needed in order to make a prison function. Mr Dunne also showed us how to bind books. He was very good to us, as he knew I was using the fact I had my own computer (with absolutely *no* internet access) to aid me in my poem business. Smithwicks' father was a printer too, and so I took the time to teach Smithwicks everything I knew regarding Photoshop, which he took to like a duck to water, designing signs and the like for his father's workshop. We were a great team. I even started getting used to being locked away at the allotted times, though that took a while.

Mr Dunne was highly impressed by our work rate, plus I began making Photoshop tutorials in Microsoft Word, using language the lads 'got' (mostly bad!) so they could make their own photo collages etc. I also designed signs to go around the prison, highlighting cleanliness and so on. Mr Dunne really appreciated all the work me and Smithwicks put in on a daily basis.

I remember one day saying to Smithwicks, 'This fuckin' print room and the computer room could do with a lick of paint, and did ya see Dunne's office? It's like a bag of fuckin' Lego in bits!' I told Mr Dunne to order the paint and let me and Smithwicks do the rest, which we did. It took about two weeks, in the middle of December, but we completed the job and the place looked great, the grey drab walls brought to life with a vibrant splash of yellow mid-sheen paint. Mr Dunne was genuinely taken aback and at tea time, on the last day of painting, he called us into his office and presented us with a Tesco bag containing two bottles of Lucozade, two boxes of mince pies, and some ready-made custard. It actually made myself and Smithwicks feel almost 'normal'. Such a nice, human gesture from an officer the likes of which were few and far between.

It was not my first time to paint for a screw, as I had offered my services to The Gaffer when I worked in the kitchen. Fitzer, being the deadly mate he is, said he was 'Fucked if I'll let ya do it on your own' so the two of us painted the entire kitchen, in our own time, as The Gaffer wanted our kitchen duties done first. He would sporadically say he would 'look after us' when the job was completed, which took about a month. Sometimes, me and Fitzer would hazard a guess at what our bounty would be on completion of the job, agreeing it would probably be a shop order to the value of €10 each, which we would have been only fuckin' delighted with. But of course, when the job was finished we got nothing but abuse from The Gaffer. I felt so bad for Fitzer, but he just said to me, 'Fuck him, he's not worth it!' And he was right.

Chapter 26

Halloween and the X Factor Tart

My days in my 'kitchen cell' on C1 were numbered, though I did last for about a month, always being overheard muttering some bullshit like, 'they won't be takin' *my* fuckin' cell'. But it was unfair on any lad who got a job in the kitchen, as he was entitled to my cell. So I knew, on that Saturday morning when the screw told me I had to move, it was the right thing to do. Plus I was only moving up to C2 so I could actually see right into my old cell from my new one. But word of my moving had spread to the kitchen, and it was music to Fitzer and The Little Fella's ears as they both enjoyed winding me up! They asked to be excused from their duties for five minutes to assist me in my move. The officer in the kitchen they asked was Mr. Sweeney, who I always got on with, so he allowed them to go.

So there I am, not overly thrilled regarding my move, lumbering up the caged-in stairwell of C Wing with a large white, see-through bag containing my clothes, and there is Fitzer and The Little Fella, standing in the middle of C1, the sun beating down through the barred windows high above us, with scarves above their heads, singing the Rod Stewart classic, 'We Are Sailing'. And the more I told them to go fuck themselves, the louder they got. Wankers, but they did make me laugh.

I soon made cell 23 on C2 my own, and began the next phase of my prison life. Antoinette was still filling me with so much joy from her amazing letters. I was, along with Smithwicks, running a tight ship in the print room, and me and Fitzer were really gelling together with our music. Prison life was becoming bearable.

There were many new characters for me to get to know on C2, none of which were the usual kitchen workers I was used to socialising with. Beside me to my left was Pops, an older, proper 'aul' Dub', a gentleman who had received a large sentence for his crime, but whose wise advice regarding prison life was invaluable. To my right was The Torment, very aptly named too. As funny as this young man was, who bore a striking resemblance to a shorter, stockier, Cristiano Ronaldo (I would later learn that he also had similar footballing skills), if you were on the receiving end of one of his pranks he was a fuckin' *torment*! All the lads on C2 were sound, sure even Cunny resided only a few cells away from me, as did No. 2, both lads being the painters of C Wing. Cunny had established himself as the actual painter for the whole prison – a feat which to this day fills me with pride as I think of all the hard work that young lad put into bettering himself.

One evening, Cunny informed me that he'd just gotten word a lad we both knew from the outside had just come in, and was waiting in reception to be housed. Cunny made a request to have this lad, Dave, come straight on to C Wing. Now this was unheard of, as C Wing was like the fuckin' Ritz compared to the rest of the kip, so you had to earn your way on to it by being drug-free and willing to work. But after some positive reassurance that Dave would be an invaluable member to C2, and the fact that Cunny was a hard-working and trusted prisoner, the decision was made that Dave was to be let up to us, on the grounds that he passed a piss test, which he did, and started work in some respect the next day, which he also did by getting a job in the bakery. And what a character he was. I mean the guy is fuckin' *nuts*, funny, but fuckin' crazy! He was in his early thirties, a stocky, short, dark-haired lunatic, with a crazy side-winding smile. Just before banging out time every night, the medic opens his office for lads to collect their prescribed meds, or to get something to quell man flu etc. Dave would firstly roar, over and over again, *'medication time, boys, medication time'*, as he'd make his way down from C2 to C1 where the medic station was located. Then, upon receiving his meds, he'd proceed to do cartwheels and tumbles back up the landing of C1. The guy was nuts!

As I said, I knew Dave from the outside, and this stood to me, as he would always look out for me. I remember my first Halloween locked up. Dave's cell came before mine, so he would be unlocked before me. At tea time, on that Halloween night, I could hear Dave roaring 'Help the Halloween party', as the screws and prisoners who could see him were falling about the place laughing. I couldn't wait for my door to be opened, and when it was, I looked to my left only to see Dave in a prison vest, a pair of prison jocks wrapped round his head, and some white shorts on with black socks and white runners! Some rosary beads hung from his neck, but in place of our Lord on the cross was a square bit of cardboard with something written on it. He was going from cell to cell, scaring the shite out of the lads, and making them give him something towards his Halloween party. As I approached him, what was on the cardboard around his neck became readable: 'Jim'll Fix It'. Yes, the news had just broken of what that vile bastard Jimmy Saville had done, and there's our Dave dressed up as him and gathering sweets and what-not for his Halloween party. Headcase.

As I said, he had nailed down a job in the bakery, and every Saturday evening, because he liked me, he'd bring me an apple tart he had baked that day, with a small pastry X on the top – my *X Factor* cake. By the way, I always found it surreal listening to some of the lads chatting about the *X Factor*, or *Eastenders*, hardened criminals debating who will win the *X Factor* or who Kat Moon is shaggin' now. Dave would make it his business to roar, so everyone would hear, 'This is for *you*, Gary, not those wankers out there, okay? I'll look after them but this is for *you*!' And every Saturday I would mill this tart while watching the *X Factor*, even though the tart was disgusting – it was the thought that counted!

Chapter 27

The Offenders' First Gig

Christmas was approaching fast. The lads and ladies from the music school, along with myself, Fitzer, Scotty – a crazy Scot in his late fifties with long flowing, greasy blonde hair, and an equally long matching beard – and assorted lads from all over Mountjoy who showed a genuine interest in music, worked frantically putting together a 'Christmas Music Extravaganza' for anybody who attended school that year. We were to play in front of about 50 prisoners, a daunting task, believe me! Myself and Fitzer worked day and night, squeezing in a rehearsal or jam at every opportunity. We got a tight set list together consisting of four songs. We were to be the main event, as the teachers in the music school saw something in us. All the other lads brave enough to face the Mountjoy crowd got up to sing a song, some while also playing the guitar. Paul, Brian and Lisa, the music teachers, formed a choir in order for the massive crescendo of Christmas carols. Rehearsals were going great – this was going to be epic.

The Offenders, at this stage only consisting of myself and Fitzer, originally had three songs to play, but at the last minute I re-wrote the classic Live Aid song 'Feed the World' and changed it to 'Free the Joy'. Fitzer was really accomplished on the bass at this stage, and his singing and voice control grew from strength to strength with each passing day. While me and Fitzer rehearsed, a small crowd would gather outside of the cell we were jamming in and just hang around and enjoy the music. They would then spread the news around the prison of how good The Offenders actually sounded – no fuckin' pressure here so.

Not surprisingly, a crowd that is solely filled with prisoners is terrifying! On the fateful morning of the gig, as we sat in the music lab, our 'back stage' so to speak, we watched with an increased beat in our hearts as the old fashioned hall, reminiscent of a primary school hall, began to fill with the over-joyous, loud, raucous prisoners who were greeted with a plastic cup of lemonade, a packet of King or Tayto crisps, and a Mars bar. Sure, they were only fuckin' delighted with life.

And so the time had come, centre stage lads, let's make this jailhouse *rock*!

And rock it did. The first couple of brave lads, who gave their renditions of an Oasis classic and a Dubliners tune respectively, set the tone for what was to follow. The crowd sensed that this wasn't going to be a comedy of errors – this was fuckin' good plus free lemonade and crisps! Scotty, our long haired lover from Glasgow, took to the stage with the music teacher Paul, who was in many ways Scotty's hero, and they jammed out a blues number that would've made Elvis nod in appreciation. A wonderful young man, Kenneth, who is sadly no longer with us as he took his own life whilst in Mountjoy, sang a mesmerising version of 'The Auld Triangle', a song penned about the very prison we were in that morning. You could have heard a pin drop as he slowly and beautifully ambled his way through its haunting verses, his coarse voice only adding to the mystery, the silence only broken as we joined him in the chorus:

> And the auld triangle went jingle jangle all along the banks of the Royal Canal.

It is a moment that is forever in my heart, and in the hearts of all the men who were so lucky to be there that day to see such a special young man do what he did best. R.I.P. Kenneth.

And so it was time at last for The Offenders.

I was shittin' but gave nothing away – if they smelt fear they would pounce! I didn't know it until later, but Fitzer was shittin' too, he just has a better way of hiding it. We opened by me introducing myself and Fitzer, A.K.A The Offenders. This got a slight cheer, well, a faded, almost mute cheer to be honest. The 'crowd' were just waiting to see what all the fuss was about – 'are The Offenders any good or wha'?' And so we began our first song, 'Doin' Your Whack', the '70's funky 'prison song' I had written at the beginning of The Offenders creation. I took the vocals as Fitzer had not yet mastered the art of singing and playing the bass at the same time, which was a pity. As I made my way through the verses, which are lined with 'prison-type' scenarios and innuendoes, I felt I wasn't getting the reaction I wanted, until I came to the last line of the second verse. I screamed, in my gravel rock voice:

> Yeah the Joy can be crazy, sometimes it has to be seen / But fuck it lads do your whack and fuck the P-19s (punishment forms).

Well a massive roar went up from the crowd, as they cheered and whistled. We'd done it, we'd won them over. The song ended to a standing ovation as did all the songs after.

I began to address the crowd to explain the name of our next song and my reasoning for writing it, and was shocked to see they were hanging on my every word. So, as Fitzer began playing his uplifting, flowing, reggae-style bass line that he had created as the song's intro, I turn to the crowd and say: 'Lookin' around this room, I wouldn't say any of you fit lookin' lads would experience the problems I had whilst out on the Dublin nightclub scene back in the day. I'd stand there, fat boy with a drink in hand, and a cracker of a bird would come over and ya think you've hit the jackpot only for her to fuck off at the end of the night when your money ran out, so I wrote a song about her, it's called "Tramp"!' This brought laughter and a massive cheer from the lads as 'Tramp' got its first airing. It's a happy, reggae-style tune, with a slight rock twist. It was a complete tongue in cheek look at my sex life which poked fun at me more than anything else.

> Gather 'round and I'll tell ya 'bout a time, a devil woman had me goin' out my mind / She walks in it begins wasp-waisted and sallow skin she throws a look, and she just blows me away yeah!

The lads find humour in this tale of sexual conquests gone awry and again we have them on their feet.

Next Fitzer hands me his bass to play, as he takes centre stage for his rendition of U2's 'With or Without You'. The lads in the crowd were clearly moved by this man's voice. Not one person shifted in his grey plastic chair, as Fitzer waltzed through each verse and chorus like he'd been doing it for years. I stood beside him, steadily keeping the famous bass line that runs through the track going, and I was genuinely stunned at how talented he was. I thought the roof of Mountjoy's school was going to come ripping off as he brought the song to a close. *Fuckin' hell!*

Last was my re-hash of the Live Aid classic. I informed the lads that I had written a 'Christmas Tune' for them, which brought some chuckles. What follows is the entire song, sung to the tune of 'Feed the World' in a flat Dublin tone to add to the humour.

> It's Christmas time Santy's not in The Joy, with his sack. / Asked him for T R (Temporary Release), he said 'Fuck off, and do your whack.' / We get a

> fry, Christmas morning well whoop de fuckin' do / Throw your arms around The Joy at Christmas time. / But say a prayer, pray they don't find our hooch, / So we can get locked run outta dust and go on the mooch. / There's a world outside our window, havin' a fuckin' ball / Eatin' their ham and turkey, they won't think of us at all. / But soon they'll run outta gargle, and that will end their buzz / But we won't so fuck them and cheers to us / And there won't be blow, in The Joy, at Christmas time / We'll ask the Priest, for his altar wine. / Yeah we know we've broke the law, but we're human after all / So to the I.P.S. (Irish Prison Service) we're gonna sing / Free the Joy even just for Christmas time / Free the Joy ...

To this day, I still can't get over the reaction we got. The place went fuckin' mental for a couple of minutes. We had truly made this jailhouse *rock*. The crowd began to disperse, but not before coming up to us, shaking our hands, and thanking us for such an enjoyable couple of hours. It was such a humbling experience, and again shows the true power of music. As myself and Fitzer made our way down the stairwell from the school to The Circle, we felt like proper, *bona fide* rock stars – that is, right until we stepped into The Circle and The Gaffer spotted Fitzer and bellowed at him to return to the kitchen *immediately*!

Fitzer turned to me and smiled as he said, 'I actually forgot we were in this fuckin' kip there for a minute, thought we might go for a pint to celebrate!'

We both began laughing, as I followed up with, 'I nicked a load of Mars Bars, so we'll have a little party later. Not really sex, drugs, and rock 'n' roll, I know, but when in Rome ...' He skipped away laughing, then broke into an amazing rendition of 'The Man Who Can't Be Moved' by The Script as he disappeared into the kitchen to go back to work.

Chapter 28

'TIS THE SEASON

Jingle bells, jingle bells ...

Waking up on the 25th of December in Mountjoy, well, it's exactly like any other day really. But, again, it's what you make of it. We get a fry on Christmas morning for breakfast. Okay, it's poxy but it's a luxury that we never get to experience at any other time whilst we are incarcerated. As I joined the queue for our festive fry that morning, it was great to see that every prisoner from C Wing had made the effort of getting up and partaking in this joyous Christmas feast. We all wished each other a happy Christmas and the general ambience was a positive, happy one.

Ohhh, the weather outside is frightful ...

As I got to the top of the queue, I see Fitzer has been chosen to work serving C Wing. This is a much sought after position in the kitchen, as the C Wing serving area was brand new so it was easier to clean. Plus fewer prisoners were housed on C Wing, as we were all in single cells, so less work. Fitzer is wearing a red Santa hat, with a snow white ball attached to its top. We had 'borrowed' a few of these hats at the school's Christmas gig, and our intention was to hand them out this morning, which I did. Any lad passing me who wanted one,

I happily obliged. Fitzer catches my eye, and signals me to come over to him. 'Here ya go, me aul' flower,' says Fitzer as he hands me a plate he had hidden under the counter. 'It's a bit more fresh than the others plus there's a few extra sausages for ya.'

'Ah, fuckin' nice one buddy,' I beam as I gratefully accept the plate. It really is the little things in life that can have such an impact. You start to think about all the things you had taken for granted for so long. It humbles you, and puts manners on you. 'What's the plan for the day Fitzer?' I enquire.

'We get off a bit earlier in the kitchen, Gar, so I'm hoping to catch the Bond film on UTV,' he laughs.

'Good stuff Fitzer, sure we'll play a few songs for the wing later, if you're up to it?'

'Sounds good, Gar, now go fuck yourself, I'm busy, bye now.' And with that he's off, singing of course!

So This Is Christmas and What Have You Done? ...

The prison regime remains in place even on Christmas day, but the screws were allowing lads to get 'banged out' together in a cell, in order to have someone to chat with while you ate like a 'king'. Smithwicks joined me in my cell, and like 'kings' we ate! We had a good laugh reminiscing about our childhood Christmas mornings waking up to the magic that surrounds Santy visiting your home while you slept, and leaving a shite load of presents for you just for being good, which most of the fuckin' time I wasn't. Magical! We both made plans to hit the yard, once my cell door was opened, and take in a Christmas morning that we have never experienced before, and never will again!

Dashing Through the Snow, in a One Horse Open Sleigh

The officer opened my cell door, wished me and Smithwicks a happy Christmas, then followed that with, 'Get out to the fuckin' yard, both of yas.'

'Not a problem officer,' I began, 'we'd be only too happy to oblige on this festive morning. And I'd say you're only delighted to be spending your Christmas day with little old us'.

'Fuck off, Cunningham, ya little bollox,' laughed the officer as he continued on his merry way.

Me, Smithwicks, Cunny, No. 2, Fitzer, The Little Fella, Budgie, Natoman, the whole fuckin' crew, assembled at the top of C Wing, and took the short, dark trip through D Wing and out on to her yard, as C Wing had no yard of its own. It was quite surreal as I gazed out on D yard that morning. A good few of the lads were wearing the Santy hats me and Fitzer provided. Another small group of lads had congregated in one of the yard's corners and were singing Christmas carols. The mood seemed so positive, such a stark contrast to how this yard usually feels. It seemed that all feuding had ceased, albeit only for one day, but it was good to see everyone just sort of 'getting on'. Our group soon became smaller, as lads broke off to join other groups to wish them a happy Christmas too. It was like when you go visit relatives at Christmas, make small talk, ask about the family, wish everyone a happy new year and then on to the next gaff. Still, it was so nice to see everyone looking so happy.

It's Christmas Time, There's No Need to Be Afraid ...

Me and Smithwicks drifted off on our own and began a few laps of the yard. As we were making our way around, we noticed that two brothers, both from the travelling community, had a large crowd around them as they held council. These two were absolute characters, extremely funny. So me and

Smithwicks join in, just as one of the brothers, Michael, is beginning his next tale in his booming 'travellers' twang:

'So as a lot of yas already know, myself and my brother here are new arrivals here in this kip ye call Mountjoy. We came all the way over from England and one of her jails, just to be in here with ye lot. Now listen here now and I'll tell yas all a true story true as I'm standing here now on the wife's bible.'

I've made my way to the top of the crowd, as I know I'm going to be hanging on to every word that comes from his mouth.

'So,' he continues, 'in the auld English jail that had myself and my brother here in, they also had an IRA fella, never saw the man but he was there. Anyways, he was to be sent back, over to here to good auld Eire, for some reason or another. So, thus begins one of the most technical, strategic operations I have ever heard of in me life, true as God! They shut down the telephones in the prison and surrounding area for a week before he's moved, so nobody can tell anyone on the outside what's going on.

'On the day of his removal there were two police helicopters deployed, hovering over the prison. They had two identical prison vans, one being a decoy, clever bastards! The IRA fella was put into one of these vans and off they went, with an escort of six police cars, each containing heavily armed officers – they were takin' no fuckin' chances.'

Michael, a short, chubby fella in his late twenties with a pudgy face and hair like Elvis, is telling this tale with so much animation and colour. He fuckin' loved the sound of his own voice, but what a bloke, so fuckin' funny.

'So they get yer man, the IRA chap, and they get him on to a private jet bound for Dublin airport. At this stage there are four armed officers escorting him on his journey back to the Emerald Isle. Soon, the plane touches down in Dublin. As the door of the jet opens, the IRA bloke is ushered out, down a flight of stairs, where himself and the British mega-force are met by Paddy the Irish prison officer. Behind him is an auld beat up Ford Transit prison van, with a driver behind the wheel. The elite English officers quickly unshackle the IRA lad, as both his hands and feet were in chains, and proceed to hand him to the Irish authorities.

'"Grand lads, fair play," says auld Paddy to the English fella. "Ain't ya gonna cuff him chief?" asks the cockney British fella. "Not at all, sure, he'll be grand," replies Paddy. He then takes the IRA dude and puts him in the back of the Transit. The driver turns over the engine and, after a few spurts, the engine roars into life. The sliding door of the prison van won't close properly, so the last thing the elite British officers see is prison officer Paddy asking the prisoner to "Give the auld door a kick shut there will ya? It's bolloxed!"'

We all fall around laughing. And the more I laughed, the more Michael would get in my face and really tell the story.

Ohhh I Wish It Could Be Christmas Every Day ...

As we headed back to C Wing, Michael's story being the focal point of our conversation, I stopped for a moment in the famous Circle of Mountjoy and appreciated the small gestures that some of the officers had made. There were bits of tinsel strewn about, and someone had erected a small Christmas tree, with lights and decorations. It made the place seem almost bearable.

We all made our way on to C Wing. Myself and Fitzer grabbed our guitars and played a few songs. It was a nice, happy time in such a dark, dank hole. Soon, we were ordered into our cells for the last time. We all said our good nights and headed into our sanctuary, or sanatorium for some. For it's only then, for the lads who are experiencing Christmas in a prison for the first time, well, it's mind-blowing. You feel the weight of the wrongs you have done that have put you here away from your family, from your kids as they wake to open their Santa presents. Family and friends united to share some quality time together, while you sit in a prison cell, ashamed, lonely, depressed. But I wanted to remember those feelings, to remember exactly how it felt to be in that poxy cell on Christmas day. For it made me want to assure myself that I’d never be back here again.

So a Very Merry Christmas / and a Happy New Year /
Let’s Hope It’s a Good One / Without Any Fears …

Chapter 29

WHOSE LINE IS IT ANYWAY?

As I had mentioned before, I had penned a 'musical', well, a bunch of songs that all related to each other and formed a story, with each song being like a chapter in its tale. I was chuffed with the results, as each song perfectly brought to life the tale of a man from birth to death. The idea I had was to create four main characters, the first being 'Journeyman', the lead role. This is the tale's main, broken character, a man who has been through a lot in his mediocre life. Next is 'The Mother', an ever-doting, over protective, loving mother, whose only point of existence is her beautiful son. We then have 'The Father', our villain, a drunk, frustrated, dark man whose disdain for our main character is ever present. And lastly, 'The One', our love interest and the object of Journeyman's affections. These all combine, through the medium of rock music, to create *Journeyman*. It only took me about three days to complete, and consisted of twelve songs, or 'scenes', although I did have quite a bit of spare time on my hands whilst under lock and key! A feat, none the less, which highly impressed my main motivator, Fitzer.

'Fuckin' great stuff outta you, Gar,' he beamed as I nervously sat in his cell, working my way through each song, frantically trying to explain what the fuck had just come into my head over the last few days. I was desperately craving his approval, which I got in abundance. 'Ya have to let Paul hear it. That'll fuckin' blow him away,' he said.

'Ya think?' I asked with a note of trepidation in my voice.

'Of course, buddy, stop fuckin' doubtin' yourself. You're always at it.'

Which is true, even to this day. I am constantly 'at' myself, never really giving myself a chance. But I think it's a form of punishment for all the pain and damage I had caused leading up to being locked up. The mind truly is a dangerous weapon in the wrong hands.

Later the next day, myself and Fitzer brought the numerous A4 sheets of paper containing my sometimes unreadable handwritten script up to Paul in the music room. (It's been said I have the handwriting of a six-year-old – I'm quite fuckin' proud of that, if I'm honest; they could have said a two-year-old!) Paul sits with great excitement, as he always did when we brought him a new Offenders' song, but today myself and Fitzer brought out a whole new level of respect from him. Fitzer had been toying around with some rough ideas for vocal melodies on some of the tracks, while the others I 'rocked' through and Paul got it. His encouragement was incredible to receive at any time, but when it's backed up with genuine praise, well, I was blown away. He has done and seen it all, so his words will stay with me forever.

'Wow, Gary, that really is incredible, just incredible! Three days? Look, there's a lady over in the Medical Unit (a separate building which housed ill prisoners and recovering addicts) – her name is Maggie, and well, she's the drama teacher over there, and she has written and directed many plays, both inside and outside the prison. I really think you and Fitzer should rough record the tracks, the 'chapters' if you will, and you should let me bring this idea to her.'

Myself and Fitzer were fuckin' delighted. 'Of course, Paul, that would be amazing,' I said with a huge smile on my face.

We grabbed our guitar and bass respectively and made our way to the ceramics room in the school, a high ceilinged, dimly lit room where men could make decorative tile pieces. The lads that day kindly gave us the room for an hour, and me and Fitzer sat between a dictaphone laying down each track roughly! And so I handed over my first ever copy of my musical, the first I had ever written, so it could be scrutinised by an accomplished playwright. Oh shit!

The next day myself and Fitzer meet at 2.00 pm in The Circle to head up to the school. I felt so nervous ascending the creepy stairwell, as I awaited the verdict on my work. When we walked into the music lab, we see Paul chatting to a small lady in sixties-inspired 'Woodstock' clothing, vibrant and colourful, her golden hair sitting atop her shoulders. She turns as we walk in, and greets us with an amazing smile.

'Ah, here's the boys now, The Offenders, Maggie,' Paul proudly declares, like a smitten father.

'Hello boys, who's who?' She speaks with a soft English accent, which only adds to the mystery of this fabulous woman.

'I'm Fitzer, Maggie,' bursts the ever-confident Fitzer, whilst he flings his arms around her in a loving embrace.

'Pleasure to meet you Fitzer, what an amazing voice you have. I was at the Christmas concert you all put on, just an incredible voice. Gary I assume?'

She turns to me and I awkwardly reply, 'Hello Maggie, very pleased to meet ya, Paul has told us some amazing things about ya.'

'Yeah,' interjects Fitzer, 'we reckon he has a thing for ya, Maggie.' Good auld Fitzer has broken the ice.

'Right,' starts Maggie, 'we've only got about an hour and that may not be long enough for me to tell you how bloody impressed I am. Wow, Gary, have you ever done anything like this before?'

'No,' comes my nervous reply, the butterflies in my stomach flapping their wings at a feverish rate.

'Well, it's just incredible, simply incredible. I can feel the pain, embrace the humour, understand the meaning. It's quite brilliantly written. And the fact that Fitzer sings all the main characters' songs, in that beautiful voice of his, while you then enter as the crazy father, screaming and shouting, it's just remarkable. We have got to do something with this. You have a real talent, Gary.'

That's it, I start to fuckin' cry, though to be honest, I'm crying as I type this (surprise, surprise). I was always more used to being told what I'd done wrong, not receiving many compliments, which didn't bother me until now.

'See Gar?' starts Fitzer, 'told ya it was fuckin' deadly!' He clatters me across my shoulders, which drags me back into the room.

'Wow, Maggie, thank you so much, I'm speechless.'

'*What?*' shouts Fitzer. 'Well, there really is a first time for everything. The Voice has nothing to say!' Fitzer is pissing himself laughing at creating what was to become my new nickname – The Voice!

Maggie informs me that it would be an amazing experience to run drama workshops up here in the school, in order to get anyone interested in starring in this play familiar with some acting principles. It was to be my mission to gather up as many prisoners as I could, the more the merrier, though it was not an easy task! For you see, 'acting' could be construed as being a 'sissy' – no 'hard man' would dare 'act'. I had my hands full!

Maggie also asked if she could offer me two bits of advice regarding the play. 'Firstly, you need some written dialogue, some spoken word.' I did this by writing a narrator's piece which assisted the viewer through the tale, and the only man who could speak these words would be Smithwicks, his silky, slightly posh Dublin accent a perfect backdrop to my tale.

'Secondly,' she continued, 'well, it's your ending, Gary, he bloody dies! You can't send people home at the end of your show depressed out of their minds!' I erupt with laughter as I had never looked at it like that. I had literally written a tale from birth to death! 'How about, birth to death to *rebirth*,' she says, whilst raising her hands towards heaven. 'He transforms his old self and becomes a new man free from the shackles that held him down.' And that is why this woman has won awards. Brilliant! It only took a small tinkering of the last song to achieve this result. She also informed us that these workshops would take place after school hours and that she was willing to give up a couple of hours of her own time in order to get this going. Simply amazing! We said our goodbyes, and as myself and Fitzer made our way back into the main jail, my head felt light. I was so proud of what we had pulled off again! Now I just had to round up a few lads – shit!

I had a good rapport with most of the lads on C Wing. I had made a name for myself by sticking up for lads I felt were unfairly treated by the officers, which was fairly seldom on C Wing. I had gained a bit of respect from some of the officers, so I knew they'd hear me out as I'd fight someone's case. I've always been a hater of prejudice, of bullying, of people's rights being taken for granted. Yes there are a million rules to abide by in prison, but some lads got treated like shit for no reason. I just didn't think it was fair and would try to speak my mind in a respectful, intelligent, peaceful way (hence my new nickname, The Voice). So winning over the lads on C Wing, with some playful assistance from a few of the officers, wasn't too difficult. Cunny had no choice, but he was still ever willing, and the rest of the lads got caught up in what I was trying to do.

I made my way to D Wing, and was delighted when a few of the lads who had taken part in the music classes happily agreed. The idea that it was an hour in the evening, which shattered the mundane humdrum of life in The Joy, seemed to be a massive factor too. This was going okay so I had an idea. I went to my A.C.O. on C Wing and asked her if I could be let on to A Wing in order to offer the lads in there the same opportunities as the lads in C and D. Now, for many a ridiculous reason A Wing and D Wing can't mix, though I suppose it's easy for me to say it's ridiculous when I haven't been caught up in a feud. It just seems so senseless to me. But I knew that this might cause problems in my attempt to bring in lads from A Wing and maybe show that as prisoners we *can* unite and bring forward something positive together! She looked me up and down and then told me to fuck off!

'Wait, Miss,' I start, 'I used to serve the lads their grub on A Wing when I worked in the kitchen, they know I'm all right. I just wanna give them the same chance to tell me to fuck off as the rest of the jail had.'

She seems to smile a little at this and says, 'Go on, but be back here in ten minutes. I'll radio around to tell them to let you in.'

As I approached the gates of A Wing I spot The Scouse, a tall, skinny lad from Southport who was a cleaner on A1. I had struck up a friendship with this lad during my time serving food on A Wing, always throwing him something extra at dinner time if the chance arose. 'Scouse, what's the story me aul buddy?' I shout to him through the deep-blue barred gates.

'All right Gar,' he replies in his Scouse accent.

'I'm gonna cut to the chase,' I begin, 'I've written a play that's gonna be staged in here so I need a load of lads to star in it. It'll be in the evenings for an hour or so every Wednesday.'

'Wooo,' he interrupts, 'every Wednesday evening? I'm in, anyways. Let's go, I've a few that'll want to do that.' And that was that. The officer allowed me access to A Wing for a couple of minutes, and myself and The Scouse rounded up another bunch of lads, all excited to see where this journey would take us. We were all set.

It took about two weeks for Maggie to get clearance from the powers-that-be to allow the school to remain open for about an hour and a half every Wednesday, but clearance she got. I will never forget those workshops as long as I live. They involved grown men, hardened criminals, partaking in a bunch of childlike games, each one with its hidden message which gave us the tools to 'act'. Games that broke down our walls and laid us bare for all to see, stripped of our inhibitions. Games like 'Zip Zap Bong', which involved us all standing in a circle, Maggie at the epicenter, as we would 'catch' a Zip and Bong it to another, who in turn would 'grab' your Bong, and Zap it to the next unwilling recipient, all this done through the exaggerated movements of our bodies as we mocked catching these unusual words, and flinging them around our circle. Some lads, the extroverts, took to this like a duck to water, but as the weeks went by, it was amazing to watch the shyer, quieter lads become more self-confident. I remember one young lad in particular, weeks after the workshops had ended, thanking me for making him realise a different side to him. It put a massive lump in my throat.

There were prisoners from all walks of life at these workshops, each incarcerated for a multitude of reasons, from drugs to violence to white-collar crime. There were a couple of lads struggling with addiction problems who became some of the funniest lads in the group. But more importantly, it brought together lads from A Wing and D Wing in perfect harmony. It was all worth it just for that!

Our last game every Wednesday evening was similar to the popular TV show *Whose Line Is It Anyway?*, and involved one of the lads being a 'host' at a house party, whilst the other lads were assembled outside the hall, awaiting their instructions of what type of 'guest' they were to be. They were not allowed to speak and had to rely on their acting skills to bring to life their character. On that first night, I was the host. I laughed as I waited for my 'guests', hearing them all breaking their shite laughing at the instructions being whispered in their ears by Maggie. As the lads came in, one by one, they each did an amazing job of creating their characters through acting alone – but one stood out

I've known Cunny all my life, and I knew how shy and reserved he was. He was always worried about what the other person thought of him. He was an amazing bloke, but this trait of his could be kind of infuriating. So when he burst into the school's old tattered hall, its walls screaming out for a lick or two of paint, emitting a roar from deep within the lower reaches of his throat, and then proceeds to roll across the floor on his side, before completing all of this with a forward tumble – well, I was fuckin' gobsmacked! I was trying to read him and his movements but that's the problem, he wouldn't fuckin' stop moving. After a minute or so I conceded defeat, and on asking what 'guest' he was he replied, 'A fuckin' stuntman, Gar, thought you'd have got that, I'm bolloxed now!' We all joined together in a chorus of laughter. It was amazing to see Cunny come out of his shell.

After everyone would leave on those Wednesday nights, and the numbers grew to over 30 as the weeks went by, Maggie would keep me and Fitzer back as she spoke of her vision for *Journeyman*. It was mesmerising listening to this soft-spoken, full of spirit English lady bring to life the characters and scenes from what had started as a few songs in my cell on C Wing not so long ago.

Those Wednesday nights offered us an escape from the tall, grey walls of Mountjoy. And Mountjoy, of course, would ultimately cause the demise of *Journeyman*, but hopefully not forever!

> I get knocked down but I get up again and you're *never* gonna keep me down.

Chapter 30

Loughan House, Can You Hear Us?

The drama workshops were coming on fantastically. Maggie had started to hone in on her choice of who was to play each character in *Journeyman*, with the idea that the lads would mime over the songs I had written. Fitzer took the lead on the vocals and, occasionally, I sang some myself, as we told this tale through these songs. The camaraderie and bond that we forged as a group of unlikely lads was truly amazing. We rarely spoke of anything else, well, except getting moved to an open prison which some of us, actually all of us, would talk about on a regular basis. Yes, for it always seemed that the grass was greener on the other side of prison life. A side which, rumour had it, included the option of readily available fresh air, to be inhaled at your pleasure, with no more locks and keys and deadbolts. Some even pondered on the prospect of better food. So, as I'm sure you could tell, every fuckin' one wanted to experience this!

As with everything in prison life, you must match an extremely high set of standards to be even considered for transfer to an open prison. These would include proving you are drug-free and that you have worked for most of your time, or partaken in the school in some way. You would have to have a clean record, which meant no fighting or giving cheek to the officers. You had to be what the prison service later called an 'Advanced Prisoner'. The lads that I spent most of my time with were all advanced prisoners, as we 'got' Mountjoy. Basically, it's a game, a game which you must play to your advantage but one where manners and a small bit of respect go a very long way. It's a game with many ups and downs, but ultimately one in which *you* are either the sole winner or loser, depending on how you choose to play it. So we got on with the game, in the hope that maybe we'd do enough to move out of this hellhole and on to the next phase of our incarceration.

One day, Cunny comes bounding into my cell. 'Me and No. 2 just got passed for Loughan House' (one of Ireland's two open prisons, the other being Shelton Abbey).

'Fuckin' brilliant,' I exclaim, although my heart sank just a little I'm ashamed to admit. Yes, of course I was happy for the lads but I'd miss them, especially Cunny! 'I'm over the fuckin' moon for ya pal, and for Ciara, Leah and Cian' (his little family). I say this and follow with a playful dig in the arm.

'Ah, we can't believe it buddy, we're fuckin' off tomorrow.' (They don't give you much notice as to when you're being transferred in case you want to try to mastermind your own escape whilst in transit, which has happened!)

'Wow, Cunny, I'm so happy for ya!' And with that we hug, like two big softies!

What happened over the next couple of weeks finally turned me off Mountjoy for good. I was always getting egged on by the lads, especially Fitzer, to 'put in' for an open prison, which involved queuing in the morning for the Governor's parade and informing him that you would like to be put up for review at the next meeting. These meetings were held at the end of the month and were designed to keep the flow of prisoners moving through the expansive wheel of the Irish prison system. But I had no yearning for an open prison. I had only my mam and brothers, and two good friends, who would visit me, my other so-called 'friends' turning their backs to me once I was locked up, which happens to a lot of prisoners. I was not allowed access to my son, and although myself and Antoinette had really hit it off, I think a visit would be expecting too much from her. I had the music going on with Fitzer and The Offenders and I had *Journeyman* going on as well. Also, I'd be fuckin' lost without Fitzer. He had, unbeknownst to himself, become someone I heavily leaned on so, 'sappy' as it sounds, I'd miss the greatest friend I've ever had. So I became the weirdo that did not put himself up for these meetings.

But Cunny's and No. 2's time had arrived – or had it? An officer appeared on C1 holding a white sheet of paper with the lads' names who were transferring printed on it. He began, like a roll call, shouting the names of the fellas who have 'five fuckin' minutes to get your stuff together, you're outta here!' No. 2 and a few of the lads let out a roar on hearing their names being announced, but Cunny's name had not been one of them. I looked at the anguish engulfing his face as he approached the officer and enquired as to why his name was not called. 'Not sure, Cunny, just says you've to see the lads in the ISM (Integrated Sentence Management, an organisation created to assist with the transferring of prisoners, among other things) tomorrow morning.'

Cunny was crushed. I had had a bad feeling this was going to happen to him, as I had stated to Fitzer earlier in the day. 'He's painting this whole fuckin' place, Fitzer, they're not gonna let such a hard workin' young fella like Cunny go that easily.' And this, unfortunately, was a regular occurrence too. You could almost be found guilty of doing too much work in Mountjoy and as a result your punishment would be that you were to be housed there for just a little longer. Cunny fell into this bracket, his hard work seen throughout the entire prison campus as he brought some life into her old stone walls, his wonderful brush strokes and rolling bringing light into some of the darkened areas of the jail. I brought him into my cell and told him not to give up, but he was distraught at the thought of having to ring his partner to tell her he wasn't transferring after all, after telling her countless times that his good behavior had granted him this move. But now he's just not going.

The next morning, Cunny bolted from his cell as soon as the officer opened his door and made his way up to the Library, which is situated beside the school. The ISM borrowed the Library's small, cramped office to hold council with the prisoners and fill their heads to the brim with bullshit. I was not a fan of theirs, as I felt their idea of 'telling a prisoner what he wants to hear', regardless of whether it's true, was not good practice. A lot of prisoners were in an extremely fragile state-of-mind, and could be drawn in by this bullshit. Cunny returned sometime later, looking even more deflated. Again, I offer my coffee-making skills and shoulder.

'They said I'm flyin' here what with the painting an' all and they don't feel that I "need" to be moved just yet. Course I fuckin' need to be moved. Everyone in this fuckin' shithole needs to be moved eventually.' He says this as the tears well up in his eyes, his broken frame slumped across my prison bunk.

'Did ya say all that to them, Cunny?' I enquire.

'Not at all, sure, ya know me, Gary, I never speak up for meself.' So very true. Not wanting to cause an argument, he shied away from confrontation. But don't let that fool ya, he's a tough guy, you just really have to push his buttons to set him off. Me on the other hand? I wasn't having it!

I stormed up to the Library, just as Officer Gobshite and Officer Clown are wrapping up after shattering another few prisoners' already damaged souls. 'May I have a word officers?' I ask politely.

Officer Gobshite addresses me as Officer Clown makes his excuses and leaves. 'Make it quick,' he says.

'Who the fuck do you think you are crushing a young man's spirit like that?' I say, as I feel my blood reaching an extremely high pressure. 'A man, I might add, who has worked tirelessly during his incarceration, Saturdays and Sundays included, to earn the right to be put forward for a meeting, a meeting which he passed, only to have you rip it from under him because of all the work he does? Are you for fuckin' real? I apologise for my language, officer.'

I pause to take a breath, when he tries to counter with, 'Now wai ... ' but I won't let him interrupt me now, I'm on a roll, in for a penny and all that. 'To me it amounts to bullying.' I leave this to linger but he doesn't like it.

'Now hang on here, nobody is bullying anybody here,' he says in his thick Cork accent, his red face giving you a glimpse of his most likely unhealthy lifestyle, his massive belly only adding to this point.

'Well, officer,' I counteract, 'I've just come from my cell and left, draped over my bunk, Cunny, who is distraught. Fearing rejection from his loved one, their relationship already frayed due to the beast that is The Joy. Confused, as he now feels cheated by the fact that fully immersing himself into prison life has somehow backfired on him. I will not sit by and watch someone I know crumble before my very eyes, over a selfish regime. There will always be other painters, granted none with the zealous attitude of Cunny, but please don't punish him for being good as that is all he is guilty of.'

I seem to get through to him, though he duly asks me to leave. I get the feeling I've wounded him a little which was not my intention. I just needed to try to help my good friend. I thank him for his audience, and respectfully leave. I say nothing to Cunny upon my arrival back to C Wing, and wait with baited breath, as there was another 'bus' departing for Loughan House the next day, which means the list will be made and called out this evening.

What happened next was kind of surreal. An officer did appear that evening with the magical white sheet of paper with just one name on it – Cunny's! But I already knew this, as about a half hour earlier Cunny had burst into my cell and, throwing his arms around me, said, 'I don't know what the fuck ya said, but thank you, thank you, *thank you*!' I was fuckin' chuffed for the lad but I did heed his following warning. 'He told me, after first saying I was going tomorrow, to tell my, quote, "large-mouthed friend" that he won't forget their little meeting, so watch out!'

As ominous as it sounded, I didn't give a fuck as the very next evening, Cunny said his goodbyes. To some of the lads it was goodbye forever, whereas for others, me included, it was bye for now. I'm not ashamed to admit I shed a tear that night when Cunny went. I was really going to miss him, but I was so fuckin' happy for him. And something told me this wasn't the end of our journey together.

The weeks came thick and fast, and one Wednesday, after our drama workshop, Maggie asked me and Fitzer to stay back as she always did, but this day she seemed sad. 'Well, Gary, we nearly did it, we nearly got *Journeyman* on to that stage'. She pointed to the rather large stage inside of Mountjoy's school.

'What do you mean?' I enquired.

'You've been passed for Loughan House, Gary, you're on the next bus,' she says.

'Get *up* outta that,' roared Fitzer, as he grabbed me in a bear hug and lifted me off the ground.

But I didn't feel happy. Number one, I hadn't even put in for the fuckin' place. 'No, your A.C.O. put you forward because of all your hard work, and the way you are with people,' continued Maggie, 'And I am so happy for you, and so proud of you. You have let me in on your life over the last few weeks, and it fills me with pride to see the changes in you, to see you reap the rewards of your actions. I just wish, selfishly, that you were staying, as I know the drama workshops will dwindle once you're gone. You drive them, Gary, unbeknownst to yourself.' She says all this with such raw emotion.

'I'm not ready to go, I don't want to go,' I start, only to be interrupted by Fitzer.

'Now, fuck all that bollox Gary. This is *your* journey. You come into prison alone, and you leave prison alone. So get the fuck outta this kip, yeah? You're very lucky to be passed to go in the first place, many aren't, and they'd give anything for your place, so be grateful.'

Fitzer always had a way of getting through to me, to getting me to cop on. I started to fantasise about life in an open prison, though the thoughts of not having a jam, or a laugh, or a chat with Fitzer seemed unbearable. But I knew if I told him this he'd rip my fuckin' head clean off! I tried to convince Maggie that the workshops would continue, that I'd ask could I stay until the play was complete, but this was met with absolute refusal. I embraced Maggie, forgetting for a moment that I was in fact a prisoner and that maybe she wouldn't feel comfortable with me hugging her, but she returned the embrace with feeling. She promised to write to me in Loughan House and I believed that she would.

And then, 'Mountjoy' happens again.

As myself and Fitzer left the school that evening, I was a rollercoaster of mixed emotions. I wasn't sure what to feel to be honest. Just as we entered The Circle, Officer Gobshite noticed me and summoned me over to him in front of the wooden officers' station. 'I believe you've been passed for Loughan?' he says, with a slight grin on his chubby face.

'That's right, officer, I have,' I say, sticking my chest out for effect.

'Won't be happening, I'm afraid,' he scoffs. 'Mary, from the school (the lady I spoke of), has asked the Governor to keep you, on account of the play plus we've seen the excellent job of painting you've done in the computer room on D Wing, and we're down a painter now, what with Cunny gone, so we feel like you'll fit right in.' He says all this with a smug, chubby grin.

'Look, ya fuckin' idiot,' I start, 'I'm not one of the poor weak lads you prey on. Mary is upstairs in the school now (I bluffed) so hang on *officer,*' and I shout to Mr. Sheridan, the school's officer, who was just about to close the barred gate that leads to the school. 'Let me back up for a sec, will ya? I need to ask Mary something of grave importance.'

'Wait, hang on, no need for that Cunningham,' splutters Officer Gobshite.

'Just as I thought,' I start. 'How dare you try to put the blame on that poor lady. You really have no morals.'

This sends him into a meltdown, as he shouts, 'You can't fuckin' talk to me like that, ya little bollox, Governor's parade immediately!' And with that I'm whisked off.

Upon my arrival at the darkened office, I'm not met by the Governor, but by a very tough Chief. 'What's going on here? You giving cheek, ya little prick?' asks the intimidating Chief, his skinny frame and round spectacles leading you into a false sense of security.

I explained what was just said to me regarding my upcoming transfer to Loughan House, and the reasons I was given for not being allowed to go.

'Well, there has been a lot of talk about this play all right, so if we want to keep ya for that we will, just like if we need a new painter we'll fuckin' do that too,' he barks at me.

'Right,' says I, 'as regards to the play, it's mine, so I'll rip up the only copy of it in front of your face so nobody will see it performed. And as regards to painting, I will go down to the computer room and, with a heavy heart, as Mr. Dunne is a rare breed in here, an actual human, I will proceed to throw black gloss all over the walls. You are promoting a regime that knocks down people who achieve, that punishes hard working men. I'm being punished for showing initiative, for not wanting to sit around doing nothing. I really feel that some of the officers in here won't be happy until someone like me scores some heroin and bangs out behind the door to rot away, slowly, piece by piece. Well I won't become another statistic, Chief, and I won't be blackmailed. I am incredibly sorry if I have shown you any disrespect, I just feel pushed to my limits. And we all have limits in this place.'

He could see I was visibly upset, and I think that saved my hide. 'Fuck off back to your cell, I'll look into this,' he replies sternly. I turn and leave, feeling like I've just fucked everything up.

But, he kept his word that Chief, and a couple of days later I was summoned to his office. 'You're going to Loughan tomorrow, that is all.' He never even looked up from the document he was reading as he uttered these words to me. I wanted to fuckin' hug him, and to this day I have a lot of admiration for him as I really feel he listened to me and spoke up for me. And so I was to be moved the very next day. No more stench and dirt. No more 'stripes' and beatings (hopefully). No more shall I be under strict lock and key. No more Tuck Shop queues and D yard with all of her madness. No more fear and intimidation. And yet I felt so very sad. Sad to be leaving some of the most amazing people I had ever met, knowing they won't be there for me, nor me for them, like we'd become so accustomed to. Plus I feared 'change'. Prison really does institutionalise you, as you become reliant on your routine in order to survive. I feared all the good work I'd done on myself would unravel, although a lot of this was also down to having very little self-esteem. I knew I needed to keep the winds of change blowing.

But as regards to saying goodbye to Fitzer? Well, that was going to be a very hard goodbye.

So on January 13, 2013, a dank, rainy Sunday morning, I packed my things and readied myself for the three hour journey that I was to embark on. I said my goodbyes to everyone, finding it hard to say goodbye to most, especially Smithwicks. Although I had gotten through to him to put in for Loughan House, too, and I'd do all I could to help in getting him there. But the hardest goodbye was the last – Fitzer. I left all my belongings at the top of C1 and ambled down its landing towards Fitzers' cell.

'Good man, Gar, ya all set?' I couldn't take it, as tears came flowing down my face. I see a slight dent in Fitzers' armour, but he soon composes himself in order to launch one of his deadly slagging rants of his. 'Go on outta that, ya big fuckin' sap ya! Cryin' an' all, bleedin' sap! Take care me aul' flower and from the bottom of me heart thanks for everything, ya made this jail very "interesting" to say the least.'

He bursts out laughing, as we both take a moment to take in what we had achieved in such a short time, all through music. We had literally brought this jail together. I thank him for all he has done for me, for saving my life, which starts the tears again (Jaysus, I'm such an aul' one). 'That's it, fuck off now, go on, now toodle pips, bye now,' he's saying all this whilst ushering me back out onto the landing. I say goodbye, but promise it won't be the last time we see each other, and how very fuckin' right I was!

I arrive at my belongings and the screw who was to bring us down to reception was becoming impatient, as I was holding everyone up. I took one last look at D Wing and told myself I'd never again lay my eyes upon its depressing decor, its grey walls a reminder of the sadness that truly does exist in Mountjoy. I take in the sensory overload that is The Circle for the last time, and watch as the officers attended to their tasks, each man and woman frantically making sure that they survived their working day unscathed in order to return home to their loved ones in one piece. As we descended down the spiral stairwell towards reception, I took one last look at the dark blue gate that, when closed, prevented entry to the school where I had so many incredible memories. It was incredible to think that there were parts of this hellhole that I was going to miss. I was institutionalised through and through.

I can't remember everyone that was on that bus to Loughan House with me that day, but Handsome was one, and I was happy about that. We were each given an extremely quick phone call to ensure that our family or loved ones knew what was happening. Then we were escorted from the reception area in Mountjoy, the very same room I had come through as a fat, nervous waster what seemed a lifetime ago, into the crisp January air. We were handcuffed and placed on the same 'prison bus' that brought me here over a year ago. I looked back at Mountjoy, and out loud I proudly stated, 'never fuckin' again'. How wrong I was.

Chapter 31

Time to Reflect

As I sat on that dark, ice-cold prison bus on that gloomy Sunday afternoon, the sounds of Gerry Rafferty's 'Baker Street' lowly transmitting from the busted up speaker (which brought me back to happier times with my eldest brother and my mother, as this was their favourite song), I allowed myself time to contemplate on the amazing lads I had met, and some of their outstanding talents.

I look out at the country landscape, the fields and mountains drizzled in dull grey and rain showers, and realised I didn't have a fuckin' clue where we were. The night before I left, I fell for the oldest trick in the book from Scotty by bringing a book with me for the journey to eat away the hours as we travelled to Loughan House. But since we were handcuffed in these dank holding compartments the James Patterson novel sat on my lap, screaming to be opened and digested, but I couldn't turn the fuckin' pages.

But I enjoyed thinking about all the positives which came from being incarcerated in The Joy. Thinking of all the incredible men I had met who had a profound effect on me, as hopefully I did on them. Remembering what myself and Fitzer had achieved through our passion for music. Reflecting on the laughs, and forgetting about the horrors of prison life. I also got to thinking of the one or two officers who were okay, who treated you with some level of respect. Actually, we had one with us this very morning escorting us to Loughan. He must sit in a chair, similar to the type an air hostess must use on an airplane, and, well, just sit there really. His only job, as far as I could tell, was manning the bus's radio. But he made a vital mistake that morning ...

Because of the fact he was, by all accounts, a really 'sound' officer, he would often let us in a little on his personal life, maybe speaking of his kids' achievements in school, or recounting a funny story about himself and 'The Wife'. But, as we boarded the Loughan-bound bus on the grounds of Mountjoy that cold morning, he informed us he had a, quote, 'killer hangover'. This was a bad move for it gave Handsome the ammunition to annoy the living shite outta him – *for the whole journey* – which he did with aplomb. It was funny, I have to say, as Handsome wouldn't give him a minute, constantly asking ridiculous, mundane questions, or requesting the changing of the radio stations. But all this poor aul' officer wanted to do was sleep. Fortunately, he did see the funny side to it.

So, here we go. Goodbye Mountjoy, hello Loughan House. What have you got in store for me?

Chapter 32

'Let's Go, Loughan, Let's Go'

As we approached the gates to Loughan House, which just sort of materialised like a mirage usually associated with a deathly hot desert, I could feel the same butterflies I had experienced when I arrived at Mountjoy. The long, winding driveway that leads from the main gate to the central area of Loughan House had many an interesting building, or equally as interesting scenery, dotted along its course. A whole new world to explore.

We pulled up outside a large, very old stone building, with a greenhouse-like porch greeting you as its entrance. Whilst I was an apprentice painter in my late father's company many moons ago, we did a lot of work in Clonliffe College, a place in Dublin that had been founded in order to provide priests for the Dublin diocese. This 'Main House', as it was referred to by all in Loughan House, struck me as somewhat similar to the buildings in Clonliffe College. The face of this Main House was covered with windows, each from the dorm-like rooms that housed the inmates. And my comparison to Clonliffe College, I would later find, was spot on. Loughan House had originally been purpose-built for the White Fathers Missionary Congregation in 1953, only to close down in 1970 and be taken over by the Irish Prison Service.

One day an inmate by the name of Peter came to me in Loughan House and handed me a black and white photo of about thirty priests and two or three nuns sitting outside a large, old stone building. They were lined up like All Ireland Champions for their team photo in the middle of Croke Park's incredible battlefield. He asked me where the photo was taken and, after studying it thoroughly, I said confidently, 'Clonliffe College in Dublin.'

'Good guess,' replied Peter, 'but, alas, you are wrong. For, you see, this photo was taken in 1968, outside of the main building right here in Loughan House, and see yer man there, top row, second last on the left? That, my dear Gary, is me!' I study the photo again, now recognising the front of Loughan's main building, and see the younger Peter who stares back at me, his thick, black-framed glasses the only thing to survive the test of time. 'Oh, how things were going to be different for me. I was studying to become a priest of all things, in the very same building that now, some forty years later, houses me as her prisoner. Crazy!' And crazy it was, wow!

I'm let out of my uncomfortable holding compartment and led off the bus, each of my arse cheeks numb to the touch. I was met by the not-so-hungover-now officer who Handsome had tormented throughout our journey, and he undoes my handcuffs. As I turned to my left, I see none other than Cunny! Just as it was in Mountjoy, Cunny was there for me as I experienced a whole new jail for the first time. 'Gar, ya look fuckin' great pal,' beamed Cunny.

'As do you buddy, I've fuckin' missed ya pal,' I offer as a reply.

'This place is amazing compared to that kip you've just come from, but hang in there for the first week, Gary, the first week is tough!' How right he was

I'm led through the massive, greenhouse-like porch into a hall. In front of me was a wide staircase and at its top was the entrance to the jail's chapel. On my left was the control room, where officers sat and kept a watchful eye over the multitude of screens showing the feeds of the many cameras that secured Loughan House. They also facilitated lads in making phone calls from this room, with you giving the officer the number you wanted to ring, and him patching you through on the phones provided down a small corridor from the office. On my right was the A.C.O.'s office, which was where I was led.

I was met by a woman and, seeing that she was an officer, realised for the first time that the officers here don't wear uniforms. I would soon learn that this small fact really does help in the process of becoming ready for life outside prison. The first thing I noticed about the lady in front of me was her kindness. Wait, she was a screw right? She was asking me things like, 'How are you? Was the drive up okay?' She introduced herself as Mrs Mulligan who would become such a massive influence in my life. I also want to add at this stage that nearly all of the officers in Loughan House were really good people. They completely rejected the 'Us vs Them' vibe that seems to go hand in hand in the lives of prisoners and officers. (And as a mark of respect to them and all they achieved by breaking down the walls between prisoners and officers, I will use their real names so they can benefit from the praise they deserve.)

Mrs Mulligan continued with her 'welcome package' speech. 'Okay, life is a little more relaxed here than in the auld Joy.' She spoke with a soft Sligo accent, her face glowing more and more with each smile, her curly brown hair bouncing on top of her shoulders. Her age was irrelevant, but she came across like the really nice aunt you had who was always looking out for you. 'Right so, ya haven't eaten so I'm going to bring you and the other new arrivals around to the canteen to get some tea, then you're free to do as you please. Here is the key to your room, which is up the stairs there, right at the top of the house. It's only two flights so not too far. You must be in your room, or assembled here in the hall, for "checks" which happen at 6.00 pm and 9.00 pm. And you must be in your room by midnight. All other "checks" are performed when you eat, so at breakfast, dinner and tea we will "check" you.' My head is spinning a little here, which Mrs Mulligan soon picks up on. 'It can be a bit daunting at first, Gary, but it all just sort of falls into place. Just stick with the system we have here, it does work, I promise.'

After we're brought to the canteen, a large dining hall with high white ceilings and bright yellow walls, we eat a meal consisting of soggy fish and mashed spuds. We were then left to do, well, whatever we fuckin' wanted. And, you see, that was the problem. We had just come from a closed jail, with all its rules and regulations, a place where routine was a key tool in your survival, and you become more and more reliant on it. You begin to abide by the rules straight away, and rely on the officers telling you what time to wake up, what time to eat, what time to sleep. You get used to it. But now, in Loughan House, an open centre that has an operational capacity of 140 adult male inmates who have been deemed suitable for such a centre, the 'game' had changed. You had almost all of your time on your hands and it was a head-fuck! It sounds like I'm being ungrateful, but that's what being institutionalised does to you. I was already starting to worry about how I was going to spend my time, what was I going to do to eat away the long hours of a typical prison day. Believe it or not, Mountjoy fucks with you so much that you actually start to think you'd be better off back there. I was very lucky I had Cunny for support.

I began wandering aimlessly around the massive grounds. Loughan House sits on an acre of land, and was actually built upon caves, making the landscape very hilly and steep. At the back of the Main House was a wide open space with massive rolling green fields, and a narrow winding path that leads to a floodlit, all-weather, eight-a-side football pitch. Out on the horizon was the calming blue flow of one of the many lakes that has made Cavan so famous. To the right of this wide open space was a separate building, a gym like every gym or hall in secondary schools in Ireland with basketball nets at either end to boot! Inside this large hall were three treadmills, two exercise bikes and two rowing machines. The hall could be dissected in half in order to facilitate a game of badminton, with its net spanning the width of the hall. In a room off the main hall was the weights room. It contained the same machines as Mountjoy, but it also included free weights, such as dumbbells and the like. The gym was the epicentre of the jail.

As you headed back to the front of the Main House there was 'The Gate' staring at you, which locked every evening at 6.00 pm. The Gate reminded you that you were still in a prison, as you could have been fooled into thinking that you had all of your freedom back. The Gate brought you back to the reality of being incarcerated. Beyond this gate, about a 30 second walk away, was the school, a newly built building which would become crucial to my stay in Loughan House.

To the right of the school was Loughan House's working farm. There were two or three barns, or sheds, down on that farm that were used for some incredible charity projects, like the 'Bikes for Africa' project which involved some of the lads fixing up battered old bikes that were only fit for a skip, and sending them like new to the needy in Africa. Incredible stuff! But as regards to the actual farm on Loughan House? Well, hailing from Dublin, my farming knowledge was at a minimum and did not increase whilst I stayed in Loughan House, but I can tell you that it was a complete working farm.

To the left of The Gate as you approach it was the Visiting Area. This was probably the main draw for any prisoner who pondered a move to an open prison – the visits. Visits in Loughan House could almost last the whole day, and you could actually embrace your loved ones, hold your kids in an almost bear-like squeeze without the intrusive benches we had become so accustomed to at Mountjoy. Governor Gavin had, quite cleverly, created a prison built on trust, and one of the changes she made was not having visitors being searched upon their arrival. This was very welcome for the people who came to visit us, as they disliked the very intrusive searching procedures required in a closed jail. Some may not think we deserved that level of human contact as prisoners, but I'm hoping I can show that we really did. The Visiting Area consisted of two large, identical rooms, filled with the grey plastic chairs I had become so accustomed to and tables. One of the rooms also contained toys and children's books, so was deemed the 'kids' area.

To the right of The Gate as you approach it was Pine Lodge. This was the 'C Wing' of Loughan House and a stark contrast to the Main House where you were housed when you first arrive. The rooms in the Main Houase were located on two identical narrow corridors, which were lined with the doors to the lads' rooms. There were two communal toilet/showering areas at either end of these halls which were disgusting. (But we soon changed that!) The rooms were a variety of shapes and sizes, some a rare single room, usually given to the landing's cleaner, but most filled with bunk beds for you and your sleeping buddy! Inside each room there was also a wardrobe, a telly and a sink. They all had large sash windows, which we could open, a luxury that I would never take for granted again. The rooms were just big enough to ensure that you wouldn't want to actually kill the lad doubling up with you. They were nothing like the disgusting conditions of your cell in Mountjoy, and were a very welcome change from 'the norm', yet everyone had the same idea – *get to Pine Lodge fast!*

Pine Lodge housed 50 inmates, and this was the nirvana everybody strived for, and Loughan House had a very clever system to allow almost everybody the chance to sample its comforts. It was a wooden-framed building, again with two floors of identical corridors. But the doors that lined these corridors led to a different sleeping arrangement. On opening one of these doors, you would be met by three more doors. A toilet was in front of you, and a door either side of that. These doors led to the single rooms Pine Lodge had to offer. It was like having a bedsit, with its bed, wardrobe, and desk coming straight from the shelves of IKEA. Again, this would stand you well as you prepared for your release back into society. So I looked forward to obtaining one of these rooms, but I had no idea how long I'd have to wait!

Cunny and No. 2 caught up with me as I began to traverse the same path again, the 'laps' in this particular jail taking a lot longer than those on D yard. 'Ya ok, Gar?' enquires Cunny.

'Bit of a head-fuck, pal, isn't it?' adds No .2.

'Ah lads, I don't think this is for me,' and that statement right there was to be the one statement I heard many a man utter after his first taste of Loughan, crazily thinking that a closed jail has more to offer.

'We all went through it, Gar, but that feeling goes after a week or so, then you'll see this place for what it really is,' says Cunny.

I'm so glad that I did listen to Cunny and decided to stay, for Loughan House made me who I am today. Mountjoy had begun the process all right, but Loughan House finished the job. But, on that Sunday night, with Fitzer and all I'd left behind weighing heavily on my mind, I didn't want to be there.

I made my excuses and headed to my room, which was located on the top floor of the Main House. I entered room 21 to see my roommate for the first time. Momo was a young lad from the traveling community, but unfortunately the first thing I noticed about him were the black smudges around his nose and on his finger tips. He had been smoking heroin. 'Ah, there ya are, I'm Momo, where ya from mister?' he asks.

'Dublin,' I reply. 'Me name's Gary and I won't be having any of that shite ya smoke going on while I'm in the room okay? I'm sorry, but you're gonna have to fuckin' respect that.'

'Oh, God, no bother, not a bother at all.' says Momo, and I actually feel sorry for the guy. You can tell he wouldn't harm a fly. I take to the grey plastic chair, and park myself down on it.

I'm only gathering my thoughts when a loud knock comes to the door. Momo opens it, only to be pushed back in by two more lads from the travelling community. Now, I spent over a year and a half living with travellers and several are close friends. But the two who barged into my room on my first night in Loughan wouldn't shine the shoes of the travellers I've met, who I'm certain would have shunned them. They immediately set about Momo, well, one of them did, a fat, horror-head of a man.

'I know ya had a visit, now give us everything ya have,' screamed this fat prick into Momo's face.

'I've nothing, swear to God, nothing,' pleaded Momo.

With that the fat bastard clattered Momo across the face. That's it, I'm on my feet, and the next thing this bully knows is he can't breathe as I held him by the scruff of his neck against the wall, every fibre of my being wanting to take my bad mood out on his ugly mush.

'Here, this (cough) has nothin' to (cough) do with you,' our fat bully offers.

'This is true, ya fat prick, but this is also my fuckin' room, and I won't have you bullying anyone in it.' My Dublin accent was enough to scare this bullying scumbag, as he didn't want the whole of the Dublin population of Loughan House on his back.

'Okay, okay, sorry boss, sorry, won't happen again,' he splutters.

'And yas both fuck off away from this young fella and leave him alone okay?' I say.

'Okay will do,' our bully sighs. And with that I threw the two of them out.

Poor auld Momo was a bit shook up, but God love him he couldn't do enough for me, as he offered cups of tea, free chocolate and sweets. I had to stop this.

'Listen, you're grand, what's done is done. Stay away from that shite you're smoking and ya won't have as many problems, ya know?'

But a couple of days later Momo and the two idiots I ejected out of our room were sent back to whatever jail they came from after being caught smoking 'gear'. Fuckin' idiots!

Unbeknownst to me at the time, though, that was to be one of the only bad nights I was to encounter inside Loughan House. The future was gonna be bright!

Chapter 33

A New Governor

I woke the next morning and met Cunny, No. 2 and Handsome for breakfast in the large dining hall. I began telling them what happened the night before, and almost immediately I regretted it. 'Only fuckin' you, Gar,' they laughed and mocked. Handsome turns to me and says, 'Pack your stuff up after we go and meet the new Governor, and move in with me, we'll have a fuckin' great laugh.' So that's just what we did.

The Governor's parade was held in the school, which was outside of The Gate but still in the confines of the prison grounds. Me and Handsome walked up to the school, its inside reminiscent of a modern college layout, with its smooth yellow walls and varnished doors, frames and skirtings. The parade was held in a corridor adjoining the school, which housed the Governor's office. A small queue had formed in this corridor, and would form every day that I spent in Loughan except weekends for the whole time I was there! God love the Governor and Chief of Loughan House. They really earned their salaries as they listened to the constant requests to be sent home, allowed temporary release, and so on.

We're not waiting long, and soon it was my turn to meet Governor Gavin for the first time. A tall lady, immaculately dressed from head to toe, she offered a massive smile – a fuckin' smile from a fuckin' *governor*! 'Hi Gary, welcome to Loughan House, I'm Governor Gavin.' She spoke with a Yorkshire accent, and her whole face seemed to smile as well as her mouth. I had heard of this lady before, but it all sounded like urban myths. I had heard of how fair and caring she was, and how Loughan House was built on trust. She allowed us back some of our 'freedom' and treated us like proper human beings. Now she had stern rules regarding your stay in Loughan House, and you were under constant review as to whether you were doing enough with regard to work or the school to afford you a chance in her open prison. And if you broke her trust there were serious consequences. There would be no pleading, no second chance. You were placed in a holding cell, located on the first floor of the Main House, and you sat in that white-walled, bare room until a prison bus arrived to take you back to the closed jail from which you came.

Loughan House had been known for prisoners absconding, and was on the verge of closure, until Governor Gavin asked to be given an opportunity to bring it back from extinction. During her reign, as she launched her 'new brand' of an open prison, one built solely on the principles of hard work and trust, there were exactly *no* prisoners who absconded. We all respected this fair, but stern woman. She, along with the equally amazing Chief Carrick, who was her right-hand lady, played a major role in the conversion of many Irish prisoners into better men.

'I heard a lot of outstanding things about you from Mountjoy,' she begins, 'from officers, from the school, you're doing good Gary, you should be really proud. I was also made very aware of the play you wrote. We have an auditorium in the Main House, and we have an amazing school on offer, maybe we could stage it here?'

I'm completely gobsmacked, her words swirling around my head. Nobody had ever spoken to me in such a positive way before, making me realise that maybe I'm not such a fuckin' waste of space. 'Wow, thank you, Governor Gavin. I'm here to grow, to use the time I have here to my advantage, and yours. I will work, and then work some more while I'm here, Governor Gavin, it's just in my make-up. I will fully partake in the school, but I need a job for the weekends, as I fear having nothing to do.'

She seemed impressed by my eagerness to work and says, 'It just so happens we need a cleaner in the Boardroom above the visiting centre, I think you'd do a great job.'

'Best job you've ever feckin' seen, Governor, I've massive OCD!'

She laughs, then follows it with, 'Can you recommend anybody from Mountjoy?'

I don't even need the time to think as I shout out Fitzer's name. She types his details into her computer, but on seeing the amount of time he has remaining her face drops a little. I need to strike now. 'Miss, I know he has a little longer left, but what is the point of an open prison? Is it not to reward the hard work you have put in whilst in a closed jail? Is it not to ready yourself for the outside world, happy in the knowledge that you're a changed man, and that you'll never return. This man ticks all those boxes and more. On a personal level, he saved my life, so yes, I'm going to speak up for him a bit more, but as regards to what he will bring this place? It's invaluable, Miss. Plus he co-wrote my play with me (I lied, sorry Governor) and I feel if you got him here, we could both achieve great things.'

'You have a wonderful way of speaking, Gary,' starts Governor Gavin. 'I had been warned that you spoke your mind, but I didn't realise you spoke it with clarity and conviction. Fitzer will be a challenge for me but I love a challenge. Plus I can put forth that on asking you to recommend someone, you immediately named him and spoke so well of him. Getting recommendations from other prisoners is a very positive thing.'

These final words are the ones that Governor Gavin would live to regret saying as it now became my mission to get Fitzer up to Loughan House fuckin' asap!

Chapter 34

It's the School Around the Corner Just the Same

I leave the governor's office to find Handsome has grown tired of waiting for me, as he's nowhere to be seen. It was still early on this bright Monday morning, so I decided to introduce myself to the teaching staff in the school and see what they have to offer. As I step through the door I'm transported again to a scene normally associated with a busy college campus. There were lads milling about the place, all heading to catch their next class, and everybody seemed in a positive, uplifting mood. I think that was the first real difference you noticed about Loughan House compared to Mountjoy – the ambience. There were men in Mountjoy who tried to bring some positivity to the place, but it was such a drab environment that it was an incredibly difficult task. But, here in Loughan, everybody seemed so much more upbeat. The freedom to walk around to get some fresh air at a time of your choosing, plus the size of the place on one acre of land compared to the confines of C Wing and D yard, helped to create a buoyant mood.

I spot a small queue that has formed outside the principal's office and decide this was a good place to start. I get chatting to a few of the lads and realise for the first time that I may be in a minority. Nearly all the lads I spoke to that morning were from different parts of Ireland – North, South, West and a few East. In Mountjoy it was a mainly Dublin population with a few culchies and some foreign lads, but here the Dubs were outnumbered. Well, at least it meant that the slagging and banter during the All-Ireland Championship would be of a particularly high standard! *Hon the Dubs!*

It was my turn to enter the office, but this was in a stark contrast to the last time I entered a principal's office! I'm met by the wonderfully high-pitched Fermanagh tones of Brenda, the school's boss. Her energy was contagious and she casts the largest smile seen this side of Cavan Town. 'Welcome to Loughan House, what's your name lad?'

'Gary Cunningham, Miss,' I reply.

'It's Brenda, Gary, and I've heard a lot about you. You've written a play?' she asks, kind of in disbelief.

'I did Brenda, well meself and a lad I'm trying to get up here, Fitzer.' I pause to let his name sink in. 'So, yeah it would be amazing to get something going with it up here with *Fitzer* involved too!'

'Well,' she enthusiastically continues, 'we have Padraig in the music room, a very accomplished musician, I'm sure he can be of help. Next door here is Mandy. She is our English/Drama/Yoga teacher and a wonderful lady. Then there's Conn, our IT teacher, a wonderful, wonderful gentleman, I'm sure he'll do what he can.'

It's like she was introducing her own family members to me, as she patiently walked through the school's corridor, stopping at each class in order to identify these teachers with their high-ranking bios.

'Facing Conn's room is Thomas, our woodwork teacher and school headcase. He's a small, bald rothweiler whose bark is way worse than his bite. He has done and seen it all, so I'm sure his wisdom will be of grave importance. Last on the first floor is Susan, our Maths and Science teacher.

An incredible, sometimes crazy woman, she would literally do anything for you. No stranger to adversity, her strength is commendable. Upstairs, first door on your right, is Mary, our Home Economics teacher, a very popular class. Mary is a fantastic cook, and her wisdom is beyond her years. Last we have Maura, our Art teacher and Vice Principal, and again we're blessed here, in good old Loughan, to have such an experienced, talented teacher amongst us. She's an incredible lady.'

I'm sold! I want in, where do I sign? This place had everything on offer for me to fulfil my 'plans', my ideas and dreams for a better future for myself. This amazing teaching staff assisted in the eventual, complete overhaul of me and my old life. The school in Loughan House was simply incredible. The staff were the sole reason for so much of the change that occured in willing prisoners wanting to become better people. I've heard the arguments on some radio talk-shows that it was disgraceful, some of the amenities offered to Irish prisoners. I cannot disagree more, for if it weren't for these incredible human beings that dedicate their lives to helping Irish prisoners we would have an even higher reoffending rate than we currently do. This school, in fact the entire complex of Loughan House, ended up creating the man that types this now ... along with Antoinette. Ah, yes Antoinette Gahan.

> Me and Ms Gahan, we got a thing goin' on.

Oh yes, we most certainly had a 'thing' all right. Now that we could hear from each other at a faster rate, well, things got interesting.

> Yeah, we got a thing goin' on.

Chapter 35

WEET-A-MINUTE ...

One of the many amazing things I was finding out about life in an open prison were the phone calls. Firstly, there was no time constraint. You could speak to your heart's content, though you would always be mindful of any queue forming behind you out of respect for the other lads. Secondly, the officers never listened in as you spoke on these calls. This was just incredible, as it was horrible knowing back in The Joy that officers were listening in as my heart shattered into a million pieces the countless times I begged my mam for forgiveness. So, being able to speak freely on the phone was incredibly liberating.

The letters between myself and Antoinette were becoming one of the most important factors in the daily routine I was creating for myself, as I sought new challenges and change. I was falling hard for this incredible, grounded, down-to-earth woman. Did she feel the same way for me? Well, I was fucked if I knew the answer to that one, as at our first meeting Antoinette had a Great Wall up similar to China's, so talking about her feelings was kind of 'off the table', so to speak! But that didn't deter me in my quest to win over this fair maiden. I worked hard every day in the gym, toning my body as best I could to no longer resemble an overweight grizzly bear, and I was seeing results! I was also constantly writing songs, poems, stories, all sent to her via letters, in the hope of grabbing her attention, maybe making her stop and 'think' about me for a second. Well, this was the plan anyway and it seemed to be working. I could sense the change in her letters to me, each one becoming more personal, letting me in past her wall one inch at a time. She always encouraged me with my ideas, no matter how crazy they were, and I really appreciated that. We were really getting on, so at the end of one of my many letters I asked for her phone number.

Well, I must have lost two stone in sweat as I frantically awaited her reply which came a week later with her number on it – result!

I'll never forget how nervous I was as I approached the control in the Main House that fateful day, with Antoinette's phone number scrawled on some torn paper and glued to my sweating hand. Mr. Camden, a crazy, hyper-intelligent officer, whose mad-cap stories would leave you bewildered, was manning the ship, and raving to another officer on the phone about some issue or another (he was also the extremely proud husband of Mrs Mulligan, the amazing lady I met on my first day in Loughan).

'Right so, I have to go, aul' "The Voice" Cunningham has just walked in, we don't want to upset the Dubs now, officer, that's right, good day to you to sir.' Camden plonks down the phone's faded white receiver, places his wide framed glasses atop his bald head, and bellows, 'Gary, me aul' flower, what can I bleedin' do for ya?' His Northside Dublin accent is quite impressive for a man who was born and reared in Cavan.

'Will ya make a call for me please, Mr. Camden?' I ask.

'Home is it Gary?' enquires Camden.

'Eh, no officer, it's a friend.'

'Oh, a "friend" now is it Cunningham? And what would her name be?' he mocks. I laugh, and this brings out his insane laugh, like a clown on acid! 'Right ya are, fire those digits at me White Boy,' he says. I did, and soon I was running for the phone down the narrow corridor beside the control room that was screaming for my attention.

When we spoke for the first time it was like talking to my best friend, someone I had spent a lifetime with. The tone of her voice only increased my attraction towards her, a silky, almost dark tone, adding to her mystery. And yet, she always spoke with such joy, radiated so much positivity in every call I had with her. Her ideas made me think. She had such a different way of looking at things, and it really interested me. She became my inspiration, a reason to become this 'new person' I kept promising my mother I'd be upon my return to society.

Her sense of humour would rival almost any stand-up currently gracing our TV screens. She really made me laugh – a gift not possessed by many whilst I was incarcerated – and this was a trait that I grew to love in her. Also, her passion for singing was engulfing. Antoinette confided in me one day that she suffered from Perthes disease, which was slowly eroding away her right hip. As a result you would think this would make life very difficult, yet she was always filling me in on the gigs she had just performed with her wedding band. Or telling me about the Karaoke nights she ran with a friend of hers named John. She'd also tell me about the gym classes and workouts she was completing on a daily basis. Something told me that no Perthes disease was going to keep this woman down and I fuckin' loved that about her. Nothing like a strong woman to set ya right, and this woman had strength coming out of her pores!

It was during one of these phone calls that she piped up with, 'So, I got a lend of my friend's guitar, and I'm gonna teach meself how to play, I'll be better than you in no time,' she laughs, as she continues, 'but yeah, sooo, here's what I was thinking. You could teach me some songs on the guitar, over the phone.'

'Can I now?' I ask, laughing as well.

'Ah yeah, sure, ya know you want to.' And she was right. I'd have done anything for her. She had made such an impact in my life. So, as the call ended that day I got my first order off her. 'Learn "Clown" by Emeli Sandé' – piece of piss.

Which it was, so the next day, as we spoke on the phone, I told her to go get her guitar, as I had learned how to play the song she wanted. Now, I had been playing the guitar since I was eight years of age and my 'specialty' was working out how to play a song after, usually, listening to it once from start to finish. I have a good ear for music, I guess. 'Clown' was not a hard song to learn, four chords, so I thought this would actually be a good start to our 'over-the-phone' lessons. Alas, it was not! Everything started well, with Antoinette listening intently, absorbing like a sponge the information I was giving her, meticulously repeating my instructions as she began forming the chords that made up the song. Day one, success. Day two? Fuckin' disaster.

I rang at the agreed time, to be met by 'Antoinette Clapton' on the other end of the line, joking that I had, 'Made a mess of that song, I'm afraid, they're the wrong chords.'

I was actually quite impressed at how straight she was, no fuckin' about here, straight for the jugular, never mind your feelings or anything like that! She really made me laugh though. 'Eh, they are the right chords, my dear,' I say sarcastically, the salty tears of laughter streaming down my face.

'Eh, no they're not, my love, doesn't sound right, ya know?' she replies.

Doesn't 'sound' right? She's crazy. But how foolish of me to think she would listen to the expert when he was telling her she was wrong. I'm not sure this incredible woman likes being told she was wrong, but then who does?

'I'm not wrong you are,' she offered. I got a pain in me arse after a couple of minutes and told her to Google the chords and see if they matched the ones I had given her. We left it there, slightly heated. Was this our first row? So I waited to see if she would come around.

She did, but on her terms. 'Right, okay, technically your chords were right, but I have to go on my ear, don't I? Isn't that what makes a good singer?'

I laughed, although I have to say I respected her answer, and nearly found myself saying 'sorry' to her. During this call, she kept referring to me as a 'prick' or, closer to the point, 'her prick!' To this day I find it strange that I felt so loved when I heard her refer to me as 'her prick' – what has she done to me!

'Go on, get off the phone, go on and stuff your face with your Weetabix.' Now she made this point in reference to a chat we'd had a couple of days earlier about how I had realised I was living almost solely on Weetabix. I fuckin' loved them. 'Yeah, go on, hang up and go stuff your face with all that wheat goodness, while I struggle away with "Clown", and the fact that it still doesn't sound right.'

'Sound right?' Cheeky cow.

My Life in Loughan was moving at a ferocious rate, as was my relationship with Antoinette as our calls became the highlight of my day. We had moved on from 'Clown'-gate, and in fact she pretty much mastered that song, and a few others, whilst listening and learning over the phone. Quite impressive!

I had begun creating new friendships with men from all walks of life. Lads like Miguel, a Brazilian-born giant of a man, his shoulder length hair adding to the impression that he was in fact a WWE wrestler in another life. Then he'd begin talking to you, and you'd feel cheated as the unmistakable high-pitched Cork tones came flowing from his mouth, having spent the last ten years living there. Great lad though. I was getting on with almost every one, bar one or two, but you'll always come across negative people and it's how you deal with them that sets you free from their tyranny.

So things were going great until I was called to the General Office one Thursday afternoon, about two months after my initial arrival in Loughan, to be greeted by Governor Gavin, Chief Carrick and an A.C.O. whose name I couldn't bear to include in the pages of my story. To say that this was a major surprise would be a complete understatement.

'Please close the door behind you, Gary,' asked the Governor, a look of concern splashed across her face. The General Office was located in the Main House, around the corner from the Control Room on the ground floor. As you walked in the office, filled with PCs and the like, you faced a massive wooden partition. There was a hatch to your right, much like the hatch that, unfortunately, most of us had the horrible experience of visiting during our time unemployed. It was from here that the office worker on duty would address your needs, or give you any mail that may have been delivered for you. On this day, though, as I walked in, the Governor was standing to my left, holding a door open in the wooden partition, with the Chief closely behind her. Our A.C.O. friend was standing behind the massive perspex screen which was built into the wooden partition.

'You have received a parcel in the mail this morning Mr. Cunningham. Were you expecting anything in the mail?' I wasn't at all. The only things I ever received in the post were my cherished letters from Antoinette.

'No A.C.O., I am as surprised as you look right now. I was not expecting anything,' I offered.

'Well,' he quickly interjects, 'this arrived for you this morning.' He held up a fairly large parcel, wrapped in brown paper. It seemed to be a box, a little thinner and smaller than a shoe box. What the fuck was this? I could see it had been opened, so I was not fooled when this A.C.O. said to me, 'Do you object to me opening it?'

'It's already open, so work away, I have no idea what it is,' I say, but I was worried. I was beginning to think I was being set up. And my fears grew when I saw what was in the brown, crumpled paper – a box of Weetabix! I immediately went into 'defense' mode. 'I have absolutely no idea what that is, Miss.'

I have turned to the Governor to say this, as I know what she, and everyone else, was thinking. Boxes of cereal are one of the ways lads use to smuggle contraband into an open prison. It seemed like I *was* being set up. I noticed that the paper used to wrap the Weetabix was actually birthday wrapping paper turned inside out, which sparked a question from this fuckin' A.C.O., who was convinced he's 'got' me now, and he'll be packing me back to The Joy in no time.

'When's your birthday, Cunningham?' he asked excitedly.

'It's on the computer screen in front of you, A.C.O., I'm not in the humour for this, it looks like somebody is trying to set me up, which I know you all think I'm only saying because I'm "caught", but I can honestly say I have no idea what's in that fuckin' box, and another thing ... ' I stop mid-sentence. I have noticed something, a yellow post-it note was stuck to the front of the Weetabix box. I get just enough of a view of it to read its brilliant comment, 'Enjoy, ya prick, xxxx Love, Mrs Cunningham'. Antoinette! The crazy lady had sent me a box of fuckin' Weetabix, the 24 pack and all! I began to smile, which the Governor notes.

'Have you something to say, Gary?' she enquired.

'In fact, Miss, I do,' I say, a little calmer. 'That parcel is for me, and all that it contains is the wholewheat goodness offered in each and every Weetabix biscuit that's inside. It was sent to me, by a crazy friend. She is half looking after me, and half taking the complete piss out of me. I can assure you you will find nothing untoward inside of that package.'

The Governor also spots the post-it and looks at me puzzled.

'Apparently, I'm "her prick", Miss,' I offered as an explanation. This has the Governor and Chief in stitches.

'Oh, thank god, we didn't want to have to send you back, we see good things in you Gary.'

Not everyone was so overjoyed though. 'I would like the Weetabix biscuits to be sent away and analyzed for traces of narcotics,' barked the A.C.O., clinging to the hope he'll find something on me.

'You can keep the biscuits A.C.O.,' I said with a heavy heart as I gave away 24 moments of pure ecstasy. 'All I want is the post-it, Miss, if that would be possible?'

'Of course, Gary, and let him have the Weetabix too,' she pleads.

'Not at all Miss,' I countered. 'Our A.C.O. won't sleep until he finds out if I am in fact smuggling drugs into the prison, through the process of bathing them in Weetabix, in order to try to fool you all. So let him run his tests. Can I go?'

'Of course you can, Gary, thank you for clearing that up. Best of luck with Antoinette ... Gahan, is it?' She read this from the back of the parcel, as Antoinette always printed her name and address on the back of her mail.

'That's her, Miss,' I reply. 'Ya never know, Miss, she could be The One.' I sling this comment over my shoulder as I turn to leave the General Office, the furious eyes of the A.C.O. like a laser-beam ripping into the back of my skull.

I tell all who will listen about the 'suspect package' sent up by Antoinette, and it's met with laughter and cheers from them all. I rang her that same night, and informed her that she nearly got me sent back to fuckin' Mountjoy! This made her laugh, which in turn makes me laugh, as I listened to her frantically apologise, and yet question the legal ramifications of receiving a box of Weetabix! She brightened up so many dark days for me, this Antoinette Gahan, her name flowing from my lips with such ease. She made me look at myself in a different light. And the funny thing was, she had no idea she was doing all this for me. She did it by being herself ... Antoinette Gahan.

Just put me wide the next time you want to send me something through the post, will ya?

Chapter 36

And the Winner is ...

I had settled in quickly with Handsome, and soon realised it was just better to do things his way. He's a great lad, but he likes things his way. I just had to adapt, and found I was becoming quite good at that particular challenge. He'd always have a little dig at me over Antoinette, like the way a little brother winds up his older sibling. 'Oh, Gar's in looovvee,' he'd mock on a daily basis, and yet I could tell he was happy for me. When you spend so much time with a person, especially in those circumstances, you begin to get an insight into his life on the outside, and you can become affected by the goings on, both good and bad. Still, I enjoyed the slagging, as it wouldn't be occurring if Antoinette was not such a major part of my journey.

I was starting to build up a rapport with most of the officers in Loughan. The major difference between them and officers from a closed jail, besides the fact they don't wear uniforms, was they were just more relaxed. They longed for the quiet life, after spending many years as officers in closed jails. So, for most of them, if you didn't give them hassle and showed them respect, then you would receive the same treatment in turn. Some were wankers, but there are wankers in all walks of life.

A few of the officers actually formed friendships with some of the prisoners. Officers like Miss Thornton, a small, fiery, very attractive lady who ran the Laundry and always had such genuine concern for us on a personal level. Or Mr. Tully, a man who became a close friend through our shared passion in music. He would often bring me in CDs from his personal collection so I could listen to and learn from the great guitar players of our time. He loved the fact I played guitar, as he was a drummer and a fantastic organ player, and on many occasions we'd jam whilst sitting in the Control Room, or down in the Auditorium, him on the keyboard, me on the six-stringer. Happy times!

I cannot stress enough how different life in Loughan was compared to the closed jail experience. If you so much as raised your hand to another prisoner in Loughan you could be shipped back to Mountjoy, whereas raising hands to prisoners there was considered the norm. Loughan House got rid of the tension you could almost taste in a closed jail. The difference between the two really was night and day.

As with the officers, my rapport with the teaching staff in the school was also growing, though one man will always stand out – Conn, the IT teacher. I ventured into Conn's room one day and was captivated by the effort this man put into his classroom. It had many colourful plants scattered around its airy interior, with Conn's desk and numerous school-like desks placed side by side around the classroom's walls, each containing a PC, about 12 in total. Music was played at just the right level in order for you to be able to hear it without it being intrusive. Conn epitomises what it means to be a proper gentleman. His full, almost snow-white beard attached to his narrow face served as a constant reminder of his natural wisdom. Sometimes, when the sun would bathe County Cavan, and in particular Loughan House, his attire would be similar to 'The Man from Del Monte', with his white straw hat worn at an acute angle on top of his snow-white hair, the 'Daz-white' short-sleeved shirt and white Chinos completing the outfit. He has some style our Conn! He spoke in almost a whisper, and I don't think I ever heard the man mutter a coarse word or get annoyed. Along with the rest of the teaching staff in Loughan House, he had a wonderful, positive outlook on things that was quite infectious.

I ambled in that day, scoping the place out to see if he too had the ancient version of Photoshop that I assumed was issued to all prisons, as I was hoping to expand my Poem Creation Enterprise into a much larger venture. I would have more time to dedicate to the creation of my new poems, and so I was hoping to get along with Conn as I planned to spend a lot of time in his classroom. I asked what courses he had to offer, and in his soft-spoken Fermanagh accent he informed me that they offer a FETAC in computers, just the basics really, and they also offered the European Drivers' License for Computing. But I had already obtained those, so I just got to the point and told him what it was I really wanted. On listening to my ramblings on my little Start-up Company he seemed extremely eager to assist. He said he had the disk needed to install the dinosaur-version of Photoshop at home, and asked if there is anything else he could be of assistance with?

'Well,' I start quite nervously, 'I'm actually writing a "book", so to speak.' Conn was the first person I ever spoke to about my book, and I'm glad he was. 'It's scribbled down on hundreds of A4 sheets, in terrible handwriting,' I continue, 'so I would love to get in into digital form to make it more presentable to someone who might want to read it, and to keep it safe from being lost or destroyed.'

I was very nervous as I told him about my 'book', hoping that he wouldn't mock me because of it. I was still struggling with self-esteem issues so writing a fuckin' book was not something I wanted the world to know about at that particular time! Yet he seemed impressed, and he quickly got me set up on one of the classrooms PCs. I informed him I would return the next day to begin the process of transferring my handwritten draft of *Joys of Joy* into digital form. And he loved the title!

The next day I arrived with the handwritten pages containing the words and scribbles that I hoped would form my book. I quickly set up a folder on my particular partition of the classroom's hard drive. I named the folder 'joys_of_joy' and set about frantically typing away, enjoying some of the trips down memory lane. Over the coming days, and unbeknownst to me, Conn had been sneaking peeks over my shoulder as I told my tale about my life in prison. He interrupted my typing one day and said, 'Gary, you can really write you know.' He states this rather than asking it, again his Fermanagh tones lingering in the air.

'Ah, I wouldn't say that, Conn, sure I've never done anything like this before, though I won't lie, I fuckin' love writing.'

'Och, aye, you surely have a wee talent there, in fact take a wee look at this, will ya?' He leans over to his messy desk of organised chaos and retrieves a print-out of the details of the Listowel Writing in Prison Competition. This was a competition designed to try to tap into the more creative sides of Irish prisoners, and to showcase what talents they might possess. I said that I was willing to give it a go! Conn informed me that Loughan House had been entering this competition for the past 10 years and had never come anywhere in the rankings – he even considered that a conspiracy had been established preventing Loughan from winning. I joked that I would change that, and I fuckin' well did!

I took a break from typing my book, and penned a short story, ensuring my word count matched that set out in the rules, involving my three most favourite things: my amazing son, my brother Noel, and the Dublin GAA Team, *the Dubs*! The story was entitled 'Sky Blue Dream'.

Conn loved it, and after meticulously and painstakingly going over it to ensure it made the grade, he sent it off and it came fuckin' *first*! I was picked as the best writer, in my category, out of every Irish jail. But on the day Conn found out this amazing news, he tricked me, the rascal. I made my way into his classroom that morning like I always did, but as soon as I entered he informed me, with a stern look on his face, that the Governor wanted to see me *'immediately!'* I was shittin' as I walked the short journey from Conn's class to the Governor's office, and upon my arrival she told me to sit. She paused for what seemed an eternity, a look of utter disappointment on her face. 'Well, Gary, what can I say?' her Yorkshire accent seeming less vibrant than usual. 'You only went and won the Writing in Prison Competition!'

'What?' says I, shocked. 'Seriously?'

'Seriously!' she exclaims. 'And a fabulous tale it is too Gary, you should feel immense pride.' She grabs me and gives me a hug, a fuckin' hug from a Governor, though it's not long before I'm (you've guessed it) crying! I can't believe I've won. I've never won a single thing in my life. The prize was a cheque for €150 and a silver Parker pen with 'Listowel Writing in Prison Winner' inscribed on it. I couldn't wait to tell my mam that at last I done something to actually make her proud.

I ended up winning the competition the following year too! But at that time, myself and Conn had forgotten all about the competition and the submission day was looming, so I just copied and pasted the 'Kitchen vs Bakery' chapter from this very book and it came first again! Fuck me! Both stories were printed in the *Listowel Writing in Prison Week*, a yearly publication that consisted of all the winning stories and poems. And they both sit on my book shelf right now. I still can't believe I achieved this.

Chapter 37

You Say You Want a Revolution ...

It's such a strange environment, this Loughan House, especially after coming from the dreary existence that embodies a typical closed jail. As I have mentioned before, Governor Gavin had based the ethos of the place on mutual trust, which mostly worked. I say mostly because Loughan House was still a prison, it still housed criminals and a small number of these lads didn't care for Governor Gavin's 'trust'. During the time I spent there, I witnessed quite a few lads abusing this trust and, as a result, getting sent back to a closed jail.

I just couldn't get my head around this as Loughan House provided you with 'semi-freedom' and, in jail terms, this was an unrivalled sensation. For some, though, who perhaps just had an anti-establishment attitude, it mattered not where they were incarcerated as they were going to 'rage against the machine', a real 'fuck you and your rules' attitude. But, as mentioned, that was not for me. I was still playing the 'prison game' and I saw Loughan House as the avenue for me to bring about the changes that were sorely needed in my life. But I did see the negative sides to the place, too, and I began to feel that certain things needed to be highlighted and maybe changed.

I found that I had a good relationship with the Governor and her right-hand woman, the Chief, although I almost ruined this rapport that we had created, and it was all down to Fitzer, though he knew nothing about it! Ever since Governor Gavin had informed me that any lads recommending Fitzer for a transfer to Loughan House would work wonders for his case, as she would have to note each and every one of these recommendations. Well, I ran with that a little too much maybe. I started going around the whole jail, introducing myself to any of the lads I hadn't gotten to know yet. I would offer my services to them to help them in any way I could, and I would, of course, be looking for something in return. All I needed them to do was to go up to see the Governor as she sat on her daily parade, and tell her they would like to recommend a lad for transfer – *Fitzer*! And each and every one of them did just that, what a great bunch of lads, but I wasn't finished.

I would always have my eye out for a bus arriving from a closed jail, and as it made its final stop outside the Main House I would greet the lads as they disembarked, introduce myself like I fuckin' worked there, and then assist them in carrying their belongings. It wouldn't take long to suss out which of these lads would be willing to mention Fitzer's name once the Governor asked them, as she always did, if they could recommend anyone that would be suitable for transfer. And a lot of them did just that! Deadly!

One day, I even got one of the lads who worked in the laundry to get me as many of the prison issue vests that they had in stock. In Loughan House, you had more room to house your own personal clothing than you would in a closed jail, so these vests were never used until I got me hands on 'em! I got a permanent black marker from the art room in the school, and scrawled in large, child-like letters across the front and backs of them: *Fitzer for Loughan.* And the lads proudly wore them around Loughan House, which was such a funny sight to see – nearly the entire jail's population sitting down to dinner wearing these ridiculous looking vests. Sure, the lads were even wearing them up to the fuckin' Governor's parade! This was the straw that broke our good Governor's back.

I was summoned to her office. 'What are you doing, Gary?' she asked, all the while holding back from erupting into a fit of laughter. 'You have made your point now, so can we call a ceasefire on the "Recommendations for Fitzer" campaign you have embarked on?'

I began to laugh. 'I haven't started any campaign, Miss,' I say like butter wouldn't melt in my mouth.

'Would ya go away outta that,' she counters laughing. 'I have to say though I admire your persistence. You have my word that I will do everything I can to get him here.' And that is exactly what she eventually did. But now I owed a lot of favours!

There were only so many poems I could write, or so many rooms I could paint, to try to pay back my debt to these lads who had helped me in my quest to get the band back together and get the greatest friend I'd ever had out of that dump, The Joy, and up here where he could bond with his son on a day-long visit, and where he could embrace his wife. I owed these lads big time, and this was when my time in prison really changed for the better!

One day, I woke up just as Handsome was coming back in from having a shower in the communal shower room. 'Some fucker is after taking a shit in the fuckin' shower!' exclaimed Handsome, his face a bright crimson from the rage brewing up inside him.

'You're fuckin' joking me,' was my shocked response.

'Look Gar, you're deadly at talkin' to the officers, you have a way with them. Forgetting the fact that some complete weirdo pooed in the bleedin' shower, them showers, in fact the whole fuckin' toilet area, well, it's disgusting! We need to sort something out between the lads and the screws. I was just talkin' to one of the toilet cleaners there, and he said he can't get his hands on any mops etc. to clean the fuckin' place. You need to have a chat with one of the screws, work your magic and get this sorted, cos this is a load of *shite*, excuse the pun!'

We both laugh, and I informed him that I would sort this out. I quickly got dressed and headed out on my mission to locate Mr. Slater, who was the head of the Industrial Cleaning Division of Loughan House. He was a fellow Dub, and a really sound guy, so I knew he'd be approachable. It didn't take me long to find him, and I immediately stated my case. 'Mr. Slater, we need more cleaning provisions for the toilets in the Main House, they're *disgusting*!' I really emphasised this last word.

'It's hard to get the lads to do the work, Gary, but yeah we could do with more provisions. But I need the lads to work with me too, you know?' He stated this more as a plea than a fact.

'I have a good rapport with the lads, Mr. Slater,' I say, 'and I think I can sell to them the idea of a cleaner living environment. I'll even go to the Governor and state that more provisions are needed if you think that will help?'

'Yeah, that would be great, Gary,' he says, following it with, 'you have a great way about you speaking up for the lads without sounding like a cheeky bollox, sure you could be the spokesman for the prisoners in Loughan House.'

He laughed as he said this, but unbeknownst to him, he'd just given me a great idea. Why not form a 'Prisoners Committee', a group of lads who would work together to make life in Loughan better for all who spent time there, including the screws! And that's just what I did with the help and support of the Governor. But little did we know what an impact our little 'committee' would have on life in every Irish jail.

Later that day, I called a 'meeting' in the auditorium of the Main House regarding the cleanliness of the landings. I was shocked to see that nearly every prisoner attended, even the lads who resided in Pine Lodge. I took to the stage and began.

'Firstly, thank you all for coming. Look lads, the toilets in the Main House are fuckin' disgraceful. I'd even hazard a guess that the jacks in the closed jails are cleaner and that's not on. I know those of you who have taken on the job of toilet cleaners are finding it hard to obtain the proper equipment to carry out what is the already horrendous task of keeping these jacks clean, but I'm going to speak up about it with the Governor and see what we can do to improve this situation.'

I couldn't believe that I had their undivided attention, so I chanced my next statement. 'Lads, someone took a shit in the shower on the first landing this morning. Now come on!' The laughter rings out in the spacious theatre, some lads pointing at others in order to 'frame' them as the culprit! 'But we all need to work together to resolve this. I can't be asking the Governor to help us sort this if we don't help ourselves. Like it or not, this is our "home" right now, this is where we live, so let's all join together and make this a clean living environment.'

They started to applaud, I couldn't believe it! 'Hear, hear,' cried a few. 'Proper order,' from some others. 'Good man, Gar,' I heard also. They listened and were willing to help, so I struck while the iron was hot.

'I am also going to put forth the idea of a Prisoners Committee, a group that can liaise with the screws, the A.C.O.'s, the Governor and the Chief and work together to better our living arrangements whilst we're housed here. We can make a difference, lads, plus it can work in your favour. If you are seen mucking in here being part of something positive, well, it can only help your case when you go and seek T. R. (Temporary Release), so fuck it lads, let's do this!' A massive roar goes up that brings to life the dull faded white walls of the airy auditorium. I'd won them over. I just hoped I could win the Governor over too!

But I had no reason for concern, as Mr. Slater and Mr. Wallace (Head of the Painting and Decorating Department) had lingered just outside the doors of the auditorium as we held our 'rally'. They then proceeded to explain to the Governor what they had just witnessed, and that they felt this could be a really positive thing. So when I stepped into Governor Gavin's office she was prepared for me.

'Funny,' she started, 'it's usually me who calls meetings in this place but apparently you drew a larger crowd than I normally do, and I have it on good authority that you and the lads are coming together to make life better in Loughan. I'm impressed, Gary.'

I was caught off-guard, everything I had planned to say evaporating into the musty air of her office. 'Well, Miss, it's not just the prisoners who have to live here, the officers do too. Why not form a committee with monthly or bi-monthly meetings that can maybe address some of the daily situations that occur here. We can all work together to make this a better environment for everyone.'

I hoped that I was not stepping over a line here until she answered, 'That is a wonderful idea, but we'd have to come up with a structure for this committee. Like who is on it, how many members and so on?'

'I'm one step ahead of ya, Miss. We should have no more than five and no fewer than three lads on the committee. In order to get committee members, why don't we hold a vote amongst us lads. Not everyone will want to run, but those who do can put their names forward, and then must rely on the rest of the prison voting them in. Everyone will feel involved.' I'm out of breath as I excitedly explain my vision to her.

'Fantastic Gary. You go ahead and organise the vote and get the word out, and anything that we can do to help, just say the word. I assume you will be running in this vote, Gary?' She asks this with a cheeky grin.

'Too bloody right I will be, Miss,' came my determined reply.

'That's what scares me,' she laughs.

And so I got the word out to the lads of Loughan about the new Prisoners Committee that was to form. I explained that the Governor would hold monthly or bi-monthly meetings with the committee in order to address our concerns, and to listen to any ideas we had to improve our standard of living. I, of course, put myself forward, as did quite a few others. I made election posters for each of the lads that were running, and we picked our voting day. It was now up to the candidates to ensure their votes. Enda Kenny, eat your black heart out!

Voting day was a bit of craic. I had set up a 'ballot box' (an A4 cardboard box) in the dining hall, and left countless strips of paper and pens beside it. All the lads had to do was write their chosen member on a strip of paper and pop it into the box. Simple!

And the results are in ...

I got in! *Deadly*! I have struggled in silence most my life trying to 'fit in', but here I was in prison getting voted as the chair of the first ever Prisoners Committee to be founded in an Irish jail. Wow! Also on board was Gym-George, a bald Dubliner who was obsessed with the gym. We had Domo, a popular lad hailing from Navan, then we had Longy, my good friend who hailed from Cork. And last we had Big Joe, so called because, well, he's fuckin' *huge* in the muscles department. He came from the travelling community and was a welcome addition, as Loughan House had a lot of travellers in her population and Joe could be their voice. So we had our committee. We got straight to work creating our 'seven commandments' of how the committee would work:

1. As committee members, we would remain drug-free at all times.
2. We could not speak up for a prisoner regarding T. R. (Temporary Release) or any type of movement.
3. We would work with the officers of Loughan House in order to make a more suitable environment for us *all* to co-habit in.
4. We would keep the minutes of every meeting held with the Governor, so as to show the rest of the lads what was being discussed on their behalf.
5. All requests will be considered except the ludicrous ones, like 'can we have a night out to the cinema' (I kid you not, I was asked to bring that up once in a meeting – some fellas forget they're fuckin' locked up!)
6. As committee members, we would be afforded *no* special privileges – we were still prisoners.
7. We would join together to better ourselves.

I even designed a logo for our 'letterheads':

It was a complete success. We got a lot done with our little committee. We had water coolers placed around the prison to provide the lads with refreshing, cold water. We got TVs into both of the visiting boxes, and I painted them as an incentive! We radically changed the cleanliness of the entire prison. We encouraged lads to get 'jobs' around the place in order to better their chances of early release, or even just T. R. To this day I am so proud of that committee and the men who ran it. But when the Irish Prison Service heard about it, well, things happened!

Governor Gavin had informed the powers-that-be in the IPS of her hardworking committee, one which had created such a 'community' vibe. They immediately wanted to know how much it was costing. 'Well, nothing,' was her surprised answer. They found this impossible to grasp, as they had looked into the setting up of a Prisoners' Committee in each of the Irish jails, based on the committees in place in British jails. Upon doing their research, the IPS found that it cost £12,000 per committee per *year*! Our committee cost the total sum of *fuck all*! This blew them away, and they sent some of their 'suits' to Loughan to investigate.

Governor Gavin called me to her office to inform me of their impending arrival. 'Let's turn it on, Gary. I want you to give a presentation, if you will. I want you to do what you're good at – knocking people's socks off!'

So that's just what I and my fellow committee members did! I typed up our code of conduct – our seven commandments – and a list of what we had already achieved in the short time since our creation in Loughan House. I also set out my ideas of how this system could be implemented in the harsher environment of a closed jail.

On the day the IPS 'suits' arrived, myself and the committee assembled outside the dimly-lit boardroom. We entered the room in our prison attire of whatever made you feel comfortable. I took the helm, as the lads were not as confident as me with speaking, and we blew them away! To this day, they use the same structure that our committee drew up for creating a prisoners' committee in all Irish jails. Amazing! *It's not the time you do ... it's what you do with your time!*

Of course, not all were enthusiastic about our committee. One officer in particular was quoted as saying, 'Who the fuck does your man Cunningham think he is?' The same officer even got our committee's name changed from Prisoners' Committee to Prison Committee. What a sad man. But I'm just glad we got up his nose.

So anything is achievable in this life. I was a fuckin' prisoner, and yet I earned the praises of the governing body of all of Ireland's jails for my work in creating a better living environment for inmates, which in turn was beneficial to the officers, since 'a happy prisoner is a quiet prisoner!' As mentioned, some weren't happy with me, but I won't lose sleep over that. I had begun to find my voice in Loughan.

Chapter 38

SMITHWICKS AND THE NEW CREW

It's funny how some people can have such a massive impact on your life, even after only a fleeting meeting. Of course, being in prison only heightens this as you are thrown together, like it or not! But I was lucky to have been surrounded by some incredible men, and although I'd made new friends and colleagues in Loughan House, I still missed some of the lads I'd left behind. It's not like you can just pick up the phone and give them a ring to see how they are, contrary to popular belief! Fitzer had handed me his wife's mobile number the night before I was leaving, which meant I could stay up-to-date with how he was keeping. I forged a truly amazing friendship with Ashling over the phone, as she filled me in on Fitzer. You could tell how much this incredible woman loved her man. She would gladly deliver my messages and good wishes to him, and in return he'd get her to tell me all his news and gossip! A great auld communication system myself and Fitzer had going on all right!

I was talking to the Governor one day, and she asked me was there anyone else besides Fitzer that I could recommend for transfer. There were quite a few, which I sounded off to her, but I saved my best one for last – Smithwicks! When you recommended a lad for Loughan, you really needed to 'sell' him, you've got to prove that he'll work upon his arrival, as this is a working jail. Smithwicks would be just as easy to sell as Fitzer, as he is a hardworking bloke with such a positive demeanour. So, when she typed his name into her PC, and upon seeing who I was talking about she said, 'Ah, yes, I've been looking at this man. You say he's a good choice, Gary?' she asks.

'He most certainly is Miss. We ran the print shop together on D Wing back in The Joy. He's a hard worker and his attitude is a perfect fit for your regime here.' I say all this as if I am Smithwicks PR agent!

'Right so I'm going to get him,' she exclaimed. And that's exactly what she did. After only a couple of weeks, she stopped me as I was making my way into the dining hall. 'Smithwicks arrives here on Friday, Gary and don't worry, Fitzer will be on one of them busses some day, you mark my words!'

I am filled with delight upon hearing of the impending arrival of my good friend Smithwicks. I find Cunny, No. 2 and Handsome sitting at one of the many round tables in the dining hall and excitedly tell them the good news.

'That's fuckin' great,' starts Cunny, 'Smithwicks is bleedin' sound, plus he's another Dub, our numbers are beginning to increase!' Which they were. Word was travelling back to the closed jails in Dublin that, although it was a long journey for your visitors to endure in order to spend some time with you, the place knocked the socks off the horrid closed jail experience. The Dubs were taking over.

Smithwicks arrival brought to an end the living arrangements of myself and Handsome. A friend of his, a young lad named Jay, very kindly offered me the room which he occupied alone, but which had bunks in it. Jay in turn moved in with Handsome, thus freeing up the space for me and Smithwicks to be doubled up. I was extremely grateful to this young lad for this act of kindness. He didn't know me from Adam and didn't have to do anything for me, but he did.

On the morning of Smithwicks arrival, I frantically scrubbed and dusted our new abode, like a 'housewife' circa 1950 – all I was missing was an apron! No. 2 had kindly given me normal bedclothes (another luxury of life in Loughan, your own bedclothes!) and so I assembled Smithwicks' bed and made the room as welcoming as possible. As I was dusting the battered wooden sill below the large Georgian-styled window, I spot a prison bus entering The Gate. Smithwicks!

I made the short trip down two small flights of stairs that led out into the reception area just as Smithwicks ambled off the bus. 'Well there ya are,' I greet my good friend in the most 'Irish' way possible.

'Ah, Gary,' he beams, it's been a while.' We embrace, albeit momentarily – we are men after all. I picked up his belongings, as he goes through the same process I did upon my initial arrival. Once Mrs. Mulligan has finished her welcoming speech, I informed her that I could look after Smithwicks from here, and she was only too happy to oblige. I brought Smithwicks into his new living quarters, and he turned to me and said, 'Could do with a clean, but yeah, it's deadly man!' The cheeky fucker! I dripped sweat all morning for him, the ungrateful swine. It's true, a woman's work is never done!

Smithwicks took to life in Loughan like a shark to the ocean. I knew he would because like myself, Smithwicks was driven by the desire to change. And in prison terms, he was in the best place to achieve this goal. I'll never forget his first visitors who came the very next day after his arrival. It was his wonderful parents, a couple very much still in love after all the time they had spent together and who really missed their only son. In Loughan, you can go out to join lads on their visits, if you're invited of course, and I was lucky to have been invited by Smithwicks on this day. I only stayed for a few minutes, and was taken aback at the thanks I received from his parents. Smithwicks had been filling them in on everything from the print room job I secured for him back in Mountjoy to the fact he was now in a better 'prison environment' up here in Loughan House. I was quick to point out, though, that Smithwicks was the creator of his own future – I just gave him a little shove.

Smithwicks was a 'foodie', his knowledge of food similar to the great Gordon Ramsay, and on his first visit from his folks that day he received his order of delectables that he had requested his parents to bring – and they had doubled the order in order to facilitate yours truly! There was Marks & Spencer's Key Lime Pie, with whipped cream to top off each slice. There was an assortment of cheeses, and a large jar containing some form of relish which I had never heard of before. Smithwicks, using the 'designer' bread that had come with his order, and adding some tuna to the wonderfully strange relish and cheese, made the most incredible Tuna Melt, grilling the sandwich on the George Foreman grill which his parents also delivered. There were sweets and cakes aplenty and, last but by no means least, they had brought the entire series of *Breaking Bad* on DVD plus an old DVD player. *Deadly*! I don't think we left that room at all that first week, except for work of course, and the daily checks that were required by the officers, as we indulged ourselves on a diet of great food and amazing TV. It really is the little things that can make the greatest difference in jail. So thanks to Smithwicks' wonderful parents – they may have added a stone to my weight but it was worth it!

Soon Smithwicks was adapting to life in Loughan, securing himself a job in the laundry, and signing himself up for the cooking class held in the school. I started bringing him around to meet the 'new crew' with some old faces thrown in, like Cunny and No. 2. These were the men with whom I spent nearly all of my time whilst I was in Loughan and what a bunch they were – all Dubs of course.

One of this crew deserves special mention – The Torment. What can I say? He was a little bollox but we all loved him. But, my *god*, did he know how to push you! As stated before, he bore a striking resemblance to Cristiano Ronaldo, not only in looks, but in footballing terms too. Behind the little annoying imp lied a caring, loving father and partner. He would do anything for you, but when he wanted to wind you up? Well, batten down the hatches! He got me on a couple of occasions, but below is my favourite.

I had been living in Pine Lodge at this particular time, and one night I did the unthinkable: I left my room door open while I headed up to Cunny for a coffee. Sarge was the guy in the room across from me, and he was usually the butt of all The Torment's gags. I asked Sarge would he be okay on his own if I headed up to Cunny for a bit. 'Course I will pal,' he answered. 'The Torment won't be fuckin' tormenting me tonight, I'm not in the humour for him.'

'Well, ya know where I am if he starts, okay?' I say reassuringly. Myself and Sarge had made a pact to look out for each other, such was the level of torments administered by the little fucker! I made my way up to Cunny's, and we chatted about fuck all like we always did but I loved those chats. I must have been gone well over an hour when I decided to head back to my own room.

Upon my return, I see my door was exactly as I had left it, and Sarge is making himself a cup of tea in his own room. 'I'll have one if you're offering buddy?' I ask hopefully.

'Nah man, gonna hit the hay, I'm wrecked Gar,' came his reply. It was a bit unusual of him to say no, but then again, this guy's bipolar personality was something to behold, soaring one minute and fading into obscurity the next. I say my good nights and shut the door. I began looking for my remote in order to turn on the TV and catch up on my soaps and after a few minutes I locate it under my pillow. I then remove the top I was wearing to get ready for bed. I open a carton of milk, and just as I place the carton to my lips, my wardrobe door flies open, and out jumps The Torment screaming, *'You shouldn't be drinking milk this late at night! Aghhhhh!*

I let out the highest-pitched scream that I have ever heard coming from my own mouth. The milk goes flying everywhere, as in my state of shock I have thrown it into the air. The little fucker! He quickly opens the door and runs from my room, and there's Sarge standing at my door in knots laughing. 'Sorry pal, I knew he was in there all along!' So much for our pact, Sarge! But you've got to hand it to The Torment and his persistence. He was almost a half hour cooped up inside my wardrobe before he scared the bejaysus out of me, the little bollox.

Smithwicks fitted right into this crew as I knew he would. It was great to have my buddy back with me, although we didn't stay doubled up for long, as after about two weeks of living together I got my chance to reside in Pine Lodge. Smithwicks was delighted for me, and soon found a suitable replacement to share his room with. Yes, it was great having Smithwicks here, but it made me miss Fitzer even more.

Chapter 39

He Was a Daytripper

Criminal Justice (Temporary Release of Prisoners) Act 2003

(1) The Minister may direct that such person as is specified in the direction (being a person who is serving a sentence of imprisonment) shall be released from prison for such temporary period, and subject to such conditions, as may be specified in the direction or rules under this section applying to that person – for the purpose of –

(i) assessing the person's ability to reintegrate into society upon such release

(ii) preparing him for release upon the expiration of his sentence of imprisonment, or upon his being discharged from prison before such expiration, or

(iii) assisting the Garda Síochána in the prevention, detection or investigation of offences, or the apprehension of a person guilty of an offence or suspected of having committed an offence.

So there ya have it, guys and gals. That is how the Irish government wants the Temporary Release Programme established in all Irish jails, but mainly implemented in Ireland's two open prisons, to work, and work it does for the most part. Yes, we could debate the Temporary Release (T. R. for short) system at great length, and some would feel that my argument in favour of it is weakened by every man or woman who has committed a crime whilst on T. R., but it really is a small number of rotten apples that spoil the whole bunch. Of course, you don't hear of the 'normal' Temporary Release situations in the daily tabloids because they are not deemed newsworthy. But, since I am trying to offer to you the 'other' side to prison life, what follows is the time I earned my first Temporary Release through hard work and good behaviour. I hope it shows that for the right recipients, ones that will not abuse the amazing chance of spending a short period of time with their loved ones, this is an invaluable treat, and one which is worth setting as your goal to be a good prisoner.

I was brought up at the March review meeting of 2013. There were officers present that day, along with whatever teachers were required to sit in on the reviews of each prisoner. Each would give their honest view of how you were progressing in Loughan House and would inform the representative from the Irish Prison Service, who ultimately had the final decision on all matters, if you were 'linking in', fully immersing yourself into prison life and being proactive. They must have said some good things about me, as I was called to the A.C.O.'s office, to be met by Mr. Duffy, a balding A.C.O. whom I got on really well with. He spoke with a Northern twang, and was always taking the piss out of us as prisoners. But he was okay. 'You got an overnight, Gary, and it must be taken by the end of the month,' he said.

'Fuckin' nice one, excuse the language,' came my ecstatic reply. This wonderful news meant I could return home, albeit for only one night, and spend time with my mam and family. You must have a fixed abode when getting T. R., as you can't just be released for 24 hours to roam the land! I was filled with so much joy and fear at the same time. It had been over a year and a half since I stood in my mam's kitchen, patiently waiting for a cup of her 'award-winning' tea. We live on a road with some of the most incredibly nosey people you have ever come across. My poor mam had to endure the shame I had brought on my family, as my deeds had become the subject of countless teatime whispers all taking place behind her back. Nosey fuckers. But it still raised my fear level by quite a bit, as I knew I would witness endless 'curtain-twitching' and throw-away whispers as I walked down my street again. Plus, I'd be *outside in the real world*. This was a complete head-fuck, trust me!

I immediately made my way to the general office, where I was greeted by Miss Doyle. A woman hailing from Cabra in Dublin, she was one of my favourites. She was a GAA fanatic, and a true blue like myself. She also ran the storehouse of Loughan, which stored everything, and would have countless Dublin GAA flags and scarves thrown around, brightening up the place. The culchies loved to hate it! She was a little older than me, but that didn't stop the playful flirting that used to take place between us. 'I got an overnight, Miss,' I stated with a smile stuck across my face.

'Ah, that's bleedin' deadly, Gary,' came her flat Dublin reply. 'When are you looking to take it?'

'Fuckin' Friday, if I can, Miss,' I say hopefully.

'Yep, that won't be a problem. Will you be getting collected?' I wasn't, as all my brothers were hardworking men, so I would never ask them to give up their day in order to bring me home for a couple of hours.

'No Miss, I've been told to get the bus?' I ask puzzled.

'No problem, I'll sort you with a bus ticket, it will get you from here to home and back again. The social welfare will give you €32 for your troubles, which will be given to you in the form of a cheque the morning you are leaving. The bus stops outside the prison on the main road at 8.10 am precisely, and will take you to Enniskillen. There you will catch the Dublin bus, which leaves at 10.20 am, and you should be in Dublin City by 1.00 pm.' She flashes her mood-inspiring smile at me, and I thank her about fifteen times and leave to find the lads and tell them my news. 'Hey Ma, I'm comin' home.'

The lads were delighted for me, and for themselves too, as many if not all of the lads from our particular group had received the same news I did. My mam was so excited as I told her on the phone that I'd be by her side in no time. She had begun the recovery process after receiving her new hip, and she was doing great. I hadn't seen her in quite some time, as our weekly visits in The Joy were cut short upon the news that the hospital was ready to operate on her. And Loughan House is nearly a three hour drive from Dublin, so I knew I wouldn't be receiving many visits. I really wanted to make the most of my time with her. And she, along with my supportive family, were just as excited to see me. Nice one!

The week seemed to drag towards Friday at a snail's pace but finally the hour had come. I packed my black Nike sports bag with a couple of changes of clothes, and headed over to the A.C.O.'s office, where Mrs Cahill, another feisty and yet friendly A.C.O., with a genuine caring nature, greeted me by handing me a pen and getting me to sign the T. R. sheet, which had a list of do's and don'ts printed on it (not to be in a public house and so on), along with my name, address and sentence. I was given a copy of this form, which must be kept on my person at all times. She handed me a small white envelope which contained my bus ticket and my cheque for €32.43 and wished me good luck. I thanked her, and started to make my way out of the prison, just as the sun was starting to peek out from atop a darkened mountain off in the distance.

As soon as I stepped out on to the main road outside of Loughan House, which was just a very wide country road with nothing but green fields as far as the eye could see, my nerves tingled a little. Here I was, waiting on a bus! Again, this may sound ridiculous, but this was fuckin' major to me! I see the bus coming my way and extend my left arm to signal for it to stop. I see other passengers, normal people already sitting on the old Bus Éireann transporter, and I'm engulfed by fear and paranoia. For those who were regular commuters on this bus, which was all of them I hazard, they would know exactly what 'type' of person was about to board their bus – a bloody criminal! I nervously stepped on to the bus and stated my destination to the driver. He punched a couple of holes in my ticket and moved me on. I found a seat on my own towards the back of the battered bus, and sat with my head firmly pressed against the cold, damp glass of the bus's window. But soon I am forgetting the feelings I have of every passenger staring at me or my paranoia that they were talking about me, as I take in the amazing sights that were emerging before my eyes as the driver makes the 30 minute trip to Enniskillen. I cannot articulate the feelings I experienced that morning, the feeling of freedom. I swore I would never again take for granted what it is to be free.

We arrived at the busy bus station in Enniskillen and the first thing I have to get use to is the noise. Cars and vans and trucks, all going about their noisy way. This felt so alien to me, as did seeing so many females! I was gobsmacked at how many women were walking around. I must have looked as stupid as I felt – I was just not used to seeing a lot of women. Plus, whilst locked up, you generally saw the same faces day-in, day-out, so even laying my eyes upon different males was a strange experience.

The bus to Dublin arrived at 10.20 am on the dot. I take my seat, and find after only a short time I am falling asleep. I didn't get much sleep the night before so I take advantage of this opportunity to drift away into a dream.

> Dreams of mam, my brothers too / All stuck together with the help of God's glue / Dreams of home of where I belong / Where these people love me in spite of my wrongs / Dreams of a future a change in my ways / Dreams of a life filled with better days ...

I wake up and am in shock as I look out my window and see the unmistakable Blanchardstown Shopping Centre as we thunder past it. I'm back in Dublin.

The bus makes its way first to Dublin airport, then into Dublin City centre, and I felt like I was viewing this incredible city for the first time. I absorb all the sights that were materialising before my eyes, wanting to imprint them in my memory forever. The bus comes to a halt in Busaras and I disembark, with my sports bag draped across my right shoulder. The bus station was as busy, well, as a bus station, and again I am transfixed by the volume of 'new' people around me. I felt scared as I stepped out on to the streets of Dublin, the sun bathing the concrete with her yellow glow. As I made my way towards the bus which will bring me to my home street, I felt so much paranoia again, like everyone who walked past me knew I was a criminal. It was so unnerving.

I catch the 83 bus, and watch with wonder as it brings me on its journey towards my house, my home. I get off at my designated stop and, after a minute or so, I was at the top of my road, the road I grew up on, played 'chasing' and football on, the road where I experienced my first kiss. As I began to make my way towards number 23, the house I can see in the distance, a few old dears walked past me. I can hear their whispers as I pass, 'Oh that's Lily's son, ohhhhh, I wonder if he's home?' It made me feel like shit! But that feeling soon evaporated as I stood outside my front door. I pressed the doorbell, and could see through the frosted glass the silhouette of my wonderful mother making her way slowly towards the door. Upon her opening that door, well, there were a lot of tears. It was a moment I'll cherish for the rest of my life.

As were the next few hours I spent with my loved ones. It was a time I would like to keep private, but one which instilled in me further that desire to change. Yes it was strange to be let out into the world and having the fear and paranoia that comes with being institutionalised consume your very being, but it was all worth it to spend some quality time with the people I loved. I even got a sneaky hour with Antoinette which was nearly as incredible as seeing my mam. We spoke, we hugged, we even had a little kiss, a kiss that will linger in my mind for all eternity. She was becoming 'The One' just like the character I had created when I wrote *Journeyman*.

I returned to Loughan House at 6.00 pm the next day, and although it was sad leaving everyone again, I had found a renewed determination inside of me. I *wanted* to change, I *wanted* to make my family proud, I *wanted* Antoinette. I was ready to work as hard as I could to achieve this. I was going to set into motion the work I needed to do in Loughan House in order to be considered in a couple of months' time for a programme. This was also T. R., but you were allowed home for three nights once a month! This was afforded to lads who were nearing the end of their sentence, and served to ready them for life on the outside. This now became my goal, and I would work as hard as I could to achieve this. Not only had I an amazing family to come home to see, but I also had a woman I needed to sweep clean off her feet.

So T. R. was a humbling experience for me. It was the tool that readied me for my eventual release and prepared me for life on the outside. Please believe me that *all* prisoners need this. And if they've worked hard enough on themselves, impressing the officers and staff, then they've earned it. I know some ruin this by fucking up once they are given this amazing opportunity, but like I said, 'One bad apple spoils the whole damn bunch'.

But we're not all bad apples.

Chapter 40

Road Trip with the Red Cross

The Irish Red Cross had come to town!

One of the amazing factors regarding life in Loughan were the countless projects that were offered to us. As prisoners we liked to work on our initiative, and during my time in Loughan I organised numerous charity projects, like 'Shave or Dye', which involved the lads obtaining sponsors, and in return they would promise to either shave or dye their hair on a designated day. It was great craic, with most of the lads opting to shave their heads but not me – I dyed my hair *pink*! We had a great laugh doing this and raised over €300 for cancer research, which was not a bad achievement while being locked up!

I also got 'Movember' going while I was holed up in Loughan, which was even better fun. Some of the officers took part in this fundraiser, and the only requirement was to grow a moustache and keep it on your face for the month of November. I would have to sell this idea to my fellow prisoners, and sometimes this could be a daunting task. Now I not only grew my 'tash' prior to the first of November, a proper handlebar moustache – I resembled one of the singers in the Village People – but I decided to go the extra mile and get a mohawk haircut as well! I was on a T. R. programme at this stage, which meant I would have to go home in this state, but I didn't give a shit which paid off with the lads as they thought, 'If this fuckin' eejit can do it, so can we.' We had a great laugh that November, as each of the lads who took part looked more and more ridiculous as their moustaches began to take shape. This was made even funnier when lads were getting visits from their partners during that time, many of whom demanded that they 'shave the 'tash' immediately! But they hung in there and again we raised over €500 for this incredible cause.

A funny thing happened to me during that Movember! Dotsy, our 'legal eagle', had secured his place in Loughan House and was fitting in well. He asked me one day if I could teach him to read music as he assumed I possessed this talent because of my guitar playing. But alas, I was a self-taught guitarist and so I replied, 'I haven't a fuckin' clue how to read music!' But on asking him why, at this stage of his life, he wanted to learn what is basically a new language, he informed me that his two young daughters, the apples of his eyes, were currently being taught the piano and so Dotsy wanted to learn all he could about music. This moved me so I brought Dotsy up to Padraig, the music teacher in the school, and signed him up for Grade 1 Music Theory. To show my support, and to actually learn what the fuck I was playing each time I strummed my guitar, I signed up too.

Myself and Dotsy knuckled down and began coming to grips with learning musical notations, scales, staves and so on. We were then informed that we were to sit the Grade 1 exam – in Dublin – on the sixth of November, my birthday! We would be escorted to Dublin, sit the exam, then be brought back to Loughan House. Logistically, this was a nightmare as the exam was held a 6.00 pm, which meant it would be near midnight by the time we returned to Loughan. Because myself and Dotsy had been passed for a T. R. programme, and the fact the we both had been home on numerous occasions without incident, we were granted an overnight from the sixth of November to return on the seventh. Great stuff!

Dotsy was going back to Dublin that morning with his wife and they very kindly offered me a lift. As we parted, we made arrangements to meet at St. Louis High School in Rathmines, where our exam was to take place.

I made my way to the school on that wet November evening, thinking this was the first time I had spent my birthday heading to sit an exam! Now I must remind you that having successfully gotten 'Movember' off the ground in Loughan, I was now sporting a handle bar moustache and a bloody mohawk! I arrived at St Louis High School, which turned out to be a girls' secondary school for affluent kids! I was soaked through with rain as I entered the massive arched doorway that led into the reception area of the school. I left my woollen hat on top of my head as I entered, and was surprised at how busy the school was. There were a lot of young schoolgirls and their parents milling about the place. I assumed there was something else being held there that evening, and so I made my way towards a lady who seemed to be directing people.

'Hi,' I start in my 'posh' voice, 'I'm here for the music exam.' She looked me up and down, paying close attention to the obnoxious 'tash that had grown beneath my nostrils.

'Are you sure?' she asked, almost sarcastically, and then follows with, 'where is your exam number?' I'm pretty sure I saw genuine shock appear on her face when I produced the exam number. I was tempted to remove my hat, though that might send this good lady over the edge. 'Oh, right,' she stammered, um okay, it's um (I was really enjoying how uncomfortable she was) up the stairs two flights, turn right, room 32.' I thanked her and skipped off on my merry way!

As I arrived at the designated room I saw Dotsy had gotten there before me. He was standing outside of a classroom, his head buried into some sheet of paper with writing printed on it. 'Howya, Dotsy,' I almost shouted.

'Not too good, Gary,' came his nervous reply. 'Take a look into the classroom there and you'll see what I mean.'

I was laughing as I removed my jacket, under which I was wearing a t-shirt which showed off the tattoos I have on either arm – my son's name and date of birth on my left forearm, and my late daughter's date of birth on my right forearm. 'What's wrong with ya buddy?' I shouted over my shoulder as I entered the room, removing my woolly hat as I did so, exposing the mohawk. I was stopped in my tracks by what I saw.

The brightly-lit classroom was filled with young girls, all around 12 or 13 who were here to take this exam. All posh schoolgirls, I might add. The look of sheer dread that showed on each of their faces was hilarious. I felt terrible that I had frightened them, but I needed to make light of the situation. The examiner, who was at the top of the class behind an old wooden desk asked, 'Can I help you?' I wanted to burst out laughing as I absorbed the look of complete shock that had hit these poor girls.

'I, along with this good man here,' pointing to Dotsy, embarrassing him further, 'are here to partake in the Grade 1 Music Exam.' I stated this whilst giving off the air of immense pride.

'Oh, right,' came the examiner's puzzled reply.

'Come on Dotsy,' I loudly ordered, 'let's grab a desk and get going.' You could hear a pin drop as we entered the classroom, and inside I wanted to die! But we're here now so let's do this. We couldn't even fit into the allocated desks as we were too big for them! After eventually squeezing into my desk, I noticed the young girl beside me slowly raising her hand for attention.

'Yes?' asks the examiner.

'Please sir, may I move seats?' the poor girl asks. God love her!

But seeing how much this poor girl wanted to get away from me made my heart grow heavy. Although she knew nothing about me – and certainly didn't know I had come from a prison! – I felt that she was just judging me solely by my appearance, which, to be fair, was a bit unusual. I could only imagine how poor old Dotsy felt!

Yep, we made some impact that evening all right. But the exam went well and though the young ladies finished long before myself and Dotsy, I can proudly state that we both passed with flying colours. This was a birthday I'll never forget!

And so back to the Irish Red Cross. The award-winning Irish Red Cross prison programme is a unique approach to raising community health, hygiene awareness and first aid in prisons using groups of Irish Red Cross volunteer inmates as peer-to-peer educators. Community Based Health & First Aid in Action (CBHFA) was originally designed by the International Federation of the Red Cross and Red Crescent Societies (IFRC) to be facilitated globally in communities in a simple and flexible way. The initiative benefits over 4,000 prisoners directly every day and 12,000 indirectly including staff and the families of prisoners. Evaluation of the programme has demonstrated high impact in terms of improvement within the prison environment and a significant increase in healthcare awareness and prisoners' personal well-being. I wanted in.

I saw this as an opportunity to amalgamate the hard work of the Prison Committee with the goal-setting of the Irish Red Cross. Anyone could join up for the scheme and quite a few did. I was voted as Loughan House Red Cross Leader, which was an honour. We had an amazing bunch of hard-working men who would attend classes designed by the Irish

Red Cross in the area of community health and hygiene awareness. We would then implement what we had learned in order to radically clean up the whole of Loughan House. Mary, the cooking teacher from the school, and one of the medics from the jail were our teachers. I designed a monthly newsletter in Photoshop for our particular faction which told of our past achievements and further goals, and we even ran a 'Health Week', where we arranged for speakers to come into Loughan to speak on a wide variety of men's health issues. We also implemented a highly successful recycling programme in the jail, which is still in place today. This all culminated in a massive presentation to be held in Dublin's Wheatfield Prison. This would bring together three representatives, including the 'leader', from each Irish Red Cross faction in all of Ireland's jails, and our job was to put forth a presentation of how the Irish Red Cross prison programme worked by giving examples of work carried out in the various jails. Red Cross delegates from all over the world would be in attendance.

Myself and two other lads were chosen to represent Loughan House. We were given instructions to set up a visual account of what we had achieved, and we were informed that our particular presentation on stage in front of not only the international delegates, but also men and women prisoners from all over Ireland, was to demonstrate the proper procedure for hand-washing (I had no idea I was washing my hands wrong all this time!).

On the morning I woke the other two lads at 5.30 am as we had a long drive ahead of us to reach Wheatfield Prison by 10.30 am. This was to give us time to set up our visual representation of the work we carried out in Loughan, and to allow us to rehearse our hand-washing presentation. However, when we arrived at the A.C.O.'s office that morning, we were informed that the jail had forgotten to apply for T. R. for the three of us to leave Loughan for the day. I was pissed! I ranted about what a stupid mistake they had just made, and stormed back to my room. The other two lads, already nervous as they were not used to public speaking and presentations (not that I was, I just had a neck like a jockey's you know what) now seemed like they didn't want to go at all. But I talked them around, explaining that it was a proud moment in their lives to be representing such a worthy cause. But they quite rightly feared that we would not get any rehearsal time, as the day had to run to a very strict clock – we were still on prison time after all. I assured them not to worry, I'd handle it!

We eventually hit the road shortly after 10.00 am! I sat in the back of the prison issue Ford Mondeo Estate, and glared out the window refusing to engage in conversation. My mood was getting everyone's attention. 'You all right there, Gary?' laughed the officer who was driving.

'Look, my mother always told me if you have nothing good to say, say nothing, so I'm fuckin' sayin' *nothing*!'

'Ah, come on Cunningham,' laughed the screw.

'Come on me hole,' I countered. 'We're going to be the laughing stock, an open prison that couldn't get T. R. for the lads? Mountjoy, where T. R. is unheard of, as is the same in all closed jails, well, I bet they had no such problems. It's a fuckin' joke, officer, and you're not the one who has to stand in front of all these people with no rehearsal and talk for four minutes!' I am seething which the officer picks up on and he ceases the mocking.

We arrive at Wheatfield Prison almost four hours late, and are directed into the massive hall which was to accommodate the proceedings. The fuckin' presentation was about to start. The hall had a large stage at its top, and placed around its walls were desks, each one occupied by representatives from the various Irish jails, which showed off their particular work for the Red Cross. I made a beeline for the Mountjoy table, and had a quick chat with their Red Cross lads, then me and my two colleagues were dragged behind stage for a crash-course in how the presentation would occur. We were to be the third last jail to give our talk on hand-washing. My two colleagues were extremely nervous, and this was only made worse as the presentations began, with each representative not only doing the jail which they came from proud, but themselves as well. Most read off sheets, with pre-prepared text set out for their presentation. One of the lads who was with me started to bottle it.

'I can't do it, Gar, we're gonna make a fuckin' show of ourselves.'

'Not on my fuckin' watch buddy,' I say reassuringly. 'Look, I'll do all the talking and you two can demonstrate the proper techniques required to achieve spotless hands. You can be my "lovely assistants"!' This makes them laugh and settles them a little.

'And next we have three young men from Loughan House who will explain to you the importance of excellent hand hygiene.' Here goes nothing.

We took to the stage, with me forgetting I was to enter stage right, and instead waltzing on stage left! My two friends were shittin'! So I knew I had to make this good. 'I would like to welcome the Red Cross delegates from all over the world, and I would like to apologise, firstly, for our late arrival here – an open prison that cannot secure T. R., great isn't it? This is a "prison joke" by the way.' I direct this last line to all the international figures sitting in the first row. But it breaks the ice a little and a laugh goes up in the giant hall of Wheatfield.

'I know it looks like we're not prepared,' I continue, 'but it's all up here.' I tap on my forehead for added effect. 'So, we have been given the very exciting opportunity to speak to you today about washing your hands because I would hazard a guess that almost all of you are doing it wrong. "Doing it wrong?" I hear you say, well let me explain.' It has dawned on me that we are the first jail not to be reading off pre-prepared sheets, as I turn to my 'lovely assistants', who are fuckin' mortified at this stage, and instruct them to apply some of the soap which we brought onto stage with us, in the correct manner. The lads did a great job of going through the proper motions of washing your hands, making sure to emphasise each movement in order to display it to our audience.

As they wash their hands I continue, 'Most of us, me included, would spend less than thirty seconds or so washing our hands – this is wrong, ladies and gentlemen. They say a good trick is to sing "Happy Birthday" whilst scrubbing, and it just so happens that one of our teachers, the wonderful Mary, who is sitting right there' – I point straight at Mary, mortifying the poor lady – 'well, it's the wonderful Mary's birthday this very day, so in order to assist my friends here as they wash their hands, and to make Mary feel special, could we all join together in a joyous rendition of "Happy Birthday"?'

And they did, it was incredible. There were well over 100 people present that day, and each and every one of them joined together in the singing of 'Happy Birthday'. On its conclusion, there was a massive cheer. I asked one of the lads to show his hands, so as to demonstrate how clean they were. This particular chap was the more nervous of the two, and as he showed his hands I said, 'Sure, Jaysus, they're still feckin' manky.' A massive cheer and laughter rang out in the large hall, and it settled my good friend who stood beside me. I thanked everyone for listening and the three of us took a bow. We were the first prison to receive a standing ovation! Wow!

When we rejoined Mary, she flung her arms around us. 'That was incredible, you blew them away, well done lads.' It felt amazing to hear all this after such a disastrous start to our day.

Mary had set up our visual presentation. The delegates made their way around the hall, stopping at each jail's 'stall' and asking questions pertaining to their projects. When delegates approached our stall, we were taken aback at the wonderful comments we received, not only for our hand-washing presentation – we were told it was the 'presentation of the day' – but for the stall which Mary had constructed, which showed a visual representation of the work we'd achieved in Loughan House.

In attendance that day was Michael Donnellan, who is the Director General of the Irish Prison Service, but when he approached our stall I had no idea who he was. 'Well done, lads,' he began. 'Excellent work. I understand you had some problems getting here this morning. It didn't show, you should all be proud of yourselves. Gary is it?' He looked straight at me, his bald head almost gleaming, his suit immaculately fitted to his frame.

'Yes sir, that's me,' I reply.

'Your report on the Prison Committee was outstanding, well done. I'm hearing very good things about you, keep it up.' He moved swiftly on to the next stall. I turned to ask the officer who had driven us that morning who I was just speaking to.

'He's the fuckin' main man, Cunningham, well done lad.' Well fuck me, wow!

We were treated to an Eddie Rockets meal on our way home, as Mary had rung the Governor in order to inform her that we had pulled it off so dinner was on Loughan House. That has got to be the tastiest burger I have ever eaten! But we earned it.

So again, me and those two lads proved that whilst incarcerated, *'It's not the time you do ... it's what you do with your time'*. It was an incredible experience and the work that the Irish Red Cross does inside of Irish prisons is outstanding.

Chapter 41

'THERE'S SOMEONE HERE TO SEE YOU'

In my role as chair of the Prison Committee, I took it upon myself to utilise my painting and decorating skills, so I painted both of the visiting areas. But what we did in the 'kids' visiting area was amazing. I say we, but really it was Beasey, who had also secured his place in Loughan. I was painting the walls of the kids' visiting area one day when Beasey strolled in.

'Great work, Gar, fair play to ya. But do you know what would be great? A few cartoon murals scattered around the walls.'

'Sounds great, Beasey,' I say, 'but I have trouble drawing a matchstick man.'

'No, ya eejit,' he interrupts, 'I'll do them if ya don't mind the help?'

I most certainly didn't, and by God was I happy he volunteered. Beasey has an unbelievable talent when it comes to art, and what he created in that visiting room would take your breath away. He brought the walls to life with huge drawings of Bart Simpson, Hello Kitty, Barney the friendly dinosaur, and all the Walt Disney classics. I painted the base coat for him, and then every evening for about a month Beasey would spend a few hours working on his masterpiece. The final result looks just as good today as when he completed it, and was a massive hit with the staff, prisoners and visitors.

Around this particular time, Loughan House welcomed another prisoner into its care. He hailed from the travelling community and was held in great esteem by the other travellers who resided in Loughan at the time. Living amongst the travelling community opened my eyes to their, sometimes secret, culture. They are an extremely loyal bunch of men, and yes they do 'stick to their own', but we always had great craic with them. It highlighted in me a prejudice I never knew existed, and I am glad that I learned more about their way of life.

Now the following story is incredible but 100 per cent true. Although you may find it hard to believe, trust me, *this actually happened*!

One particular traveller had arrived in Loughan, and almost immediately he had a mission to be released asap! He was nearing the end of his sentence already, but jail had obviously worn away at his patience and he wanted out *yesterday*! Big Joe, a fellow committee member, invited me into his room for a coffee and a chat one day.

'See yer man the traveller who has just arrived? He is going to do everything in his power to get under the Governor's nose, in the hope she'll send him home early. But, I've just been told what he has planned for this Friday and you're not going to want to miss this.' Big Joe winks at me, with devilment etched across his face. 'Oh, yes,' he continued, 'the fuckin' madman thinks what he has planned will aid him in early release, a madman!' I'm intrigued. 'Just make sure you're around the visiting areas on Friday, Gar,' laughs Big Joe. I'm very fuckin' intrigued!

Friday came, and what I witnessed was unbelievable. This traveller in question had decided to invite his *whole family* up on a visit. Now, as I'm sure you know, a traveller's family can be considerably larger than that of an 'average' family. Most lads in Loughan would have at max four or maybe five people up on their visit. This man, well, he had at least 40 visitors! It was fuckin' hilarious! Myself and the Dublin crew, Cunny, No. 2, Handsome, Sarge, The Torment etc. all sat under the shade of a massive oak tree that faced the visiting area. It was a sight to behold as all these travellers basically took over the grounds of Loughan House that were open to the public. There was a large car park just outside the school in Loughan, and it's here that your visitors can safely park their vehicles. But on this day, it was crowded to capacity with mobile caravans and cars, all belonging to the people connected to the traveller in question. They brought KFC, McDonald's, Burger King, you name it, and they were offering these fast food treats to anybody who wanted some. The atmosphere was electric and fuckin' crazy! I remember one of the lads from Loughan, an older gentleman by the name of Fran the Lamb, who was a con artist almost by trade, well, he turns a corner and is carrying as many KFC family buckets as he could manage. He arrives at our tree and offers us one. 'Sure it would be rude not to lads,' said auld Fran. We fell about laughing.

It was incredible watching the goings on of this particular visit. There was no hint of trouble or aggravation, they all just came to see their husband/father/son/uncle/cousin or whatever fuckin' relation he was to all this congregation. But the look on the officers' faces? Well, that was fuckin' priceless. There was nothing they could do, as technically he was not breaking any rules. There was no trouble, they just took over. But one particular highlight was when the visit was drawing to an end, which was nearly the end of the day as they arrived first thing that morning! The traveller in question made his way to the entrance of the car park at the school, and waited as each and every mobile caravan, now I mean *all* of them, wheel-spun out of the car park, as if they were putting on a display for him before they left. I'm not sure if you have ever witnessed a mobile caravan doing a wheel-spin, something you would usually associate with Jeremy Clarkson of *Top Gear* fame, but it has got to be one of the funniest things I had ever seen. When the mobile caravan 'spinning show' had ceased, and his final visitor had left, this traveller made his way from the school car park, back to the visiting area and made a beeline straight for us!

'Well, Dublin Men,' he started – he would always refer to all Dubs as Dublin Men – 'the auld Governor, she'll have to send me home early now, won't she?' We all break our shites laughing. But alas, it blew up in the poor fucker's face!

The following Monday, after being informed what had happened on Friday, the Governor did summons him to her office only to inform him that she won't be pressured by anybody into making a decision, and because of his blatant flaunting of the visit rules and of her trust she had no choice but to send him back to a closed jail. This really was a kick in the teeth for the poor auld fucker! He would now have to do his remaining time to the day! But, along with his extremely large family, he gave us one of the best laughs we'd ever had in Loughan House!

Chapter 42

A SAD TALE WITH A HAPPY ENDING

A rumour was spreading through Loughan House that, amazingly, none of the prisoners or the staff for that matter wanted to believe. We were set to lose our leader, the person who had looked after us so well. We were about to lose the one individual who had achieved something that nobody else could during our incarceration, as this person believed in us as human beings, she 'trusted' us – yes, Governor Gavin was set to leave! It is unheard of for a prisoner to be upset at an officer resigning, and even more preposterous to think, as prisoners, we would 'miss' a fuckin' Governor, but miss her we would.

I really didn't want to believe this, thinking it was just a bad rumor. But I needed to know so I asked for a meeting with Governor Gavin. I gave the false impression that there were some 'pressing prison issues' that needed to be addressed. She granted my wish for a meeting, and when I walked into her office that day, well, I knew solely by the look on her face that this was no rumour. Shit! I immediately pressed her for answers, answers I wasn't sure I was ready to hear. 'Is there any truth to the whispers lingering around Loughan, Miss? Are you leaving?'

She begins to tear up a bit as she softly explains the situation to me. 'Yes, Gary, the IPS has done a "Godfather" on me, just like the legendary Marlon Brando, they have "made me an offer I can't refuse".' I am stuck to the plastic grey chair in her small, dusty office. 'I am moving to a much better position in Portaloise Prison and, well, I'd be crazy to pass up on this incredible opportunity.'

I'm not sure if it was the look of utter disbelief that my face couldn't hide, or the fact that she had said it out loud to someone, but something snapped inside of this incredible strong woman. She began to cry, as did I! Crying over a fuckin' Governor? Even as I type these words I am still shocked at what an impact her decision had on, not just me, but the entire population of Loughan House.

'Oh God, Gary, I can't believe how upset I am,' she weeps. 'I have grown to actually love this place and that is all down to the hard work of each and every one of you. I trusted you all, and only a very small number let me down. I had a vision of how this place could work, and you men allowed my vision to become a reality, along with my wonderful staff. We have broken down the barriers between officers and inmates.'

An amazing example of this was when we held a football tournament, an eight-a-side battle for supremacy, and the officers of Loughan entered a team. That took balls from these officers, and the craic and banter that was had was second to none, but alas they were annihilated in almost every game. Well, they *had* to be or we could never show our faces around Loughan again, which could prove a bit difficult since it is required to show one's face whilst locked up! Still, the coming together of officers and inmates was incredible.

I am clearly moved, and Governor Gavin can see this. 'Stop it now, Gary, you'll have me in floods,' came her stern warning to me. I compose myself and ask the question I know will be on the lips of every person who either resides or works in Loughan: who is going to take her place?

'Governor O'Reilly, Gary,' she says. 'He has been the Governor of Castlerea Prison for over 15 years, and I feel he will be a suitable replacement.' I wasn't so sure, as his name had accompanied the rumours pertaining to the departure of our beloved Governor, and there were mixed feelings. Only time would tell and it did! Governor Gavin asked me to finally dispel the rumours, and in my capacity as Chair of the Prison Committee it was to be my duty to inform the lads of Loughan this sad news. But this is Governor Gavin we were talking about, and she had one last parting gift for us all.

I gathered all of the lads of Loughan in the auditorium of the Main House. Its walls never seemed more drab than they did that day, as I stood on the large wooden stage to deliver the news. 'Right lads, look, it's true. Governor Gavin is set to leave.' I paused to let this sink in, and I am stunned to look at the shock on each of the lad's faces, the look of actual heartbreak. This woman had been like a surrogate mother to some of these men, myself included. And yet I was speaking about a Governor! Incredible! 'Governor O'Reilly will be taking over.'

This is met with a mixed reaction, as the lads who had arrived from Castlerea Prison shifted nervously on their plastic chairs upon hearing the name of their former Governor. 'Well, that's the end of the happy vibe at Loughan,' piped up one of these men.

'Look lads, we've got to give this guy a chance,' I say. 'Governor Gavin has created an incredible ethos here and you know the aul' saying, "If it ain't broke, don't fix it". We need to see how he gets on plus, like it or not, he is going to be the new gaffer!'

You could cut the atmosphere with a knife, so I try to lift the mood by informing the lads of Governor Gavin's parting gift. 'As you all know, Governor Gavin believes in each and every one of us. She sees the good where others only see the bad. She has worked tirelessly to fight our cases with the IPS, in order to grant each and everyone of us T. R., or to try to get lads we recommend from the closed jails up here to Loughan. And she's not finished yet. She has invited Brian Murphy to Loughan House for a walk-around, though this is only a decoy, as she will make sure that those who are entitled to T. R. will be granted an audience with him.'

A massive cheer erupts in the dreary auditorium as I finish this announcement. At the time Mr. Murphy was Director of Operations in the IPS. The main responsibilities of the Directorate include prisoner progression through sentence management, the control of prison population numbers, maintenance of good order and discipline, and the security of the estate and prisoner transport services. This man had almost the final say in a lot of what happened to you whilst in prison, from the granting of a move to an open prison to allowing T. R. He was, in many prisoners' eyes, like Santa Claus with a jolly belly to match! The mood has lifted amongst the lads as they leave the auditorium, almost all of them daring to believe that they might just have a chance to speak with Mr. Murphy in order to show him they should be granted T. R. Governor Gavin had done it again!

And so a couple of weeks later, true to Governor Gavin's word, Mr. Murphy arrived at Loughan House. I had never seen the place looking so well. Every corner of the jail glistened and gleamed. Every prisoner looked as well as they could in the clothing they had received from their visitors. The atmosphere was filled with nervous energy. I took it upon myself to paint the auditorium, creating 'waves' on the walls of this magnificent room with two different shades of blue. I wanted to impress Mr. Murphy as well, as I had a request of my own!

All of the lads began congregating outside of the visiting area, almost forming a queue as they waited for Governor Gavin and Mr. Murphy to emerge from her office, which was located above the visiting area. Soon, the small white door opened, and out stepped Governor Gavin and the rather intimidating frame of Mr. Murphy. I was coming out of Pine Lodge just as this was taking place, and noted the fear on all of the lads' faces. Nobody wanted to be the first to approach him, so I did! I made my way towards them both, dressed in my painter's attire as I had just come from painting the auditorium. Governor Gavin already knew what I wanted to say, and as I grew nearer I could hear her say, 'Gary Cunningham, Brian, our "voice" of the prisoners.' This made me a little nervous, but nothing would stop me from saying what I wanted to say.

'Mr. Murphy, it is an honour to meet you sir.' I extend my right hand as I say this in order to provide the most 'manly' handshake I can muster.

'Mr. Cunningham, the feeling is mutual,' comes his reply. This stops me in my tracks. 'I've heard quite a lot about you, and your report on Prison Committees was incredibly impressive.' He says this with a massive smile forming across his well-groomed face.

'Thank you so much, Mr. Murphy, but nothing we achieve here in Loughan would have been possible without the amazing woman standing behind you.' I look at Governor Gavin as she stands slightly behind Mr. Murphy, and see she is moved. But she offers me a reassuring wink and nods confirmation that now is my time to make my request.

'So Gary, sell yourself to me. Tell me why I should grant you a full T. R. programme,' he says.

'I am not here to speak about myself, Mr. Murphy,' I begin, 'I am here to speak on behalf of another prisoner who I feel would not only benefit from a move up here to Loughan, but who would also become an integral part in the continued growth and progression of this open jail.'

'Oh, right,' he says surprised, 'I'm not used to hearing lads speak up for others rather than themselves. Go ahead Gary, give me his name.'

I nervously give the full name of the greatest friend I've ever had, Fitzer, only to be stopped in my tracks!

'I am very surprised with you Gary,' starts Mr. Murphy, 'surprised that you would associate yourself with such a man. He has been nothing but trouble since his incarceration, and has spent his time trying to rule with intimidation.'

I am shocked to my very core, as is Governor Gavin. Who the fuck is he talking about? Has Fitzer snapped in The Joy? Has prison turned his funny character, and 'do anything for you' demeanour into that of a troublesome prisoner? I feel my blood pressure rise. I cannot believe the words I'm hearing to describe my amazing mate! Just as I'm about to interject, Mr. Murphy asks, 'And how long did you spend in Castlerea Prison in order to form a friendship with this man?'

Castlerea? What the fuck is he talking about? I've never set foot in the kip! Thankfully, Governor Gavin has spotted this and speaks before I do, as I was scared of what was going to come out of my large gob! 'No, no, Brian, wrong Fitzer, we're speaking of the Fitzer currently in Mountjoy,' she says.

'Ohhh, right, sorry Gary, my mistake.' I feel I have lost a stone in weight from the sweat my body has produced, but thankfully my heart rate has begun to slow down. 'Go ahead, Gary, tell me about him,' he says.

I compose myself and begin. 'He is an incredible individual, Mr. Murphy. A hard worker, he has held his position in Mountjoy's kitchen since the first day of his incarceration. Extremely popular with both inmates and staff, his positive attitude is infectious. He has amazing musical ability, both as a bass player and a singer, his voice is incredible, Mr. Murphy. He also saved my life when I was at my lowest ebb, and I will forever be in his debt. He is a family man, with an amazing wife and a wonderful young son. This little boy was only brought into the world slightly before Fitzer's incarceration, and I know he finds it hard to bond with him through the visits in Mountjoy. I think that is my biggest reason for nominating this incredible man, Mr. Murphy, the chance for him to experience the visits here in Loughan House. But don't get me wrong, he never moaned about the fact he got locked up, as he knew it was nobody's fault but his own. He helps so many people, Mr. Murphy, that I nearly feel it is my obligation to put forth this man to you and beg you consider him for transfer up here to Loughan. I can reassure you he will not let you down.' I feel tears forming on my lower eyelids as I finish my pitch.

'I have spoken to you many times about this man, Brian,' starts Governor Gavin, 'I even had the pleasure of meeting him on my last visit to Mountjoy. I made it my business to meet him actually, after all Gary had told me about him. And Gary wasn't wrong, Brian. He's a lovely guy, and I heard nothing but good things from the staff of Mountjoy about him.' I fuckin' *love* Governor Gavin!

'Yes, you have spoken of him a few times with me Governor Gavin, and Gary, you should be very proud. I don't think I have ever heard a prisoner speak so well of a fellow prisoner,' says Mr. Murphy.

'He saved my life, Governor, he's me best mate.' My tough exterior begins to show signs of cracking then it almost comes completely apart.

'Gary, he still has a bit of time left to do. I'm not sure about this one. But promise me you'll keep up the good work. You are an inspiration Gary, keep it up.' And with that Mr. Murphy turns and makes his way towards his nervous audience that has assembled to meet him.

Fuck you! were the words that came screaming into my head. Governor Gavin looks as saddened as I do. She was about to offer words of support until I interrupt her. 'Please Miss, don't say anything. I need time to digest this. I just really miss him, and I know how much he'd benefit from this place.' I don't wait for a reply, as I turn and make my way back to the auditorium to finish my painting job. My heart was shattered!

I arrived in the auditorium and began applying the final coat of white Satinwood paint to the skirting boards. I had a Sony Discman (remember those?) placed inside the leg pocket of my overalls, and I was listening to the quirky EP myself and Fitzer created back in The Joy. I soon realised this was a bad idea, as the unmistakable intro to Fitzer's wondrous, haunting tune he wrote for his wife and child brought tears to my ears. As he began the first verse I felt the might of my sadness as my heart grew heavier and heavier.

I am startled by the sudden appearance of Governor Gavin and Mr. Murphy. She had brought him down to show the unusual painting job I had done on this weathered room. But I saw this as my final opportunity, and so I leapt to my feet and rushed towards Mr. Murphy, who was dressed in one of Louis Copeland's finest. I removed the paint-splattered, over-sized earphones from my head and plonked them on to his – what the fuck was I doing? Oh well, here goes nothing!

'What the fuck are you doing Gary?' demands Mr. Murphy.

'That voice singing that song, that's Fitzer, Mr. Murphy. He actually wrote this song about his wife and son, and we recorded it in Mountjoy.' Governor Gavin looks like she was about to burst out laughing. There I was, covered in paint, standing in front of one of the most important men in the IPS, as I forced my earphones on to his head. I needed to almost stand on top of him, as the wire from the headphones was quite short, but he loved the song. He listened to it in its entirety, amazed by Fitzer's incredible voice, and blown away by how good the song actually was.

'Mr. Murphy, I am so sorry, getting him here just means the world to me.'

I'll never for the rest of my days forget his cryptic answer. He winked at me and as he walked away with Governor Gavin and said, 'It's done, Gary' ... What's fuckin' done? Could it be?

The weeks fly past as Mr. Murphy's visit becomes the stuff of folklore. He had granted T. R. to almost everyone who qualified for it. But I had given up on my good friend. Maybe it was too much to ask, maybe Fitzer had a little too much time left, maybe I'd never see him again.

One day A.C.O. Duffy asked me if I'd mind talking to a young lady he had coming in. This young woman was a playwright and was in the process of creating a play about prison life. Mr. Duffy had told her about my own musical and the fact I was writing a book, which intrigued her. I gladly accepted the chance to talk to her and we chatted for hours about my time spent in prison. I explained to her the meaning of some of the prison slang, like Balls Rough and so on, which she found very funny. I also spoke of Fitzer and his voice, how he brought to life the characters in my musical. Amazingly, this talented young lady did in fact complete her play, and she called it *Balls Rough*! It was staged in London, and she wrote to me sometime after thanking me for inspiring her. Isn't that fuckin' mad?

Mr. Duffy appeared and told us it was time to wrap it up, and as we were leaving the auditorium, I asked her if she would like to read the synopsis of *Journeyman* and listen to the songs that bring the story to life. She gladly accepted, and so she waited for me in the A.C.O.'s office while I ran to my room in Pine Lodge in order to grab a copy for her. I re-enter the A.C.O.'s office and find herself and Mr. Duffy having a chat. 'Here you go, Miss,' I say as I hand over *Journeyman*.

'Now I feckin' need that back okay?' She laughs and tells me not to worry. 'Oh, and the singing voice you will hear? That's the guy we've been talkin' about for the last feckin' hour.'

'I can't wait,' came her eager reply.

'Who is this singer, Gary?' asks A.C.O. Duffy in his harsh Fermanagh tone.

'Fitzer, Mr. Duffy, the lad I've been trying to get transferred here since my first day.'

'Sure, he'll be here next week,' said Duffy .

Wait ... *What*? ... Duffy had a reputation of ripping the piss out of us prisoners, finding great joy in winding us up. 'Fuck off, oops sorry about the language, Miss, but *fuck off Duffy*, really?' I ask this in dire hope.

'Close the door Cunningham, and tell fuckin' no one I showed you this,' he says sternly. He turns to the PC on his desk and frantically types away. Upon finding the email he required, he turns the monitor towards me and asks me to read out the email. 'I, Brian Murphy, request the immediate transfer of "Fitzer" (his real name was used obviously) from Mountjoy Prison to Loughan House Open Centre.' *Jaysus, he's fuckin' coming*! 'He should be here as early as next week Gary, well done.'

I erupt with tears (how surprising), tears of complete happiness. The young lady in the office has even been swept up in this raw emotion. 'Aw, I am so happy for you Gary, the band will be back together,' she says with a smile.

'Thank you Miss, I'm sorry, but I have to run, there's someone I need to talk to. Thank you Mr. Duffy.' I plant a massive kiss on his bald head, which doesn't go down too well, but I'm gone before he can berate me.

I run to the control room and request a call. I give the number to the officer and sprint towards the ringing phone. I pick up the orange receiver, and hear Fitzer's wife's voice. 'Ah, howya Gar, ya all right?' she said.

'Fitzer is fuckin' coming here, he's fucking coming, Ash, as early as next bleedin' week!' What happened next will stay with me forever as she wept tears of absolute joy down the phone. I don't think either of us spoke for a minute or two, we couldn't!

'Jesus, thank you so so much Gary,' she gushes.

'Fuck that, Ash, he deserves it. He has earned it himself! I just brought his name up once or twice.' We both begin to laugh. 'Plus he saved my life, Ash, I owe him, I fuckin' love him. And I now get to put a face to his wife's voice and to meet his deadly little boy.'

'Here, fuck off,' she laughs, 'it's me that loves him okay?' We are both in stitches, then she finishes with, 'I can't wait to put my arms around him, Gary, I'll never let him go.' That's it, I'm fuckin' sobbing!

I say my goodbyes and thunder to the Governor's office, and catch her as she leaves. 'Thank you, thank you, thank you, *thank you*!' I almost scream, as I give her the biggest hug my body will allow. I don't even wait for her reply, not wanting to hold her up as she was leaving for home, instead telling her I'd see her in the morning. I turn and sprint towards Pine Lodge in order to tell the Dublin lads, but I tell my favourite Dub first, Cunny. Me, Cunny and Fitzer have a very close bond, so when I tell him he's blown away.

'How the fuck did you manage that, Gar?' he asks in shock.

'I have no fuckin' idea, but I'm not gonna question it,' I say.

Everyone is delighted with the news of Fitzer's pending arrival, with The Torment saying, 'Deadly, free gigs, The Offenders are back together'. Little did The Torment know how much truth there was in that statement!

Chapter 43

The End of One Era ... and the Beginning of a New One

And so, sadly, the last hours of Governor Gavin's reign in Loughan House drew ever closer. There was a strange atmosphere hanging over the jail, with inmates and staff alike not really knowing how to feel. We all wanted her to stay, and yet we all wanted her to be happy with her decision to leave as we knew it was one of the toughest decisions she has ever faced. Myself and the committee came up with the idea of having a 'whip around' amongst the inmates in order to purchase a bunch of flowers for this magnificent lady. Of course, as prisoners we had no access to actual money, but we had our 'grat', which at the time I think was €12 a week, put into our prison accounts.

We approached Chief Carrick and asked her if it would be possible to set up some sort of way where the lads could contribute a few euro to the purchasing of flowers or something along those lines. She thought this was a wonderful idea, but stressed that no prisoner *had* to contribute, as some lads relied heavily on that €12 a week. I reassured her that no man would feel pressured into handing over any money. She then handed me a sheet, similar to a charity sponsor card. Any of the lads who wanted to give a couple of euro would simply sign their name on this sheet, along with their prison number, thus allowing the powers-that-be access to their accounts in order to obtain the allowed amount. I had thought to myself that if we got over half of the jail to give even €2 it would go along way towards a bunch of flowers and maybe some chocolates.

But what the men incarcerated in Loughan House did, well, it was incredible. Every single one of them made a contribution, averaging around €10 each, with some only able to spare €2, but every inmate made a contribution. It blew me away, along with the officers and staff of Loughan. We raised enough to buy a wonderful crystal bowl, which Miss Thornton kindly went out and purchased for us along with a beautiful bunch of flowers. I would like to point out to any man who I served time with in Mountjoy, who didn't make it to Loughan House, that this was not bullshit. Every prisoner housed in Loughan wanted to be a part of this. I know that for most of the Governors we were used to, well, you wouldn't be caught dead buying them a penny jelly, but trust me, this Governor was different.

And so the day had come, Governor Gavin's last one at the helm of Loughan. I woke at 4.30 am and began my sit-ups like I did every fuckin' morning. I gazed out of the window in my room and watched the sun rising from its slumber off in the distance. I felt like today was going to be special. Ever since I had got word that Fitzer was coming, I became more and more excited. Nobody had any idea when he was arriving, so I became the butt of many jokes as I would run out every time I saw a bus come through the gate in the hope it contained my good friend. Some of the lads, Sarge and The Torment in particular, got great pleasure informing me that a bus had just pulled in with a Dub on board, only for this to be complete bullshit! Fuckers!

Chief Carrick summoned me to her office early that morning. 'Right, Gary, today is a big day, albeit a sad one.'

I could see how upset she was. Herself and Governor Gavin were like sisters. They ran an amazing jail together but I had my faith in Chief Carrick that the good work would continue whilst she was still here. 'So,' she continues, 'I was thinking I could get the Governor into the dining hall at about 2.00 pm. I'll tell her she can use this time to address the jail for the last time, but I want you to try to have everyone in the dining hall for 1.30 pm. I'll get the Governor there early, and then boom! *Surprise*!' She raises her hands high above her head as she says this.

I'm in! This will be great. 'I was thinking of writing a poem, Miss, chronicling her time here in Loughan. Of course I would use this opportunity to slag off all the officers, but all done in good taste.'

'That sounds great, Gary,' came her happy reply. 'Right, let's do this.'

And do it we did!

We got the lads assembled in the dining hall, every single prisoner who was in Loughan House that day was there. Mrs Mulligan and Miss Thornton had arranged the flowers, chocolates, and our crystal bowl in a lovely fashion at the top of the room. We were given the warning that she was on her way, and so you could hear a pin drop as we stood in silence awaiting her arrival. As she walked through the door of the dining hall, we all screamed *'Surprise!'* She was blown away. Immediately, a waterfall of tears streams down her face. She was in total shock.

Chief Carrick, who was also clearly moved, composed herself enough to begin proceedings. 'Thanks, lads, job well done!' She looks at Governor Gavin and says, 'We've been planning this for a while Governor, and the gifts you see before you were bought by the prisoners themselves.'

That's it, Governor Gavin was sobbing. In fact, I don't think there was a dry eye in the dining hall that day. All the officers and staff of Loughan were moved, too, as was one man I had never seen before. He was an older gentleman, dressed in a long black crombie jacket, with a perfectly groomed goatee beard. He resembled 'Zod' from the late Christopher Reeve's *Superman* movie. I assumed it was our good Governor's husband.

Chief Carrick then calls upon me to speak on behalf of the prisoners. I thank the Chief and then proceed to inflate the ego of one of the most incredible women I have ever met. I offered thanks from myself and every prisoner present for the tireless work that she has put in as she prepared us for life outside of prison. I then informed her that I have written a poem of sorts which tells the tale of her time here in Loughan. I catch the eye of every officer and A.C.O. present and warn them they ain't gonna like this!

I then proceed to tear strips out of every officer in Loughan. My particular favourite couple of lines pertained to Mr Slater and Mr Wallace, heads of the cleaning and the paint workers respectfully, who were hardly ever spotted without the other at his side.

> Wallace and Slater, walk around like the Legion of Doom / So Mr Wallace, Mr Slater both of yas get a fuckin' room!

This resulted in a loud cheer. As I brought my poem to an end, I dedicated the last couple of verses to our amazing Governor. I struggled to finish the last few lines as I wished her all the best for her future, but I got there and the poem ended to a massive roar from the Loughan lads.

Governor Gavin, clearly touched by the gestures from us that day, embraced me in a hug and whispered into my ear, 'See your man there in the black crombie? Just so you know, he's the new Governor!'

Ah *fuck*! Here I was slagging off every single officer in Loughan in front of the new boss? Shit! I approached the new Governor in order to introduce myself, and offered my sincere apologies, but I'm met with, 'Gary, I've heard a lot about you. Interesting poem, but not to worry, it was all in good taste.' Thank fuck for that.

Governor Gavin tried to address us, but was too moved to speak, so we all just stand and clap for what feels like hours, but by God did this woman deserve it. The next thing I witnessed will stay with me for a long time. The inmates all formed an orderly queue in order to shake the hand of the woman who looked after them so well, and to give their personal thanks to her for all she had done. It was an amazing sight.

The dining hall began to empty, and myself, Cunny and No. 2 headed back over to Pine Lodge for a coffee. We arrived at my room, when The Torment comes bursting in. 'Gar, a bus with Fitzer on it, just got word off an officer. *Quick*!' He was out of breath as he says this, or was this just part of the ruse?

'Fuck off, Torment.'

'Gary, on my kids' life, I'm not lying.' He did look sincere, but this guy was the best wind-up I've ever seen.

But next thing I know Longy sticks his head into my room, and in his broad Cork twang he says, 'Bus just arrived from The Joy, there, lads, maybe it's your mate, Gar.'

That's it, I'm gone like Meatloaf's *Bat Out of Hell*! I sprint towards the Main House and true enough, there stands a prison bus. I run past the congregation that has gathered around Governor Gavin as she says her final goodbyes, even ignoring a request from an officer to stop and chat. I arrived at the prison bus. The windows were blacked out so I couldn't see anything, then I hear a voice coming from inside the bus.

'Gar, me aul' flower.' *It's fuckin Fitzer! I can't fuckin' believe it!*

The officer seems to take an eternity to open the door, but when he does there at the top of the steps that descend from the bus was the greatest friend I've ever had. He's still in cuffs as I fling my arms around his neck. 'Jaysus, Gar, you'll fuckin' choke me, ya bollox,' laughs Fitzer. He looks great, obviously still attending the gym whilst in The Joy. And I spot in the background his wonderful black bass and another rather large guitar case. He notes that I've spotted the case. 'I only went and bought Paul's 'White Lady'.

'No fuckin' way,' comes my reply. This was a custom-built Fender bass guitar, snow-white in colour, a real beauty! But forget the fuckin' guitar for a minute. *Fitzer is here!*

'It's great to see ya, me aul' flower,' he starts, 'how the fuck did ya manage to get me here? You're a mad bastard, buddy, but honestly, thanks, it means a lot. Now fuck all that soppy shite, what's this place like?'

I find I'm having difficulty arranging my words into coherent sentences. 'I'll give ya the grand tour in a second buddy, first I just want you to know how happy I am to see ya. The first week is a pox, Fitzer, but hang in there, okay? Sure, I'll be by your side doin' your nut in so don't worry.'

Fitzer was then asked to enter the Main House by Mrs Mulligan to be processed. But I ask her can I have him for just one second? There was someone he needed to meet before it's too late, the other person responsible for him being here this early in his sentence – Governor Gavin. As we approached Governor Gavin she was surrounded by staff and friends, all wishing her the best. I catch her eye, and then she spots Fitzer!

'Excuse me one moment,' she says to her colleagues. And what happened next was one of the most special moments of my life. Fitzer and Governor Gavin shake hands and have a quick chat, I'm not sure what about as it was their moment. She then turned to me and said, 'I told you I'd get him here, Gary.' What an incredible woman.

Chapter 44

For Those About to Rock, We Salute You

And so Fitzer was in Loughan. Straight away he 'got' the place, understanding that it was a far cry from the depressing D Wing of The Joy. He quickly secured a job, and found his nirvana in Tom's woodwork class up in the school, where he spent most of his weekdays. He is gifted at woodwork, and this was something that Tom noted straight away. It wasn't long before he offered Fitzer the position of 'woodwork-room cleaner'. This afforded him extra time in the woodwork room to work on the various projects he was making, which ranged from lamps and jewellery boxes to a child's chair made for his son.

The inmates and staff all took to him right away, which was never something I was worried about. He'd do anything for anybody, and never looked for anything in return. But he would never let anyone take the piss out of him. He would never resort to violence, but he'd make sure you knew if you'd pissed him off!

I'll never forget his first visit in Loughan House from his wife and their son. They made the journey from Dublin, early one cold bright Friday morning, arriving in Loughan House at around 11.00 am. Although Fitzer is a private man, and not one to speak openly about his feelings, just one look at him that morning told a million stories. We didn't see him for the whole day as he absorbed his first non-intrusive visit with his family, though he did ask me to come out to meet his two 'reasons'. This was something I was about to do, until I caught sight of Fitzer and his two-year-old son playing just outside the kids' visiting area. It stopped me in my tracks, as this was one of the first times Fitzer had a real opportunity to bond with his son without the intrusion of a wide wooden bench keeping them apart. He hadn't spotted me, and so I turned and headed back to my room in Pine Lodge. I was fuckin' delighted for the guy. Fitzer deserved this.

So Fitzer fitting in or taking to Loughan House were never concerns. What did concern me was what he had left behind, the music class in Mountjoy. For it was there he became the incredible bass player that he is today. It was there that he got to jam with other musicians. It was there he met Paul, the music teacher. Fitzer had become Paul's prodigy and they had formed an incredible connection. Unfortunately, the music class in Loughan House paled in comparison, but this was not the fault of Loughan House – even a music class on the outside would find it hard to compete with the one in The Joy. So I needed to create a good 'jamming' ethos for us, which I did.

We actually put on our first gig in Loughan a week after Fitzer arrived. I spread the word that we would be playing in the auditorium at 7.00 pm one evening, which was well received, as Loughan House can become quite dull unless you keep yourself occupied. Another thing that Loughan lacked was stage equipment. We had no mics and no amps for our electric guitars. But we had an acoustic guitar and bass, and we had Fitzer's voice, so we'd be grand for now! That first gig felt good. All the inmates from Loughan filled the newly painted auditorium that evening, and respected the fact we had no amplification. So as we worked our way through our set list, which included the perfect blend of cover songs and original material, they would remain quiet to enjoy what was being presented to them. Although once the lads heard Fitzer sing he did what he always did – he blew them away! We'd won over the Loughan crowd. Result!

Fitzer came to me one day with some thoughts. As he entered my room, he is met by myself and Cunny. 'Just about to stick the kettle on me aul' pal, can I tempt ya?' I ask him.

'Sure, why not Gar, wha?' laughed Fitzer. 'Here Gar,' he began, 'there has to be a drummer amongst the population here in this mad aul' jail.' Myself and Cunny laugh at Fitzer's accurate description of Loughan.

'I did put out the word some time ago,' I say, 'but no one got back to me.' Then the funniest thing happened as me and Fitzer continued this chat. Cunny, not really interested in this particular topic as he's not a musician, was sitting on my bed playing and keeping a steady beat as he quickly hits his hands of his thighs and then his chest increasing the speed, then decreasing it all just to relieve the boredom of the conversation between myself and Fitzer.

Fitzer notes this and pipes up, 'Would ya look at your man here, fuckin Animal from *The Muppets*, there's a drummer right there!' We both look at Cunny, who seemed confused. Fitzer explains in a way only he could. 'You're gonna teach yourself the drums, Cunny, okay? In fact, you don't have a choice. Someone will have a bongo or something at home that they can bring up on a visit. Or we could see if we could get one of those 'beat-box' things, you know the ones, Gar, when a band is playin' acoustic, the drummer will sit on it and hit it in a very fuckin' similar fashion as to the way young Cunny here is hitting his fuckin' thighs!'

We fall around laughing, but then something incredible happened – Cunny wanted in! I have spoken before about this guy's confidence issues, how he never felt good enough.

Try as I might I could never get through to him just how amazing he truly was. But he was still reserved around people he didn't really know, and so joining a 'band', and learning possibly the most difficult instrument of them all, was going to be an uphill task. But something snapped inside Cunny that day. He really wanted in. And what he was to achieve next in his life was truly astounding.

Since mine and Fitzer's first gig in Loughan, word had spread to the officers of how good we actually were. If it sounds like I am 'blowing the trumpet' for The Offenders, well, I am. Firstly, we were honestly bloody good. But also, like Cunny, I have never felt like anything I had done was good enough, but here I was in a band with my friends, and we were making people happy. Prison had done enough to me to *never* want to return, and yet this band had given me hope for a new future, it had shown me that I can achieve good things with a little hard work. So apologies if I seem 'big headed' as this is most certainly not my intention. I'm just so proud of what we had achieved to date and excited about what we could achieve next. Though none of us could've predicted what was to become of our little 'prison band'!

We got talking to Mrs Mulligan one day, who had fallen in love with Fitzer's voice, having heard us jam in the auditorium one afternoon. She was delighted by the fact that we wanted to start a 'proper' band, not just the two-piece me and Fitzer had been since our first meeting. We explained to her that Cunny was willing to audition for the role of the drummer in this new band, though he had no fuckin' idea how to actually play the drums. I told Mrs Mulligan I could keep a beat on the drums, having been in a couple of bands in my youth and always watching and learning from the drummers. So I was sure I could assist Cunny in his quest to become the next Keith Moon. Mrs Mulligan told us that her teenage son was a budding musician. He had started out on the drums, but his passion lay in playing the guitar. As a result, she had a Cajon (this is the 'beat-box' Fitzer was referring to earlier, a wooden box that a drummer sits on and keeps a steady beat) which she was willing to lend to us. Fitzer quickly jumps in. 'I reckon I could make one of those meself Miss up in woodwork. If you could bring yours in, and maybe Google how they are made for me that would be amazing.' And that's just what she did. She also told us, as she left that day, that there was a battered drum kit in her home. It was sized for a teenager but beggars can't be choosers. She told us to see how Cunny got on with the Cajon, and then we'd take it from there. Grand!

Mrs Mulligan kept her word, and the next day she brought in a wonderful light-oak Cajon. She also printed off a 'Wiki-how-to-do' set of instructions in order for Fitzer to make his own. He would have all the materials available to him in the woodwork room, everything except snare string, which was the string that sits under a snare drum and gave it that rattle, and served a similar purpose on a Cajon, giving it a 'snare' sound. But on closer inspection of the 'how-to' list, we saw that snare strings could be replaced with some guitar strings which we had plenty of. So using Mrs Mulligan's son's Cajon as a template, and reading his Wiki instructions, Fitzer created his first Cajon and it was breathtaking. It had a factory finish, and while sitting on its top, and striking its front, you could hear how authentically he had created it. It was a masterpiece. Even Tom the woodwork teacher was impressed, stating that Fitzer could actually mass produce these and sell them. He made one for each of The Offenders, and ones for a couple of other lads too. We would trace art or whatever they wanted on its front as a decorative piece, then I would apply a few coats of oil-based varnish to keep them pristine. But the life of The Offenders took on a pace of its own over the next eight months or so, which hindered Fitzer's time spent in woodwork, thus not allowing him the chance to mass produce these amazing instruments he had created. But fuck it, The Offenders were worth it!

Fitzer proudly handed Cunny his very own Cajon after its completion and, amazingly, after a few sessions where I tried to explain the fundamentals of drumming, he took to it like a nervous first-time swimmer to water. And of course the more he practiced the better he got. We started jamming as a threesome and became really tight in no time. Cunny was now an official member of The Offenders and I couldn't have been happier!

We played our first gig as this new line up, and Cunny was incredible. I thought his nerves would get the better of him, and although he looked like someone had poured a bucket of water over him with the amount of sweat his body had produced, his playing was wonderful. Myself and Fitzer, along with all the lads who attended that night, were blown away, as was Mrs Mulligan. She happened to be on nights that evening, and after the gig she praised us for a great show, but she took extra time to make sure Cunny knew just how good he really was. She then informed us that we could have the old battered drum kit she had at home. Now all we had to do was show Cunny how to play an actual drum kit. Simple!

Now that we were getting a drum kit, it highlighted the fact we had no other equipment. And so I took it upon myself to try to sell the idea of getting a PA system – an electronic sound amplification and distribution system with a microphone, amplifier and loudspeakers, and a bass amplifier – to Governor O'Reilly. His reign was of stark difference to Governor Gavin's, with Governor O'Reilly ruling with more of an 'iron fist', but I found him to be approachable. He took to the Prison Committee meetings well, and assisted us in everything we were still trying to achieve to improve the living conditions of Loughan. But one thing I didn't know about the man, which turned out to be an amazing bonus for

The Offenders, was he had a massive passion for music. He also had good taste, and liked the songs that myself, Fitzer and Cunny were producing.

So when I requested that he might look into sourcing a PA system from somewhere in the IPS, he was only too glad to help. He also loaned us a large oversized speaker that he had at home, which had once been part of a 'stack amp'. Alas, the controls (or the 'stack' part) had been lost through the years. But A.C.O. Duffy informed us that a friend of his was clearing out his house, and he was pretty sure he had seen something similar to what we needed sitting on the skip in this man's garden. He brought it in the next day and after removing the layers of dirt that the skip had coated it in, we plugged it into the Governor's speaker and hey, presto, it fuckin' worked. Fitzer had a bass amp!

Now we had a PA system – which in the end Governor O'Reilly had paid for himself – which had three mics, a board, and two large speakers. We had the large 1960s speaker from the Governor's home combined with the stack removed from A.C.O. Duffy's friend's skip. We had the Cajon Fitzer had made, and we had the funniest looking drum kit you have ever laid your eyes upon. It was sized for a teenager and consisted of a busted snare, two thrashed toms and a battered floor tom. It also had a busted and bent crash cymbal, and a hi-hat which remained closed as it didn't work. The kick-drum pedal was temperamental and as for the actual bass drum? The front of its skin, which is the part everybody sees, had a bunch of 'Dora the Explorer' stickers strewn about its face! But we had two drumsticks and Cunny behind the kit, although his massive six foot muscular frame, sitting behind a tiny battered drum kit, was a sight in itself but, fuck me, he made it sound good.

We began setting up our equipment like the way any professional band would. We were ready to take The

Offenders to the next level. Me and Cunny spent every waking minute on the battered blue 'Dora the Explorer' drum kit, as he began mastering the art of timing. Mr. Tully, the officer who I enjoyed many a jam with before Fitzer arrived, was an actual drummer, and he spared us his personal time in order to teach Cunny a thing or two. We had a system, myself and Cunny: 'Bum' meant 'use the kick drum' and 'tit' meant 'hit the snare', and as silly as this may sound it worked ('bum, tit, tit, bum, tit'). After only a month, Cunny was able to play 'Coming Back to Life', one of Pink Floyd's most incredible tracks, in its entirety.

Cunny's first live gig was in front of about 120 prisoners and a few prison officers, and although I thought he was going to pass out from the stress, he was fuckin' great. He got the biggest cheer of the night as the lads started chanting his name, all knowing this was the guy's first ever gig playing the fuckin' drums! Here was a young man with confidence issues, who had never played any musical instrument before, holding his own as the drummer in a bluesy rock 'prison band'.

We started to write more original material which Cunny would lay down his own drum beats to. Our jams were becoming more and more expansive as we experimented with this new material. The residents of Loughan House would respect our rehearsal times, and leave us to it as we took over the auditorium and bashed out our songs. We began to feel like *bona fide* rock stars! But we were becoming a good tight band, wrote some great tracks, played everybody's favourites and gave it our all each and every time we played. Fitzer was even getting better at singing and playing his bass at the same time. Sometimes we would have 'guest appearances' from other lads, like Do'Di, a fine whistle player. He had made the move to Loughan, and we were honoured to have him on stage with us as we'd provide the backing track to his rendition of 'The Lonesome Boatman'.

It was amazing but what had started as a means to relieve the boredom associated with prison life was becoming something we might make a career out of. We were impressing inmates and officers alike. Governors, Chiefs and A.C.O.'s were singing our praises. Word was even travelling back to Mountjoy and other closed jails about this exciting, tight band, a band who wrote their own songs, had a guy on bass who was taught in prison, and a self-taught drummer. We were getting up off our arses and creating something remarkable in what was the worst time in each of our lives.

So the closed jails were hearing about The Offenders. I wonder what would happen next?

Well, we only went and wrote ourselves into the fuckin' history books of the Irish Prison Service as the first 'prison band' to be transferred to different closed jails in order to play gigs. We played two incredible gigs in Castlerea Prison which almost took the roof clean off. Our equipment would be loaded onto a prison bus, and we'd be put into a separate prison bus and transferred to these prisons – now is that not rock 'n' roll? We really wanted to show as many incarcerated men as we could that there is a different way to 'do your jail', that if you put your mind to it you can achieve anything.

I am so proud of The Offenders, or The Off#enders as we are called today, as there already exists a German Ska band by the name of The Offenders. Mr. Camden, our crazy, kooky officer, made the suggestion that since 'everybody is "hash-tagging" this or "hash-tagging" that, just hash-tag the name!' Brilliant, although I think he meant #The Offenders, we just preferred The Off#enders. And then we were overjoyed with the arrival of Sweeny-Todd to Loughan House, as this young lad was a fantastic rhythm guitarist. He was a shy lad, but Fitzer worked his magic and soon Sweeny-Todd was to become the fourth and final member of The Off#enders.

Before I continue to the next instalment of this book which, like my sentence at the time, is coming to an end, I must describe a truly moving and quite incredible experience that happened to me and Fitzer, all down to The Off#enders. There was a musical priest who would come every Saturday evening and Sunday morning into Loughan House. His parish church was actually facing the main entrance to Loughan House, which is the Blacklion parish church in County Cavan. He had been informed of The Off#enders, and although some of our songs may not go down too well with his congregation on a Sunday morning, he did see a guitarist and a bloody good singer that he could maybe put to use.

Christmas was fast approaching, and the biggest difference between a closed jail and Loughan was that if you were on a T. R. programme, you could ask to be sent home for a couple of days over the Christmas period. I was actually offered the chance to go home, but after a wonderful chat with my mam, I informed the IPS that I just wasn't ready to go home during the festive season as there might be too many temptations.

So the priest then asked myself and Fitzer if we'd be interested in partaking in the Mass to be held in Blacklion parish church on Christmas Eve night. I was to play the guitar but the main man, Fitzer, was to be the star of the show, and bejaysus he was!

We were brought over, under escort, on a couple of evenings leading up to the Mass to rehearse with the women's choir in this wonderful, old church. Fitzer took to the choir without a hitch, and I accompanied them all on my guitar. This was going to be good. On Christmas Eve, myself and Fitzer were escorted over to the church for the 10.00 pm Mass. The whole church was filled to capacity and lit by what seemed like thousands of flickering candles placed all around. We felt a bit nervous as we were welcomed by the priest, who informed the congregation where we had come from – a prison! But we got a lovely, warm 'Christmas' welcome, which put us at ease, and we were extremely grateful for this act of kindness.

The highlight of the night was when Fitzer and this amazing four-part harmony women's choir did an incredible version of 'O Holy Night'. Fitzer sang the second verse and chorus while standing on the candle-lit altar, accompanied by the choir. It was the most moving experience of my life. There was not a dry eye in the church that Christmas eve as Fitzer commanded the attention of all. After the Mass, every parishioner took the time to thank us both, but mainly Fitzer. Even celebrity TV chef Neven Maguire, who lives in Blacklion, requested a selfie with us. The choir then gave us little parting gifts of aftershave and chocolates. We were moved, as were they. They informed us of the dread they experienced on hearing two prisoners would be singing and playing at the Mass. But they soon saw that not all books should be judged by their covers!

So The Off#enders had re-written the history books of the IPS. We had broken down some walls and made some headway in changing how people from the outside viewed prisoners. We even invited all of the older folks who lived in Blacklion into Loughan House for a Christmas feast prepared by the inmates, followed by a Christmas show put on by The Off#enders. It was magical. We were achieving great things, and all the while we were getting a glimpse of a brighter future, a future we never could have imagined on our first day in Mountjoy.

Chapter 45

A GOOD CHOICE IN *THEORY*

Before I provide the last instalments of The Off#enders tale, and my own as well, I must describe something that Mrs. Mulligan organised in Loughan House that had such a positive effect on a lot of prisoners, myself included.

One day Mrs. Mulligan approached me with her idea. 'Gary, I am looking to set up a group and, yes, this could be misconstrued as "group therapy", but it is so much more than that.' She emphasises the 'group therapy' part because she knows that not many prisoners feel comfortable 'opening up', and even less comfortable doing so in a group environment! 'It really is so much more than that Gary. It is something I am a true believer in, in fact I am studying to become a spokesperson on this very subject. It's a different way of thinking, Gary, known as Choice Theory.' Choice Theory, I hear you ask? Let me try, with a bit of help from Google, to explain what this Choice Theory entails.

Choice Theory, developed by Dr. William Glasser, is the explanation of human behaviour based on internal motivation. As Dr. Glasser explains it, all of our behaviour is chosen as we continually attempt to meet one or more of the five basic needs that are part of our genetic structure. These needs are as follows:

- *Power,* which includes achievement and feeling worthwhile as well as winning
- *Love and Belonging,* which includes groups as well as families or loved ones
- *Freedom,* which includes independence, autonomy, your own 'space'
- *Fun,* which includes pleasure and enjoyment
- *Survival,* which includes nourishment, shelter, sex.

One of the core principles of Choice Theory is that, whether we are aware of it or not, we are at all times behaving to meet these needs. The ten axioms of Choice Theory are as follows:

1. The only person whose behaviour we can control is our own.
2. All we can give another person is information.
3. All long-lasting psychological problems are relationship problems.
4. The problem relationship is always part of our present life.
5. What happened in the past has everything to do with what we are today, but we can only satisfy our basic needs right now and plan to continue satisfying them in the future.
6. We can only satisfy our needs by satisfying the pictures in our Quality World.
7. All we do is behave.
8. All behaviour is Total Behaviour and is made up of four components: acting, thinking, feeling and physiology.
9. All Total Behaviour is chosen, but we only have direct control over the acting and thinking components. We can

only control our feeling and physiology indirectly through how we choose to act and think.

10. All Total Behaviour is designated by verbs and named by the part that is the most recognisable (see more at www.brucedavenport.com).

Yep, bit of a mouthful, isn't it? But trust me when I say that it *works*. Choice Theory speaks of our 'Quality World', or our perfect world, and how we struggle every day to fill this 'Quality World' with perfect plans and ideas. But it's not always that easy to achieve, as life has a way of fucking with you at every twist and turn. So it all boils down to the choices we make. Forget the choices we've made as these are gone forever. We control our own future with our choices. If you find any this of interest I urge you to Google the William Glasser Institute of Ireland to find out more. Right, back to the tale.

Mrs. Mulligan sold this to me and anything that encourages the betterment of yourself as a person was right up my street. I told her I'd sell it to the lads. She said she needed 12, and it would take place over two days in the auditorium. I set about finding lads to take part, and luckily for me the lads were ever willing, as they knew I always had their best interests at heart. I made Fitzer and Cunny do it – they had *no choice*, ironically enough!

As the 12 Choice Theory men assembled in the auditorium that first day, the air was filled with trepidation. Lads were beginning to worry that they might have to open up about things. I told them that there is nothing wrong with this basic human emotion, but they worried all the same. Next in walked Arnie, our Choice Theory teacher. His attire was similar to an actor playing a typical teacher in a British school, patches on his elbows and brown corduroy trousers to match! He had tight grey curly hair, which almost looked knitted to his scalp. His goatee matched his hair colour, and he spoke in a posh Dublin tone, but the guy was incredible. Over the two days, he taught us everything he knew about Choice Theory. He gave us the tools to think about the choices we make, not just as prisoners, but as normal people. He gave us ideas that didn't seem unachievable and, most amazingly of all, he got each and every man in attendance to open up! This was a humbling experience.

I broke the ice by talking about the death of my beloved daughter and the 'bad' choices I made after she died. I laid myself bare, and poured my heart out onto the floor for all to inspect. But, seeing me like this gave the other lads the courage to bring forth what may have been holding them back for so long. I am honoured to have shared those two days with that group of prisoners. We shared our deepest and darkest secrets, our hopes and dreams, our nightmares and shame, but we shared them amongst each other, and through this two-day course we were given the tools to make better choices in our lives.

The course was a complete success, which made Mrs. Mulligan happy and it was worth it solely for that! But she wasn't finished, in fact she'd only begun. 'I feel Choice Theory would be an amazing addition to the curriculum of every Irish jail Gary. It is filled with so much positivity, and not bogged down with mumbo-jumbo bullshit. I really think it could work,' she said enthusiastically.

'I agree Miss one hundred per cent,' I reply.

'Well, how do you feel about standing up and doing a talk in front of a delegation of like-minded people and some higher-ranked staff in the IPS as I try to show them how invaluable this course could be for prisoners?' she asks.

'Not-a-feckin' bother, Miss, anything for you, ya know that,' I jest.

'Oh, thank you Gary. The talk is next Saturday in St. Patrick's College in Drumcondra. I'll get you an overnight so you can attend.'

'Not at all, Miss, sure I'm home that weekend on T. R. so I'll pop down. I don't live too far from there,' I say.

'Really?' she asks surprised. 'You would give up one of your days home to do this?'

'Sort of Miss, I'd give up one of my days home to do this for *you*!'

She was ever so grateful, but as I've said before, this woman deserves an award for the tireless work she puts into reforming prisoners.

But on the morning of the talk, I was as nervous as a condemned man heading towards the gallows! St Patrick's College in Dublin was where young men and women go to become teachers. As I entered the large hall that was to hold today's talk, with its rows of chairs ascending upwards towards the ceiling, I immediately note that the majority of the audience were women, some a bit older than me. As I entered, there was a man with so many letters after his name it looked like the fuckin' alphabet. What the fuck was I doing here? Sarge, who was also out on T. R. at the time, came along with me to offer moral support. 'Jaysus, Gar, rather you than me pal,' he laughs. Cheers for the moral support, ya bollox! Mrs. Mulligan finds me and calms me down in a way only she could manage. She explains that I'll be getting up after the 'doctor', a fuckin' *doctor,* who is currently addressing the crowd. Oh shit!

The crowd of around 100 people clap on the completion of the doctor's speech, then Mrs. Mulligan takes to the podium to introduce me. I can't remember all she said that Saturday afternoon, but I know she ended it with, 'Yes, Gary is a prisoner, yes, he has lived in Mountjoy, although he now is incarcerated in Loughan House. I just beg and implore you all to give this young man a chance. Remember, *anybody* can become incarcerated. It could be your son, or your grandson. Please allow this wonderful young man, not only explain how valuable Choice Theory would be in prisons across Ireland, but also allow him to tell you about what he's achieved since his incarceration. I think you'll enjoy it!'

And so, there I am standing atop this expansive stage, shittin'! The room was silent and I could feel their judgmental eyes make up their minds about me before I utter a word. I've got to win them over, I've got to for Mrs. Mulligan.

'Good afternoon Ladies and Gentlemen, could I just have one more round of applause for our last speaker, in fact for all of today's speakers.' A large burst of clapping starts, and as it draws to its conclusion I say, 'Yes, I am a prisoner, yes, I have spent time in Mountjoy, so keeping your handbags close to you at all times is to be advised!'

That did the trick, the ice was well and truly broken. I speak of the reasons for my incarceration, how selfish I was. I tell of the hurt and shame I brought on my family. I describe what I have achieved whilst in prison, putting a lot of emphasis on the 'choices' I've made which leads me to Choice Theory. I explain how I feel that it would be an amazing course to run for prisoners, as it gives willing participants new ways to better themselves. I speak of Mrs. Mulligan and her tireless work, of her vision of allowing all Irish prisoners access to Choice Theory. I explain how Choice Theory has vastly improved my life, and I feel as my sentence nears an end that it has helped me in so many ways. For example, I can 'choose' not to drink, or if I find myself in a heated conversation with a fellow prisoner I can 'choose' to just walk away. It has given me another set of tools I can use in order to change and reform. It offers such a simple way of thinking, and makes you aware of all the choices you have, good and bad, that ultimately dictate your life's path. Choice Theory all the way!

Upon reaching my talk's conclusion, I thank everyone for their time, and as I set about leaving the stage, I'm stopped in my tracks by the standing ovation I am receiving. I'm moved to tears. I thank them one and all and quickly take my seat next to Sarge. 'Fuckin' amazin', Gar, well done, pal,' says Sarge. The floor was then opened to questions, and myself and Sarge saw this as our chance to leave, as we had missed the start of the day so we didn't know what the other speakers had talked about. That is, until every person in the audience starts to direct their questions towards fuckin' *me*! There are doctors and professionals aplenty which these people can choose for their questions, and yet they choose the prisoner! Mental!

One lady in particular blows me away. 'Hi, Gary, I just want to say, I know your mother Lily very, very well. You have done her proud here today. Well done, and all the best for the future.' Have a guess what I did next? If you guessed 'cry like a fuckin' baby' then please collect your prize!

Mrs. Mulligan grabs hold of me before I leave and gives me a massive hug. 'Perfect, Gary, though I never doubted you.' This was too much for me. Having lived a life with few or no compliments, I assumed the days of receiving praise were long gone. But I had done so much work on myself, and my appetite for change and for a better life was voracious. Maybe it wasn't too late for me. Maybe I could win back the trust of my brothers, Gerry, Noel and Jason. Maybe I could make my mam proud of me, and start to heal the damage I had caused her through my incarceration. Maybe Antoinette and I could live happily ever after, as I show her the 'New Man' that I have become. Maybe I could build a bridge between myself and my beloved son. Maybe ...

Chapter 46

LAYING DOWN TRACKS

My prison life had become all-consuming. I was still running our prison committee with as much dedication as I could muster. I was still fulfilling my duties with the jobs I had secured in Loughan, such as opening the gym at 7.00 am each morning, cleaning the gym and helping out with any painting jobs that needed my assistance. But what truly consumed my prison life like a lion that consumes its prey was The Off#enders – and I loved it!

Sweeny-Todd had become a most welcome addition to the band, as good a fit as Cinderella's glass slipper. He had asked his brother to bring his electric guitar and the small Fender practice amp he had from home on his next visit. The amp would prove invaluable to our gigs as it meant I could use it, thus leaving only Sweeny-Todd's guitar running through our PA. But the guitar which Sweeny-Todd's brother brought was something special. It was a copy Fender Stratocaster with a light-oak neck which was polished and waxed to perfection, thus allowing great ease as you worked your way along its smooth surface. It was flame-burst in colour, and, well, I was in love. It was the coolest guitar I had ever played and it encouraged my quest to become a more accomplished lead guitarist.

After the success of the gigs we had played in Castlerea Prison, all of which went off without a hint of trouble, it got me and Fitzer thinking whether we could go back to Mountjoy to play for the lads we had left behind? Could we meet the school teachers, Brian, Lisa, but most of all Paul, and show them how far we have come from that first day they heard us? We dreamed of this gig, and so set about trying to convince Governor O'Reilly that it would be an amazing accomplishment. He agreed but he warned us that this would be an extremely difficult task and he didn't hold up much hope for it. Still, one can dream.

One day, whilst in the auditorium jamming a new track I had written, 'Can You Hear Me', a belting rock track with a high energy feel and pace to it, Fitzer could tell I had something I wanted to say. 'Spit it out, Gar,' he laughed.

'Right lads, you all know I can have crazy ideas.' All three of them start to laugh.

'Crazy is one way to describe them Gary,' joked Sweeny-Todd.

'Fuck off,' I counter as I follow it up with, 'why don't we record an album?' This stops the laughter. I can see the hamsters in each of their heads running around their little hamster-wheels at a blistering pace!

'A fuckin' album?' asks Cunny bewildered.

'Well, I'm glad you are the first to ask Cunny,' comes my reply. 'You are nearing your release date and will be reinstated back into society very soon, and although words cannot describe the pride myself, Fitzer and Sweeny-Todd have for you and all you've achieved, you have no "proof" that you accomplished this amazing feat. The only one who can back you up is your girlfriend, Ciara.'

The reason Ciara could back up his 'drumming tale' is because she actually got to see him play live, as did Fitzer's wife Ash. The two women had become very close during the time of Cunny and Fitzer's incarceration. They both had sons named Cian who were the same age. The two women would usually come up to visit their men together (I would play the role of babysitter towards the end of these visits, allowing the couples some quality time). It was on a rare midweek visit, as the girls usually came up at the weekends, that I had an idea. I approached A.C.O. Cahill, the only female A.C.O in Loughan and a really nice lady, and asked her for the unthinkable: would she allow the two girls and their sons access to the auditorium for a couple of minutes to see their men in action? Both Cunny and Fitzer had learned how to play their instruments whilst locked up so neither of these ladies had ever seen the two lads perform. Plus, Fitzer had informed me that only on a rare drunken occasion, when he was a free man, would he sing at the odd karaoke or house party. This particular fact blew me away – his wife Ash had never heard how good he actually was!

Mrs Cahill was sceptical, but after reassuring her they would be out as quick as they had come in, she granted them five minutes. I frantically set up our equipment with Sweeny-Todd, and then proceeded to run out to the kids' visiting area to inform the ladies that they could sneak in but we had to be quick!

We played 'Look at Me That Way', and at its conclusion, well, they were stunned. Cunny's partner was actually in a state of disbelief. The tears of pride began to flow down her face, and as Cunny left his position from behind the drums to embrace her, I turned to Fitzer and said, 'Let's play "Stay" (the Rihanna song).' And so I picked up Sweeny-Todd's acoustic guitar, and we produced one of the most memorable versions of the song we had done to date. You could feel the pain in Fitzer's voice as he sang straight to the most important person in his life, his wife. In hindsight, it probably wasn't the best song to choose as Fitzer's wife was sobbing! Hindsight really is 20/20! But she did add humour to these tears by saying, 'Fuck sake, Gar, the amount of times I'd tell him to shut up singing in the shower or the car, well, I'll never tell him to stop singing again!'

So Cunny's partner was the only proof he had of his own 'hero's journey'. 'If we could pull off an album, well, that would be amazing,' beamed Cunny.

'Too-fuckin'-*right* it would,' came the enthusiastic reply from Fitzer. 'Only problem is, me aul' flower, we don't have anything, not one fuckin' thing, to record this album on. Sure, look at our fuckin' equipment!' he laughed. As a band, we all stopped to survey the battered equipment we used to produce our music. In fact, Sweeny-Todd's guitar and amp actually stood out, as they were in good condition! We all break our shite laughing.

'But we did those gigs, and wrote these songs, with this very equipment, so not too shabby really when ya think about it,' I say with pride.

'Hear, hear,' pipes up Fitzer.

'Anyway,' I continue, 'there is an iMac computer sitting up in the music room in the school, and when I asked Padraig (the music teacher) how proficient he was using it, he quite honestly told me he hadn't a fuckin' clue.' It had been donated to the school in 2008, and basically has only been powered on once or twice. I explained to him I had been doing a BA in Creative Digital Media in the Institute of Technology in Blanchardstown before my incarceration, and we almost solely used these iMacs, in fact we had 'Mac Labs' containing 12 of these incredible machines. So he tells me he'd be only delighted to give it to us in order to try to record some songs. I also know the machine comes pre-loaded with an incredible bit of software known as GarageBand, which was basically a recording suite.

The look of pure happiness on Fitzer's face makes me want to continue. 'I have a good understanding of GarageBand, we have a PA, we have mics, what the fuck is stopping us?' Straight away the lads buy into it. 'When I'm home this weekend, I'll spend some time on the internet and I'll Google how to set up the iMac to the PA. I'll put my findings on a memory stick, print out what I can and, sure, Bob's your uncle!'

'Fuckin' deadly, Gar, *let's do this lads!'* roars Fitzer. Which we did, but my God did things change after this album!

Recording our album became the only thing The Off#enders thought about. We knew we needed to get Cunny's drums down, as he could actually be sent home any day now as he had been passed for Community Service. I quickly got to grips with the GarageBand software and in no time we had created a 'recording studio' in Loughan's auditorium. We finalised the track list for our album and set about recording the guide tracks for each song, which involved the whole band playing live whilst we hit the record button! We then began the painstaking task of recording each drum, guitar, bass and vocal track separately, all of which would culminate in a polished, finished product. That was the plan anyway! None of us had ever recorded before and not one of us had Music Producer as a skill on our CV, but we had time on our hands and the determination for this album, in both songs and production, to be the best we could possibly achieve.

Cunny and Fitzer set about laying down the drum tracks. We placed the now even more battered and worn 'Dora' drum kit on the floor of the auditorium, and positioned three mics around it – we only had three remember! Cunny then set about laying down his beats. But, alas, he was finding it hard to keep the timing at the perfect level that an album demands. This was beginning to chip away at his confidence, but one must remember that at this stage the lad had been playing the drums for a grand total of six months! But we needed help, so in steps Fitzer! For a chap who would not be 'computer savvy', it was incredible how quickly he took to GarageBand and eventually became a master of the software. He had found 'drum loops' embedded in the numerous options available to a GarageBand user, and came up with the idea of finding a loop that matched a particular song we were to record. This loop would be in perfect time to the track, and so all Cunny had to do was play along to the loop thus ensuring better timing, and it bloody worked! I can still feel a smile on my face when I remember watching the massive frame of Cunny sitting behind the teenage-sized drum kit surrounded by the three mics. He would have a set of earphones attached to his head, and he would lay down his drum tracks with aplomb! It was incredible to watch.

But, alas, prison and her rules cared not for our album as the day we all knew was fast approaching had arrived – Cunny was to be released! This was to be the end of an incredible chapter in our lives, having known each other since birth. Don't get me wrong, we were all over the moon for the guy, especially me. Cunny has always been a huge part of my life. I had seen him in his 'addiction days', at his lowest ebb, and I knew of his confidence issues. Yet the man who was to leave Loughan House for the final time was someone who had completely turned his life around. We all shed a tear that morning, as his father Gerry came to collect him, but they were tears of joy. We wished him the best, and as I gave him my final hug, I said to him, 'Remember what you've achieved. Hit the ground running out there. You are an inspiration and we all love you dearly. I look forward to seeing you on the outside as free men!' And with that Cunny had 'left the building'.

Cunny had only laid down drums for 8 of the 20 tracks we had chosen for our, as yet untitled, album. And although the sound quality from these tracks was only at 75 per cent because of our lack of mics to record his drums properly, his playing on these tracks was brilliant. But now we had no drummer! But this wasn't going to deter Fitzer. He came to me and explained, 'Ya know the drum-loops which Cunny was playing over, well, we could just use these drum-loops for the remaining tracks. I know the sound quality will be 100 per cent better than the ones with Cunny playing on them, as the drum-loops will have more clarity, but we are in jail after all. It's not like we can just hire a fuckin' drummer to stand in for Cunny!'

As always his eagerness was infectious, and so that was exactly what we did. Fitzer or myself would find a suitable drum-loop to the track which we were to record and the final result was stunning! It sounded like a proper, polished album that you would purchase in HMV. Myself, Sweeny-Todd and Fitzer spent countless hours laying our guitar and bass tracks down, and soon we had 20 incredible songs ready for vocals. And this, as they say, was when the 'magic' happened.

I was to sing on a few tracks, well, 'shout' is more accurate as I was the 'rocker' in our set-up, but I gave it my best shot. I even penned and sang a song for the woman in my life, Antoinette, entitled 'Rub Me Up the Right Way'. I just hope she likes it! But it was Sweeny-Todd who shocked us all. Fitzer had caught him singing in his room one day and was blown away. Sweeny-Todd, like the rest of The Off#enders, holds Paolo Nutini as one of his biggest inspirations and had that same quirky tone to his voice. He was a bit 'rough and ready', yet he had a lovely tone to his voice. But he was a shy lad until Fitzer got hold of him!

'Look, man, you're singing on the album okay? If ya don't you will regret it for the rest of your life!' Thankfully, Sweeny-Todd bought into Fitzer's enthusiasm, and ended up singing three songs! One was a song I penned for my son called 'Walked for Miles', which told the tale of the last day I spent with him before my incarceration.

> On the day that we walked for miles and miles /
> I had no money but we spent so much time.

I had arranged this song on the album, having learned that you can create a 'string section' comprising violins and the like in GarageBand. I was so proud of the guitar and bass tracks that we put down for this song, with a wonderful flowing drum-loop accompanying them. We had played this song countless times live, and I could sing it without a hitch, but when it came to recording it? I simply couldn't. I was too attached to the lyrics and found that I could not hold back the tears as I tried to tell the song's somewhat sad tale. But Sweeny-Todd, quite bravely, offered to take the lead and I am forever grateful that he did!

Sweeny-Todd also wrote his very first song! It was a haunting and extremely moving tune entitled 'In My Dreams', all coming from our shy and quiet guitarist.

Next to lay down his vocals was Fitzer and he knocked them out of the park! One of the two tracks that Fitzer penned himself on our album was entitled 'Scream My Name', a song again dedicated to his wife Ash. This song was to change all our lives for the better, for so many reasons.

One of the tracks on which Cunny played drums is the hard-hitting 'Can You Hear Me', which I wrote and sang (shouted), and though the sound quality is not as good as the tracks with drum-loops, please remember we were in prison! In fact, please take into account, if you do decide to have a listen to these tunes (most can be found on YouTube), that prison gave The Off#enders lemons and we made the best lemonade we could!

So The Off#enders, after many long nights and even longer months, completed our album, which was entitled 'Released'. I came up with the idea of flooding each and every Irish jail with this CD, which also included two songs that the lads in Mountjoy recorded and sent to Loughan House via email. The album would cost €5 with the proceeds going to three charities, shown at the bottom of the album cover, which were very close to The Off#enders' hearts. I designed the album cover in Conn's classroom with Photoshop.

We'd done it! But my next idea was to change our lives forever!

One of the songs we recorded was Paulo Nutini's 'Iron Sky'. In the short time I spent trying to obtain my BA in Creative Digital Media, I had been shown how to use another of the iMac's pre-loaded software, iMovie, which was a video editing program. So I got to thinking about creating a music video, filled with Google images and some free videos I obtained from YouTube, for our version of this incredible song. Every time I was permitted home, I would trawl through Google images, upload appropriate ones to a memory stick and bring them back to Loughan in order to create my 'vision'. The final result made people stop. No one could believe that, firstly, the song was recorded in prison, but secondly, so was the accompanying video. The vocals are the unmistakable Fitzer, but the 'speech' in the middle? That's me! On the original track, Paolo Nutini uses the actual speech, which is Charlie Chaplin's speech from *The Great Dictator*. But on this track, it's good auld Gar! (Again, available on YouTube.)

People were starting to pay a lot more attention to this prison band! We even did a presentation to members of the hierarchy of the IPS, where we sold them on the idea of selling each album in all of Ireland's closed jails. We played the 'Iron Sky' video for them and it blew their Brown Thomas socks off! Alas, the logistics of mass producing our album and getting it into the jails was a step too far, but maybe some day!

Word had quickly spread to all of Ireland's jails about The Off#enders. We were told that we had inspired lads to do likewise and try to set up their own bands. Myself and Fitzer had given up hope of our dream of playing a gig in Mountjoy, until one day a phone call came to Loughan House that would change everything, and the phone call was for me! It was a fuckin' A.C.O. from Mountjoy who was in the process of putting on a show that would be attended by members of the Irish media. Unfortunately, it was a sad occurrence that led to this gig. Philip Chevron, the Irish singer-songwriter best known as a member of The Pogues, and regarded as one of the most influential figures in Irish punk music, had sadly passed away. But, incredibly, in his will he had stated that he wanted his three favourite guitars to be donated to the school in Mountjoy and they could not have found a better home for them. Billy Bragg, the English singer-songwriter and left-wing activist, was a close friend of Philip Chevron and was to be the guest speaker on the day. But with all the hype surrounding The Off#enders, and the fact we had already played in other jails without incident, we were to be the 'surprise' act to perform! Fuck me!

Unfortunately, we had no drummer available to us, as Cunny had been released, and Sweeny-Todd refused to go back to The Joy as he 'never wanted to see that kip again', which was totally understandable. So it looked like it was to be just myself and Fitzer, as it was at the beginning, that would fly The Off#enders' flag. Incredibly, though, Mountjoy actually hired a professional drummer to jam with us. We got the school in Loughan House to email this drummer the two tracks we were to play, so he could become familiar with them.

To say myself and Fitzer were excited was the understatement of the year. We'd get to jam with the lads in the music 'lab' of Mountjoy again one last time, and would get to show Brian, Lisa, and Paul how far we'd come. Fitzer also pointed out that we should bring copies of the album with us and the video to 'Iron Sky'.

'Sure, ya never know who might be there that day, Gar!' said my good friend.

Oh, how fuckin' right he was!

Chapter 47

Back to The Joy

So the morning of our trip back to Mountjoy had arrived. Mr. Nolan, who has got to be the one of the quietest officers I have ever met, was to be our escort. It seemed like the whole population of Loughan House had gathered outside of the Main House to wish us luck. It felt so good to know we had the lads' support. Fitzer had the brilliant idea of donating his own handmade Cajon to the school of Mountjoy, and I was only too happy to double that donation and give the lads the one he made for me too. We filled up the Ford Mondeo estate car with our guitars and the Cajons, say our goodbyes and set off for Dublin. Destination Mountjoy!

We had a good laugh in the car with Mr. Nolan, as myself and Fitzer drew out more and more of his personality. I think he really enjoyed that long drive with us as we cracked jokes and told our 'prison tales'. We arrived at the famous gates of Mountjoy at around noon and, well, it felt very surreal for me and Fitzer. We had both sworn we would never see this vile building again, and yet here we were re-entering her walls voluntarily! As we stepped inside the massive arched gate, each of us carrying our guitars and Cajons, we could feel the looks of the officers on gate duty that day – in fact, we hear one of them mumble, 'Who the fuck do they think they are?' It's amazing how many people would rather you didn't reform whilst in prison! Fuck him!

Next, we experienced for the first time what every visitor who visited us whilst we were caged in this dungeon had to go through – the search procedure. Our guitars and Cajons were run through an x-ray machine to make sure we weren't trying to smuggle in contraband. We were then searched and presented to the sniffer dog, who does her job of checking us out. We pass with flying colours!

As we leave the search area, we're met by an A.C.O., the man who was running the show that was to be put on the next day, but something seems off. Firstly, he informs us that we would not be permitted to go straight up to the school, as he had promised. This was to be the first of many promises that this A.C.O. would not fulfil for us.

Fitzer smells a rat. 'That's all bollox. He told us on the phone how we'll have ample time to jam and get our sound right. How he had arranged for us to be left in the school while the rest of the lads were on lockdown. Something doesn't feel right here Gary!' How right he was.

We were brought into the main building of The Joy and, unfortunately, it felt like I was only there yesterday. The unforgettable stench seemed as rank as ever, and the chaos that occurs in this jail on a daily basis was taking place right in front of our eyes. I have never appreciated Loughan House and the ethos it offers more than I did at that very moment, as memories of how life was spent in this ageing jail came flooding into my mind.

The A.C.O. turns to us and says, 'Right lads, firstly, thank you so, so much for agreeing to come from Loughan House to do this. As you know, you will both be staying here tonight, and unfortunately we have no choice but to put you both on The Block.'

Wait, *what*? The fuckin' block? This particular disgusting area of The Joy is located in the prison's bowels and is reserved as a punishment area! This is where you go if you've been a really bad boy in The Joy. It housed Mountjoy's most troublesome lads, who were left on 23 hour lockdown. And that's where they're putting us! I whisper to Fitzer, as we were led towards this stomach-turning part of the prison, 'What the actual fuck, Fitzer? The fuckin' Block?' I say, my anger levels reaching a height I didn't feel comfortable with.

'I know, buddy, but look, it's only for tonight so fuck it, don't show these pricks that it's getting to us, don't give them the satisfaction.' Wise words from a wise man, but we were about to be pushed way beyond our limits.

We arrived at the disgusting cells which we were to be housed in, and were informed we've missed dinner, so 'tough shit lads'. Our cells faced each other, and as we get settled inside these filthy rooms, I catch sight of Fitzer and his face was telling a thousand stories.

'What time will we be let out in order to go up to the school to meet the lads and run through our set?' I ask the skinny officer who was about to slam my cell door shut, but he completely ignores me! Arsehole! I feel like Fitzer and myself were yet again being punished for showing initiative. You must remember, we volunteered to return to this vile kip! Don't get me wrong, we were not under the impression that we would be put up in luxury, with four-poster beds and room service. We just assumed, *like we were promised*, that we would be housed with the general population, thus allowing us to be treated the same as all the other prisoners. Fitzer, who was sitting behind a cell door across the landing from me, knows what I'm like, and I know what he's like, so I knew we were both freaked!

After what seemed like an eternity, another officer opens our cell doors and orders us up to the school. Fitzer was clearly irate. 'Fuckin' *wankers,* Gar. I'm tellin' ya, I feel like tellin' 'em to stick their "gig" up their hole and get us back to Loughan! Fuckin' lying bastards!' It was very rare to see my good mate this irate, but for no reason whatsoever, at least none that we could think of, we were being treated like 'punishment prisoners'.

We were taken from the depths of The Joy up into The Circle, which hadn't changed one bit! The officers' station was still a hive of activity. The same surreal feeling washes over me as I set my eyes upon this massive structure once again, but soon our mood lifts! We were led towards the blue barred gate that grants access to the school, and this alone would be enough to lighten our mood, but guess who walked past myself and Fitzer as we waited for the gate to open? None other than The Gaffer from the kitchen.

'Well, would ya look who it is, the f-f-fuckin' Off#enders, or whatever yas are c-c-called. Yas must think you're b-b-both really special, do yas?' came the stammered words from this gobshite's mouth. Amazingly enough, after just a fleeting glance at each other, myself and Fitzer do the exact same thing at the exact same time – we completely ignore the man. As Fitzer said to me many moons ago, 'He's just not worth it!' But The Gaffer's words were starting to put the pieces of the puzzle together for us. Some of these officers thought we had a high opinion of ourselves, and though nothing could be further from the truth, our guard would need to stay up!

Then we walked into the hall of Mountjoy's school and all the bullshit we had just encountered from the officers completely evaporated. There on the stage was Mountjoy's new band and they were fuckin' *great*! Scotty, our long-haired lover from Glasgow, was the first to greet me.

'Look at you, Gary, all fuckin' slim,' he says, sounding remarkably like Billy Connolly.

'Scotty, ya mad bastard, man, is it good to see you,' I reply. We hug it out, and I continue my trip down memory lane as I shake the hands of some of the most amazing lads I have ever met in my life, realising I never thought I'd see them again!

I look across the hall and see that Fitzer was in his element. He was with his mentor, Paul, the music teacher, and I tell myself not to intrude on their catch-up.

After a few minutes of chit-chat, Paul says the words we all wanted to hear, 'Let's have a jam, lads' and fuck me did we jam! We didn't play anything in particular, we just played. The unity we shared that evening was something I'll take to the grave with me. Myself and Fitzer then let the lads hear some songs from the album which they all loved. Fitzer asks Paul about the drummer arranged for tomorrow.

'Look, lads,' he starts, 'he was never sent your songs. I'm sorry, lads, it has nothing to do with us. But he'll be here first thing in the morning, and I know the guy, he's incredible, and will pick up the songs in no time, so don't worry.' Another lie from the now infamous A.C.O.! He told us the drummer actually liked our songs! Fuckin' hell!

Soon an officer appears to inform the lads of Mountjoy that it's time to wrap it up. Myself and Fitzer say our goodbyes and tell the lads we can't wait until tomorrow. We're going to show the outside world what reform-willing prisoners can do! Myself and Fitzer then head back to the stage, as Fitzer wanted to spend a bit of time getting our sound right. But as we make our way towards the stage, the overweight officer pipes up, 'Eh, are yas fuckin' right or wha'?' he drools.

'The A.C.O. said he got clearance for us to be allowed up here to ready ourselves for tomorrow,' I say.

'Did he now?' comes the sarcastic reply of the officer. 'Don't mind him, there is no fuckin' way yas are staying here, *so come on the fuck*!' He bellows this last line at us.

I see that Fitzer was being pushed, as was I, but again, we chose not to lower ourselves. As we are led back to 'the dungeon', Fitzer says to me, 'That A.C.O. can fuck off, man, the fuckin' lies he's told us! Look Gar, the gig is early tomorrow, so they'll have to let us out early for it. We'll get up to the school, I'll sort the sound, we'll jam with the new drummer and we'll blow their fuckin' heads off!'

'Damn straight buddy,' I reply fervently.

We are returned to our filthy cells and I shout good night over to Fitzer. I enter the cell, and see that someone has left whatever was for tea on a plastic plate on the battered MDF table which belonged to the cell. The plastic plate was covered by another, and when I remove this plate, I'm met with ice-cold curry, which has started to congeal! The fuckin' pricks! Again, we didn't want any preferential treatment. We had no delusions of grandeur. We just thought we'd be treated like every other prisoner, and not like we were being punished. Loughan House seemed a million miles away as I sat at the edge of the steel bed, its scruffy duvet cover omitting an awful stench.

If I could pause here for a moment, I'd like to make something clear. Despite the success of The Off#Enders, it wasn't as if I thought I wasn't incarcerated anymore. Ultimately, the band became one of the biggest factors that led to me becoming a reformed character, however if I had ever lost sight that I was a prisoner – which as I say I never did – this fuckin' hellhole was making sure I knew I still was. I felt so low as I sat in that freezing cold cell that night, my only company a fuckin' huge cockroach who had taken up residence in one of the corners of this depressing cell, and knowing that my best friend was going through the same bullshit across the landing from me. My heart had gone out of playing the gig. Fuck you Mountjoy, and all the shite you stand for!

But maybe all was not lost ...

Chapter 48

'Here's Your Breakfast, Rock Star!'

I didn't sleep a wink that night, I just couldn't. I began doing countless push-ups and sit-ups to try to tire myself out in order to fall into a slumber, one that would remove me from this cell momentarily as I was taken away on whatever dreams my subconscious permitted, but it wasn't to be. Dawn had begun to break as a small amount of a new day's light crept through the window of my cell. I could hear an officer make his way from cell to cell delivering what I assumed was breakfast, and I wasn't wrong! The lock turns in my cell door and on its opening, there stands an officer with a white plastic bag in his hand. He throws the bag towards me and says, 'Here's your breakfast, rock star!' The bag lands on the cold grey floor as he smirks and slams shut the cell door once again.

I am seething! I pick up the bag to examine what delectables await me, only to find that the impact of the bag hitting the floor has caused the milk carton inside to burst, thus soaking the small packet of Weetabix and slice of bread contained inside. He ruined my fuckin' Weetabix! This would usually be enough to send me over the edge – my fuckin' Weetabix! – but I needed to calm down! Myself and Fitzer were here for a reason and I would *not* let these narrow-minded screws destroy what looks to be an incredible day.

I sat on the freezing cold floor and started to control my breathing. I zoned out of the walls of this prison cell, and allowed my mind to wander. I thought of what The Off#enders had achieved in order to be here today. I thought of the lads housed in Mountjoy, and how they must adhere to the strict regime of this jail on a daily basis. I fully appreciated Loughan House and realised how lucky I was to become one of her inmates. I focused on the upcoming gig and ordered myself to give the performance of my life. Sure, myself and Fitzer would be out of here today after the gig, and on our way back to Loughan House. Or would we?

After a couple of hours, I hear movement outside on the landing of The Block. I hear my good friend's voice, 'Ah, howya, officer, it's been a while,' he laughs. Somehow this man always manages to be positive, even in such a negative environment. But the officer ignores him as he makes his way to my cell door to open it. When he does, I see that it is an officer myself and Fitzer knew from our kitchen days.

'Morning officer,' but he has turned away.

'Officer, can we have a shower please?' requests Fitzer. Again he is ignored. I walk the short trip over to my good friend to see how he is. 'Look man, they're fuckin' with us, we need to realise this and just let them get on with it. If we react then they've won,' he says. But again, they were pushing us very hard!

We were still seeking permission to use the showers, but this was falling on deaf ears. We were about to blow a fuse when the officer returns and orders us towards the shower room located at the end of the landing. Myself and Fitzer don't speak as he leads us into this blue-tiled room. We were just happy to get a shower to be honest! Upon entering this freezing cold shower area, the officer proceeds to slam shut the gate that we've just walked through, thus locking us inside.

'Fuckin' great this is, wha'?' laughs Fitzer, followed by, 'Fuck them Gar, today is going to be a *great* day!' He's still laughing as he enters the shower but his laughter subsides a little as the ice-cold water hits his already shivering body. *Jaysus* that was one cold shower!

We decide to wear our smiles for the rest of the day no matter *what*! As we dry off, we see no sign of an officer to let us out of the shower area. A prisoner was mopping the large landing of The Block and I ask would he tell any of the officers on duty that we were ready to come out. He does, but the officer in question seems to take a lifetime making his way towards us. But Fitzer has a plan. Upon unlocking the barred gate, Fitzer turns to the officer and with a huge smile on his face says, 'Thank you very much officer, much obliged.' I also thank this officer in the same upbeat manner. We were going to show them that we would not be affected by the bullshit that they were creating around us. Fitzer whistles as he heads back to his cell to change into his clothes.

'This is going to be an amazing experience buddy,' I chirp to my good friend, raising the level of my voice for added effect. This was prison life, we were in The Block where it seems to be the norm to treat the prisoners like shit. So we would put up with it, and do ourselves proud in front of the unnerving crowd that was to gather in Mountjoy's school hall. Members of the media, Billy fuckin' Bragg – we've got one chance to show these people what we're about, and we were going to grab this chance by the scruff!

We were led back up to the school, and all the lads attending that day were milling around like ants frantically ensuring everything was in order. 'Ah, howya lads,' beams the music teacher Paul. 'Did yas sleep okay?' Myself and Fitzer don't answer and instead we both fall about laughing.

Paul, looking a bit confused, then proceeds to introduce us to our drummer for the day. This man was in his mid-forties and looked like the quintessential rock star! His black hair was spiked and 'messed-up', but was done so on purpose to create a 'look' that probably took him some time to achieve. He was exuding 'coolness' from every pore of his skinny frame.

'Hi lads, right, let's just get to it. Why don't you two set up and show me these tunes?' he asks, smiling. Myself and Fitzer comply and soon we were jamming with this absolutely fantastic drummer. We had chosen 'Look at Me That Way' and 'Room for One More', the latter being a song that Fitzer had co-written with another inmate whilst in Mountjoy. The drummer loved the tunes and after only a couple of run-throughs he had them mastered. Excellent!

The hall in Mountjoy had never looked so good. The floor was gleaming. The walls were covered in fantastic art that was created by some of the jail's inmates. There was a small kitchen area just off this hall which was as busy as a beehive! To see how hard the chosen inmates had worked in order to assist in the making of the food for today's presentation was commendable. There were 'French Fancies' and exotic cheesecakes, and there was finger food that Neven Maguire would have been proud of!

And so the time had arrived. The Off#enders were to be the last act of the day. As the media started to fill the hall, they were met by the Irish Prison Services Press Officer who duly informs them that all prisoners were off limits, there were to be exactly *no* interviews with any of the inmates! This press officer also tells myself and Fitzer to just stick to singing our songs and to leave 'chatting with the crowd' whilst on stage to a bare minimum. Eh, we'll see about that Mr. Press Officer, for I had something up my sleeve!

I see one of my heroes enter the room, Newstalk's very own Tom Dunne! Although he is now a radio presenter, I knew the man from his days as the singer/songwriter with the incredible Irish band Something Happens that were around during the mid-1980s and early '90s. I approach him nervously to introduce myself, but he seemed preoccupied so I leave him to it.

'Is everybody in? The ceremony is about to begin.' Here goes nothing ...

Brian Murphy, the very man who I threw my headphones on in order for him to hear Fitzer sing, and who allowed Fitzer a transfer to Loughan House, begins proceedings. Mr. Murphy had recently taken on the daunting task of becoming Governor of Mountjoy. He welcomes the attendees and gives a quick synopsis of how the day will run. The first person to speak was the sister of the late Philip Chevron, Deborah. She seems nervous as she takes to the constructed podium that is placed stage-left. She begins to speak of her brother and his amazing career, allowing all that were glued to her words access to some of the more private sides of this remarkable man. She tells of how imperative it was for Philip in his dying days that his favourite guitars be presented to Mountjoy. She seems sad as she speaks so fondly of her beloved brother, and it moved both prisoners and 'free folk' alike. I was lucky to speak to Deborah later that day, and she informed me that she was terrified whilst speaking to us all ... wow!

Just before she left the stage, she introduced the next speaker. 'Ladies and Gentlemen, Mr. Billy Bragg!' I have been a huge fan of Billy Bragg for a long time so I'm quite taken aback. Again, his words regarding Philip Chevron were both insightful and amazing. He spoke of some of the funny times they shared when they gigged together. But he put a massive emphasis on the presentation of these three beautiful guitars. Billy Bragg explains that he runs a charity in England called 'Jail Guitars', or 'Guitars Behind Bars' as it is sometimes known, which provide guitars and instruments to the jails of England. He tells of how he would love to bring this scheme into the jails of Ireland, and tells of the conversations he had with the late Philip Chevron pertaining to this very subject. He feels that was why he was chosen to stand in Mountjoy that day. He then shows the guitars, and as a guitarist myself, my breath was simply taken away! They were absolutely beautiful.

Billy Bragg then jokes, in his 'cockney' twang, 'Well, I better make sure they work,' and proceeds to pick up the only acoustic guitar of the three, and plays a beautiful rendition of 'Redemption Song' by Bob Marley. He ends his talk by explaining how he feels music can heal the damaged, how it can give prisoners a different focus. Hear, hear, Mr. Bragg, that is the mission statement of The Off#enders! He leaves the stage to a standing ovation. I will never forget that moment, sitting beside my best friend and band mate as we listened to the incredible Billy Bragg talk and sing. Again, wow!

Next to take to the stage was the Mountjoy band, accompanied by Paul and Brian from the music school and by God did they rock! The played a blistering version of 'The Bucket' by Kings of Leon that nearly ripped the roof clean off! You could sense their nerves, yet you could also see they had rehearsed their arses off for this! They can forever hold their heads high as they brought a massive cheer from all that were lucky enough to witness their show.

'And now, Ladies and Gentlemen, we have a couple of members of a very exciting prison band that was actually formed here in Mountjoy many moons ago. They are currently housed in Loughan House Open Prison, but willingly came back to Mountjoy to perform for you today. There has been great excitement surrounding this band, and so without further ado I present to you ... The Off#enders!'

We take to the stage, and I feel sick with the nerves. Ever since my first day in Mountjoy I have sporadically experienced butterflies in my stomach for many different reasons, and although I love the beauty of butterflies, I just wish they'd fuck off out of my stomach! I introduce myself, Fitzer, and Paul the music teacher who has kindly offered to take the role of lead guitar, which I am only too happy to oblige. Nothing quite matches jamming with this guy, so it's an honour. Myself and Fitzer have one last consultation with our stand-in drummer, then we begin.

'Look at Me That Way' was unbelievably well received. The drummer was *incredible*. I have never felt so alive inside as when I looked out at the gathered crowd and absorbed their applause. I turn to Fitzer and he simply smiles and winks! Next was Fitzer's own song, 'Room for One More', a moving bluesy number which shows off this man's rich, deep voice. Again, the drummer jams with us to perfection, as does the music teacher Paul. I cannot fully articulate my true emotion as the song drew to a close. They were on their feet, *on their feet!*

I turn to Fitzer and give him a 'man' hug. 'We fuckin' did it, Gar, even after all the bullshit we've been through over the last 24 hours, we still did it!' he whispers to me. Now for my surprise ...

I walk towards the mic to address the audience. 'If I may, I would like to say a few words.'

The look on the face of the IPS Press Officer was priceless. He was heard saying, 'Get your man *off* that fuckin' stage!'

You can hear the gathered media scramble to get their dictaphones or smartphones ready, hoping I would say something controversial or damning about Mountjoy or the Irish Prison Service in general. But nothing could be further from the truth.

I began, 'Firstly, thank you Deborah for your amazing talk at the beginning of today's proceedings. You have a beautiful way of speaking and I think everybody in this hall today was honoured to walk with you through your memories of your incredible brother, so thank you.' There was a wonderful round of applause for this special lady.

'Also, a massive thank you from us prisoners and fans to you Mr. Bragg. You are an inspiration to many, but your kind words and feelings regarding prisoners is something we're not used to hearing, so thank you. Oh, and not a bad version of Bob Marley's classic too.' This brings laughter and applause.

'Also, a massive cheer should be afforded to the Mountjoy band that played for you today, simply incredible lads,' I say. Again, the applause rings out as these men get the praise they deserve.

'Myself and Fitzer would now like to present two Cajons to the school of Mountjoy, both of which Fitzer hand-made in Loughan House Open Prison, where we are currently held.' We hand over the Cajons to Rob, the drummer of the Mountjoy band, as again the crowd begins clapping.

'I would also like to give praise to the amazing teaching staff here in Mountjoy.' And in truth, this was my sole reason for taking to the stage to speak that day. In attendance was the Director General of the IPS, and many of his staff. The Governor of Mountjoy, Brian Murphy, was also in attendance, and we had the Irish media gathered, so what better way to highlight these three individuals and what they do! I then proceed to read out a chapter from this very book which speaks of their amazing work, and it does the job. There was a massive round of applause for these three lovely individuals as I brought the chapter to a close, and they fuckin' deserved it!

Lastly, I draw everyone's attention to the large projector screen the lads had set up for Fitzer and me. It was attached to a laptop that contained the DVD copy of my video to 'Iron Sky'. The Press Officer frantically makes his way towards us to try to stop us, but he's too late, it's begun. The room was as dark as we could create it as the video to 'Iron Sky' gets its first airing. Myself and Fitzer stare at the screen, afraid to turn around, but when it ended? Well, nobody could have predicted what happened! The look of shock that has spread through each face in the audience was actually quite funny. There was a split-second of silence then a huge cheer and loud clapping!

'It's all right, isn't it?' laughs Fitzer, nonchalant. We were surrounded by all in attendance in order to pick our brains as to how we recorded the song and made the video. Tom Dunne approaches me, and congratulates me on what he described as, 'An incredible cover of an incredible song, but that video? Wow!' Tom fuckin' Dunne!

The IPS Press Officer deals with the media's queries and then pulls myself and Fitzer to one side. 'I thought I was going to have a heart attack when you began speaking, Gary, you're a very bold boy, but everything you said was perfect.'

'I'm really sorry I didn't tell you, officer, but I was afraid you wouldn't permit me to praise the teaching staff here,' I offer as a reply.

'It was perfect, Gary, but that video? Fuckin' hell! Well done lads. But look, they all want a piece of yas now, so just watch what you say okay? Don't speak about why you're in jail, and don't mention any prisoners by name, okay?'

Fitzer turns and says, 'They'll have to get out the aul' IPS history books, again, Gar me auld pal, sure, they can just dedicate a section to us in it. Fuckin' *hell*, Gary wha'?' We both start to laugh. Yet again, we'd done it!

I then noticed a well-dressed man lingering around who has avoided us to allow us to answer any questions that we were allowed to. Eventually, this extremely confident man approaches and introduces himself as Mr. Brian Whitehead, CEO of the Olympia Theatre in Dublin, head of MCD Music promoters, and singer/songwriter Ryan Sheridan's manager!

He says, 'Look lads, I don't get impressed that easily but you two have fuckin' blown me away. The production of the song, to be achieved in prison, is simply incredible and as for that video? Wow lads!' Is this really happening? He's not finished. 'I've done my research and I know you have a bit of time left, Fitzer – by the way, some fuckin' voice ya have there – but you are nearing the end of your sentence Gary?' This was true, my incarceration was drawing to a close. 'Well Gary, when you're out I want you to come to my office in The Olympia and bring that album with ya. Well done lads, incredible!' And then he just walks off. Myself and Fitzer are too stunned to talk, so we just start laughing yet again!

The day was a complete success and as we said our goodbyes to the Mountjoy men for the final time, well it was a moving experience. We wish the lads well, as they do us, and we thank them for looking after us. We also thank the amazing teaching staff, with Fitzer making sure to inform Paul that he was the sole creator of the amazing bass player that he had become. We pack our guitars and bass away, only to be met by the 'lying' A.C.O. 'Lads, I'm sorry. You have not been treated well. I know this and I'm sorry.'

This takes stones, and so we are about to accept his apology until Fitzer says, 'Sure look, fuck it, we're heading back to Loughan now.'

'Well,' he interrupts, 'I can't get yas an escort until tomorrow morning.'

'Ah *fuck off*,' I shout as I turn away from him.

'Gary, fuck it,' starts Fitzer, 'one more night, fuck it! None of these can take away from what we achieved today, so let them have their fun!' Again, such wise words from my greatest friend!

I actually slept that night. A combination of lack of sleep from the previous night and the incredible events of the day we just had brought on a very welcoming slumber. The officers who open the doors of our cells in The Block the next morning were of a very different nature.

'Morning lads, you're the talk of the town. Fair play to yas lads, well done,' says the friendly older officer. 'Grab a bit of brekkie if yas like, but you're both out of here in the next few minutes.'

I amble over to Fitzer. 'Did ya sleep pal?' I ask.

'Eventually buddy. That was some fuckin' day, Gar!' says Fitzer which he follows with, 'I'm just finding it hard to get rid of the bad taste this place has put in my mouth over the last couple of days.'

'I know buddy, but fuck it, come on, let's get the fuck outta here before they decide to keep us!'

We again make our way out of Mountjoy, this time both of us confidently knowing we will never return. A very small number of small-minded officers had tarnished what was a life-changing experience for myself and Fitzer, but the officer who brought us back to Loughan was nothing like them. Jolly Officer Kelly will always go down as one of the nicest officers myself and Fitzer had ever come across. He was definitely hand-picked to escort us back to Loughan in order to repair some of the damage Mountjoy had inflicted on us, and I would say it was the A.C.O. who had lied to us so often who arranged this particular escort. So to that A.C.O., I forgive you. I understand you wanted the best show possible and you wanted to highlight the talent that exists in an Irish prison, but here's the funny thing. If you had been straight from the start and told us what we would have to endure, we would still have come!

Chapter 49

'Mama, I'm Coming Home'

We received a hero's welcome upon our return to Loughan, although Chief Carrick was not pleased that they kept us an extra day. We could have spoken of the shite we'd just been through, but we decided not to. Instead, we tell our amazing tale of what happened that day. Chief Carrick mentions that we were the topic of conversation on some radio talk show, but she can't remember which one. But she said it was nothing but positive feedback and she informs us that she was filled to the brim with pride. She then pulls me to one side. 'Well, Gary, next Monday is *the* day. You'll leave here for the last time a free man.' It felt strange hearing these words as they pertained to me. 'Are you feeling okay leading up to Monday, Gary?' asks Chief Carrick.

'Ah yeah, I'm grand Miss,' I lied. For I was far from grand. I was filled with fear of what was to become of me. I was 100 per cent institutionalised. I had used my prison routine as a way to focus my energy and put in the hard work that was needed to change my life. But what would become of me once I was released? Would I fall at the first hurdle?

I'm sure Chief Carrick notes this, but she decides to leave it for now. 'Sure, I'll talk to you closer to Monday Gary,' she says reassuringly. I turn away from her and head back to my room in Pine Lodge, the air seeming frost-filled on that gloomy Friday afternoon.

On the Saturday morning I decide to walk the entire complex of Loughan House on my own. I put earphones on my head, which in fact were connected to nothing at all but gave the impression I am listening to music, thus informing the lads to leave me to it. I just wanted to experience this on my own.

I start in the Main House and admire how clean it is thanks to the amazing work of not just the exceptional cleaners, but of the Prison Committee and the Red Cross, both of which I am proud to say I was a part of. I enter the dining hall and think of the laughs we had as we sat around one of the many round tables. I make my way to the gym, which I had grown to love. Not only was I responsible for the opening and closing of this gym, which was a role I was honoured to have held, but I was also the cleaner and it was fuckin' spotless. I head out to the visiting area and reminisce on the few visits I received from my mam, each one as enjoyable as the last. I take a peek into the kids' visiting area and marvel once more at Beasey's creations which adorn the walls. I am moved.

I head up to the school and thank its walls for providing me with the tools I needed to fulfil my dreams, my hopes for a brighter future. I think of the times I attempted woodwork, only to be told to 'leave it to the experts' on more than one occasion. This brings a smile to my face. I allow myself to reminisce about Mary, our Home Economics teacher, and the lady who did the impossible – she taught me how to cook something! But she was so much more than just a teacher, she was a friend. I'm really going to miss her. And I was also going to miss the man who encouraged me the most, Conn the IT teacher. This man was the reason you are holding this book (so you can blame him). He was a constant stream of support and I am forever in his debt. He actually bought me a parting gift, Stephen King's *On Writing: A Memoir of the Craft*, in which Mr. King takes a break from scaring the shite out of us and gives his 'guide' to writing. As I turn the cover of this amazing book, I see Conn has written me a little message: 'Gary, this is one of the most interesting books I have read, and I hope you enjoy it – I also hope it inspires you to keep writing along with all your other creative activities. You have a multitude of talents to draw on to make your future bright. I wish you the very best of luck with everything – Conn.' I am (drum roll, please) fuckin' bawling. Below is a picture of the amazing man himself, along with the wonderful head of the school, Brenda, who was always on hand when I needed her the most. This was the day I won the 'Writing in Prison Competition', as they handed me the book in which my story was published and my winner's pen, which my mam now gets great use of as she attempts to break the fuckin' world record for 'Most Word Search puzzles done *ever*!'

I turn and walk away from the school with a heavy heart.

Upon my return to Pine Lodge, I can see what my final few hours as a prisoner will entail, basically, getting the shite slagged out of me. The lads were going to torment me! But this was the done thing, in fact, I've done it myself countless times when one of the lads was nearing freedom, and so I just take the abuse, all friendly in manner, in my stride. The notable absentee was Fitzer, as he had been granted an overnight, which I was delighted about as he'd get to wake up with his son. My buddy Gaga made a wonderful feast that night, and we all sat around the table telling stories about the times we'd shared together during our 'whack'. It was a great laugh.

I awoke that Sunday and wasn't sure how I felt. Of course I was excited to be going home, but prison has had its effect on me. I spent the day mostly on my own. I knew Fitzer would be back later that evening and we would have a good auld chat, but I wasn't ready to say goodbye to him again. And this time there was no chance that I might see him again soon. I would not be permitted to visit him as I will have become an ex-con. I would be able to ring the prison to talk to him, so this gave me a little comfort, but I knew I couldn't start sobbing in front of him as he's not into that shite. In fact, I wonder how he will take to reading what an impact he had on my life ... if he even reads this fuckin' book! So, I come up with a plan.

I head to the auditorium, firstly to soak in the ambience of the room, and to let my mind wander to the countless gigs we had performed in this wonderful theatre. I think of all the people we made happy through our music. I think of the countless, sometimes frustrating hours spent recording our album. I make my way to the stage and power up the iMac that is sitting on its own on an old wooden table. I use the camera that was integrated into the iMac and make short 'goodbye' videos for the lads as a bit of a joke, that is, until I make Fitzer's. What starts off as me slagging him and 'having a laugh' quickly descends into me becoming an emotional wreck. I cannot emphasise enough how upset I was. The last time I shed tears in this manner was when my beautiful daughter died, so here's the thing – why the fuck am I crying like this? Because if it wasn't for this bloke, for his friendship,

I don't think I would have made it through prison. He saved my life in more ways than one. And just look at the incredible journey we both had! I contemplate deleting what has now just become a video of me crying my bloody eyes out, but choose not to, as I want him to see how thankful I am for his friendship.

When he arrives back from his overnight that evening we don't speak of my Balls Roughness. Instead he fills me in on his last 24 hours spent with his family. Midway through our chat, I am summoned to the A.C.O.'s office. I tell Fitzer I won't be long and make my way over to the Main House, only to be stopped in my tracks by Chief Carrick – on a Sunday? The Governor and Chief of Loughan House have the weekends off, so this has shocked me. She directs me to her office above the visiting area which is next door to the Governor's.

'Right, Gary, I'm going to make this short and sweet. From the bottom of my heart, thank you for all you have created here in Loughan House. Your work has been incredible and you really made a difference to life here. I can't actually believe I'm saying this, but I'm going to miss you, in fact we all are.'

I am stunned! Again, speechless! She hands me a 'Good Luck' card and wishes me all the best for my future. I offer her a hug, which she accepts. Chief Carrick gets my eternal thanks for always believing in me.

I return to Fitzer's immaculately kept room in Pine Lodge and tell him what just happened. 'Fuckin' hell, but it's nothing you don't deserve, Gar. You have affected a lot of people since ya got yourself banged up, me included pal.'

I successfully quell the tears as I thank him for such kind words. We take a trip down memory lane, and what a lane it was. I say my goodnights and head to my room, and as soon as I close the heavy wooden door, I begin to let the tears flow. I'm really gonna fuckin' miss him just 'being there', miss his support, miss the fact that he is a crazy, funny headcase – I'm just really going to miss him!

I woke up and told myself to begin right now to embrace the new Gary and to face the world with my head held high. I only pack my clothing as every electrical appliance, or anything else I have, I leave for Fitzer and the lads. My brothers Noel and Jason were arriving shortly in order to bring their baby brother home. I make my way out on to the landing and am met by my truly great friends. I'm not going to be able to stop these fuckin' tears. Fitzer carries my bags, and as we step outside I see my brother Jason's unmistakable black van, with its multi-coloured sign advertising his painting and decorating company. I embrace both of my brothers in a way I never have before. I'm so happy to see them! Fitzer meets my brothers for the first time and they chit-chat, while I go about saying my final goodbyes. Mrs. Mulligan gives me a tear-soaked hug and wishes me all the best. She then strangely asks my brother Noel for his phone number. I don't pay this much attention, as I firstly say goodbye to Gaga and thank him for all the laughs ... and the fuckin' slagging! Next was Sweeny-Todd. I simply hug the life out of him and thank him for what he brought to The Off#enders. I know this guy will be a huge success in his life. Then it's Fitzer.

I grab hold of him and hug the life out of him. I don't care who is looking at me, but I need to think of Fitzer, too, so I let go. 'Thanks, Fitzer, thanks for fuckin' everything!' I say through tear-filled eyes.

'Fuck that Gar, thank *you*. Look at what ya offered us! You're a mad bastard but you're *our* mad bastard.' He says all this with his usual enthusiasm. 'And one last thing,' he continues. 'You better make fuckin' sure you ring Antoinette as soon as you get a phone. She's "The One", Gary, just like in *Journeyman*.' God, I hope he's right, for I have fallen hard for this amazing, caring woman – but does she feel the same?

I'm so proud of what my two brothers did next. Jason, who was the singer in our family, begins, 'Fitzer, firstly what a fuckin' voice, me and you have got to jam someday, and secondly, thanks for lookin' after the little bro.'

Noel then chimes in with, 'Yeah, Fitzer, we've heard so much from Gar about ya, you're a really cool guy, man, so from all our family, thank you and we look forward to seeing *you* as a free man.'

I give Fitzer one last hug and tell him to 'keep fighting the good fight' and then I jump into the van. I can't take it any more. I'm finding it too hard to say goodbye. My brothers jump in and before you know it I'm leaving Loughan House for the last time. I am leaving prison *for the last time* ('Yes it's good, oh it's good, it's good to be free').

I am crying, my supportive brothers allowing me the time I need to adjust. Suddenly, Noel hands me his phone and tells me to, quote, 'Have a read of fuckin' that!' It was a text message from Mrs. Mulligan. I would like to keep the contents of this text message private, but one thing she did say, which blows my mind, was that I stopped her from retiring. She had fallen out of love with her job, and felt maybe it had run its course until she met me! Fuckin' hell! I plonk back into my seat and try to fully absorb these words.

And soon I'm home and there, standing in the kitchen of the house I was born in, is my mother Lily. All who know her would tell you just how wonderful she is. Along with one other equally special person, she was the driving force in my need for change. I love this woman so much. I had let her down with my actions almost three years ago – I served a total of two years and nine months – and yet her love and support for me never wavered. And so, as I embrace her in our kitchen, the sun setting behind the shed in our back garden, I look into her vibrant eyes and say, 'Mama, I'm home.'

Chapter 50

The Beginning, Not the End

So there you have it. I have just realised that I have completely laid myself bare for all to inspect and dissect. I have put out to the universe my most personal thoughts, dreams and fears. How will it be received? I have no idea. I wouldn't blame anyone for thinking I was glamourising prison life, but I promise you I am not! I couldn't blame anyone for thinking, 'Jaysus, he had a great fuckin' time,' because in many ways I had. And that is the strangest thing. In the first couple of months of my release I actually longed to be back! Loughan House had become my 'home'. I was *someone* in there – Chair of the Prisoners' Committee, guitarist in an amazing band. I had a job that I got paid €12 a week for and I earned every cent of that!

But out here in the 'free' world? I felt I was nobody. I was of no importance to anyone. I started to slip back into drinking heavily. I was self-medicating, trying to quell the thoughts I was having about prison, about myself. Everybody was always telling me that it was amazing what I had achieved 'inside', but I felt worthless out here on the 'outside'. It felt more like the 'outside of life' to me as I was feeling more and more like I wasn't fitting in. Mountjoy has made my OCD a million times worse, as I am always haunted by the memories of the filth and the smell, the cockroaches, never wanting to be surrounded by dirt again. And I'm sure my mam was sick of buying packets of kitchen rolls upon my release, as I got through them like mad. And the drinking. It needed to stop. I was losing the battle to keep the new and improved Gary going. I knew I'd never again commit a crime, solely for the reason that I *never* want to see the inside of Mountjoy again, so that wasn't an issue. But my drinking could become a big issue until the intervention of the person who would ultimately change my life for the better – Antoinette Gahan.

Antoinette was aware that I would need time to adjust upon my release so she gave me my space for the first few weeks. But I missed her, and I will never forget my nerves when I finally dialled her number one sunny Saturday evening. I asked her out, she said yes, and the rest is history. But it almost wasn't, as the damage prison had done to me was starting to consume me further. I knew the drinking itself was a problem. But what shocked me the most? I was going to lose 'The One', Antoinette. I loved this woman with every fibre of my body. And though she never once asked me to stop drinking, she made it clear it didn't suit me. And so I stopped!

It was tough at the start but I am over a year sober now and I will never revert back, all thanks to Antoinette. She was the one who made me feel like 'someone', like I mattered. Antoinette would sit and listen to me for hours as I told her most of the tales that make up this book, a book I had given up on completing until Antoinette pushed me to finish it and made me fall in love with it again. And I have, I love this aul' book. As I've said, some may feel that it's a view of prison life through 'rose-tinted glasses', some may even find it disrespectful. To anybody I have offended or annoyed I am truly sorry. I had been the most negative person that God had created before my incarceration, and I really wanted to show how positive I have become since my release.

I could have filled a book twice as big as this one with all the dread I felt on a daily basis in Mountjoy. Filled it with the fights and drug abuse and suicide. But I chose not to. I chose to try to put a positive spin on the most negative time in my life. Mountjoy is vile. If you are a young man reading this then please heed these words: *No matter what the crime is, it's not fuckin' worth it.* Yes, you will more than likely survive your time spent in prison, but at what cost not just to you, but to your family too? I urge you to heed these words.

I just wanted to try something I felt hadn't been done regarding a true story about someone's experiences in an Irish jail. I really wanted to try to open people's minds about 'ex-cons' and I know I'll always have my work cut out in this regard. But I long to break down the walls of judgment and prejudice that people hold against ex-prisoners. Not all of us are rotten to the core. Many of us will carry the shame of being a prisoner for the rest of our lives, but we just want a chance to get on with things. I have spoken on talk shows about how I cannot find employment due to my record. I have served my time for the crime I shamefully committed, and I'm still paying for it now that I am free. But this won't deter me. Someone will give me a chance and that person will be very lucky, as I will give them my all.

So trust me when I say that prison has done damage to me, but it also has given me the tools to be the guy who is typing this very conclusion. I helped to start a movement, the Prison Committee, that has improved standards in all Irish prisons. I wrote a musical that was very well received and I was part of the greatest ever 'prison band' created in any of Ireland's jails. I made a decision in prison to change, and parts of the prison system assisted in this change. For people who think prisoners should not be afforded educational rights and stimulating activities, I urge you to read this book through different eyes. I beg you to see how reformed I am since my release, thanks in large part to the help and guidance of some of the officers and staff I met along the way. Sure, I even wrote a fuckin' book! But I have loved every cramp this book caused in my hands as I frantically wrote the first drafts until the ink ran dry in my blue Bic pen.

How are the other members of The Off#enders you ask? Cunny is doing great. He hit the ground running and hasn't stopped. Sweeny-Todd likewise, though I never doubted Sweeny-Todd would do anything less. He is co-running his own company at the time of writing. Amazing stuff from an amazing lad. But what about Fitzer? Well, I speak to the greatest 'male' friend I've ever had (Antoinette is my best friend too ... I just don't want the two of them fighting over me!) almost every day on the phone. Fitzer is doing brilliantly I can happily report. He is due home in a couple of months and I couldn't be more excited. He is still the same amazing upbeat character who I met on D1 serving breakfast many, many moons ago. He still is the best bass player I've ever had the pleasure to play with, and his voice is still incredible. He is also still the man who saved my life and I would not have survived my sentence without him.

And as for The Off#enders? I made that trip to Mr. Whitehead's office and he was very impressed. I don't want to say too much, as nothing can be done until Fitzer is home, but the future is looking fairly bright.

As is my own. I am still looking for that elusive job, but I know it will come. My mam is so proud of me, and this makes me feel on top of the world like I can achieve anything! She is so astounding that I wrote a song about her, which is on The Off#enders album. It's called 'She' (so-called because she hates being referred to as 'she' – 'Who's she? The cat's mother?' – so of course I called it 'She'). In the first year of my release I created a video for this song as a Mother's Day gift to her (available on YouTube). As for the next steps? The top of one mountain is the bottom of the next for me, as I strive to be the greatest son/brother/uncle/cousin/boyfriend that I can be. I am the happiest I have ever been in my entire life, and one line from the song for my mother has never had a truer meaning than right now:

> If this is lost, I don't want to be found.

I have been the proud partner of Antoinette Gahan for over a year and a half. The way we met is crazy, I know, but she fills my heart with such joy and happiness on a daily basis, and I'd be lost without her. She has torn down my 'prison' insecurities and made me feel like I'm the only man on the planet. She has travelled this crazy journey with me, and has never judged me for the wrongs of my past. She inspires me through her determination and lust for life. Her strength is unbelievable, she is the blood which courses through my veins. Now that I'm in, I never want out.

Above all, I have such a longing inside me to succeed so I can one day become the greatest husband my beautiful Antoinette, my soulmate, could ever have wished for.

I wonder if she'd say yes? I was in prison after all ...

ACKNOWLEDGEMENTS

I would like to take this opportunity to thank a few people:

To all the lads I did 'me whack' with, thank you from the bottom of my heart. We became a family and I cherish every memory we shared together (good and bad). Especially 'Black-Git', K. 'Insanity' G., 'Gorgeous-Luke' and 'Scully', Ian, Redmond, Mick Smull, Tooee, Big Joe and Big John, Eddie Scott and, of course, the Bakery Lads ... I can't wait for the rematch of our football game! Although you lads don't feature heavily in this tale, you all did and still do feature heavily in my heart. Thanks lads.

To the teaching staff, firstly in Mountjoy. *Wow*! These dedicated individuals come into what can be an extremely hostile environment and give us their undivided attention as they provide us with the tools to radically change ourselves. Their patience, kind hearts, and the fact that they go out of their way to make you feel 'normal', and not like the social reject that you have convinced yourself that you are, is simply astounding. And to Maggie ... I don't think you will ever know what you meant to me and to the *Journeyman* crew. You are a very bright light in a very dark place and I feel blessed that I got to meet you, and even more blessed that you are still part of my life. Thank you for everything Maggie.

The same goes for the phenomenal teaching staff in Loughan House. It's not just a job to these people. They have a way of making you feel like you are their only student. They deal with all walks of life, all cultures, and do so with aplomb. Their dedication at times left me stuck for words. Also a massive thank you to Sorcha and Jackie ... you are both simply incredible women.

To Governor Gavin and Chief Carrick, thank you for believing in me. You are both equally amazing, strong women. And to Mrs Mulligan, a true lady. Choice Theory all the way Miss!

I would like to thank Derek and Joe for sticking by me and not turning their backs on me. Both of your friendships mean the world to me.

To my nephews and nieces, Mark, Alan, Jennifer, Sean, Sarah, Conor, Luke, Adam and Dylan, for their support and food. I love you all so much.

To Ash and Ciara, 'prisoners wives', you are both amazing ladies and the strength you gave 'your men' was simply astounding. Oh and Ash, you're a bleedin' headcase!

To my beautiful, strong, sisters-in-law Barbara, Bernadette and Niamh for their constant care and support. You are amazing women, thank you.

To my amazing brothers Gerry, Noel and Jason, you are all an inspiration to me and you had your little brother's back, even though I fucked up. I know I let you all down, but you never let me down and I love you all so much for that.

To Mr. A. Kennedy and Mr J. Dixon (and Katie of course!). You showed me unbelievable support at a time when I deserved to be judged, and have always been incredible to me. Two great lads ... thank you. And to Mr. N. Boylan. Similarly to the lads, you and your team (especially Helena and Garrett) have been incredible to me ... but you allowed me in as a friend. Your words of encouragement and offers of help and assistance are things I will never forget. I feel very lucky and proud to call you my friend. Thank you.

To Deborah ... I will never forget your strength the day you spoke about your incredible and extremely talented brother in Mountjoy. You made a massive impact on my life, and I am so proud that I can now call you my friend ... and you better keep writing! You have a gift.

To Brian Langan. We never met face to face but your kind words and constant stream of support are something I will remember forever. And a special thanks for pointing me in the direction of David and The Liffey Press.

To Frank Shouldice. I initially dreaded our first meeting, but the advice you gave me that day is evidenced in this very book. A true master of your art and a really cool guy. I am honoured. Thank you.

To Darina. I sometimes feel I owe you the most thanks as I know you spoke up about the publishing of this book, and I know how much your husband values your opinion. And of course, you are the true voice of "Amy!" A million thanks to you Darina, a.k.a., *The Agent!*

To David Givens and The Liffey Press. I could not have hand-picked a better person or company to oversee the reading, dissecting, and final completion of this book. As a man you are a complete gentleman (funny too!) and like Frank, you too are a true master of your art. Thank you for having faith in me, and for taking a chance on me. From day one you made me feel so at ease. I am so grateful and blessed to have met you, and I don't think I will ever be able to fully show you how grateful I am. You are amazing! (This 'amazing' is to be left in, DG (lol)).

To the first incredible woman I know, my mam. Words cannot describe how much you mean to me Ma. I'm so sorry for letting you down, but the Gary who writes this story has changed and I promise that this is how I'll stay. You are the strongest woman I know and I love you with all my heart.

To the second most incredible woman I know, Antoinette, my soulmate. What can I say, but *thank you*! You are incredible and the support you have given me has made me who I am today. Also, your tireless work as you read and re-read this book, giving your critique and checking my spelling was invaluable. I simply adore ya!

Lastly, I would like to thank you, the reader, for sharing this most personal of tales. My intention was never to offend, but instead to maybe give people a different perspective on some of the men and women released from prison. I hope I have given you some food for thought.

If anyone would like to hear some of The Off#enders tracks and to see the 'Iron Sky' video I created, please head over to YouTube and simply search, 'Gary Cunningham The Off#enders'.

From the bottom of my heart, thank you all.

Gary Cunningham
(Prisoner No. 77615)